ECONOMICS, ETHICS AND RELIGION

By the same author

ISLAMIC BUSINESS: THEORY AND PRACTICE
ISLAMIC FINANCIAL MARKETS (*editor*)
CYPRUS AND THE INTERNATIONAL ECONOMY
ECONOMIC DEVELOPMENT IN THE MIDDLE EAST
TRADE AND INVESTMENT IN THE MIDDLE EAST
THE ECONOMIES OF THE MIDDLE EAST
BANKING AND FINANCE IN THE ARAB MIDDLE EAST
BANKING IN THE ARAB GULF (*with John R. Presley*)
GULF TRADE AND FINANCE
POLITICS AND THE ECONOMY OF JORDAN

Economics, Ethics and Religion

Jewish, Christian and Muslim Economic Thought

Rodney Wilson
Professor of Economics
University of Durham

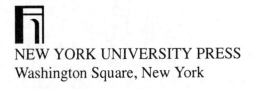

NEW YORK UNIVERSITY PRESS
Washington Square, New York

© Rodney Wilson 1997

First published in the U.S.A. in 1997 by
NEW YORK UNIVERSITY PRESS
Washington Square
New York, N.Y. 10003

Library of Congress Cataloging-in-Publication Data
Wilson, Rodney.
Economics, ethics and religion : Jewish, Christian and Muslim
economic thought / by Rodney Wilson.
p.   cm.
Includes bibliographical references and index.
ISBN 0–8147–9313–4
1. Economics—Religious aspects—Judaism.   2. Economics—Religious
aspects—Christianity.   3. Economics—Religious aspects—Islam.
4. Economics—Moral and ethical aspects.   I. Title.
BM509.E27W55   1996
291.1'785—dc20   96–21422 (Rev.)
                                                              CIP

Printed in Great Britain

Contents

Table and Figure List

Acknowledgements

I would like to thank two of my colleagues in the Department of Economics in Durham, Professor Denis O'Brien, who read and commented on Chapters 1 and 2, and Professor Peter Johnson, who read and commented on Chapter 3. Professor Françoise Deconinck of the University of Paris X read Chapters 2 and 3, and made very useful suggestions.

Some of the material in Chapter 4 was presented at a seminar at the Islamic Foundation in Leicester in November 1995. I would like to thank the participants for their questions and comments, notably Dr Umer Chapra of the Saudi Arabian Monetary Agency, for his comments on my treatment of Ibn Khaldûn, the Islamic philosopher and economist. I have learnt much from discussions there, and at a seminar during December 1994 at Universiti Sains Malaysia in Penang on Islamic Political Economy.

I alone am responsible for the text of this volume, and those acknowledged may not share the views expressed. It is hoped, however, that this work will encourage others to work in the field of economics and comparative religion, and that the bibliography will prove useful.

1 Economics and Ethics

The interest taken by economists in ethical issues and beliefs, and that taken by moral philosophers and theologians in economics, have both revived in recent years. This book is intended to make a contribution to the cross-fertilisation of ideas that is occurring where these disciplines meet. One aim is to provide a literature survey, which will be useful for further work in this area. For this reason this study contains an extensive bibliography. At the same time the author attempts to evaluate the major contributions to the literature, and place them in the context of related writings. Hence the work of theologians and moral philosophers is juxtaposed with the contributions of economists, which results in some interesting comparisons.

The study could have been confined to economics and ethics, with no reference to the work in this field by economists with strong religious beliefs. Theological contributions could have been ignored, as is largely the case in the business ethics literature. It is the author's belief that such contributions should not be neglected, even in the context of increasingly secularised societies. An understanding of religious teaching helps put ethical issues, including those involving economic relations, in a fuller perspective. Religion has a profound influence on personal and social values, which affects even those without beliefs. The social theologian, Charles Davis, sees fact and value as inextricably intertwined in the social sciences, so that non-trivial judgements of fact always presuppose some prior judgements of value.[1] Yet scientific methodology cannot answer questions of value governing human action. These can best be addressed through religious and philosophical argument. As Davis asserts, empirical investigation can produce only probable findings, not ultimate truths.

Modern societies are pluralist, with not only the secular and different levels of religious belief coexisting, but also many different religions. There is no study of comparative religious

---

[1] Charles Davis, *Religion and the Making of Society: Essays in Social Theology*, Cambridge University Press, 1994, p. 31.

1

teaching on economics in a single volume, perhaps because the task of writing such a book was seen as too daunting. For an exhaustive study encompassing all the world's major religions this would certainly be the case. This study is confined to an investigation of the view of economics in the world's three major monotheistic religions, Judaism, Christianity and Islam. It would have been interesting to look at Hindu, Buddhist and Shinto views on economics, especially in the light of the enormous economic changes that have taken place in East and South East Asia, and to a lesser extent in South Asia. This would have been too wide a remit however, especially given the diversity of beliefs within and between Eastern religions.

The author in any case has more knowledge of religions of Middle Eastern origin, having worked on the economic development of the region for over twenty-five years. This included work on Islamic economics; researchers interested in Middle Eastern economies know just how much economic behaviour in largely Muslim countries is influenced by religious beliefs and values. As a Christian who has participated in interfaith dialogue with Muslim economists at numerous conferences and seminars in the Middle East and elsewhere, the author believes he has a contribution to make, based on his own experiences. Judaism is included as it is possible to define a Judeo-Christian tradition in the economics sphere as in other areas. Nevertheless it is important to be aware of both ancient and modern Jewish writing on economic matters, and not simply Old Testament teaching. The author also has first-hand experience of Israel and its economic problems, and attempts to discern in this study the extent to which it has a distinctive Jewish economy, especially given its claim to be a Jewish, indeed *the* Jewish state.

The views of Judaism, Christianity and Islam on economic issues are analysed in Chapters 2, 3 and 4, and there is a discussion of the way in which these relate to business ethics in Chapter 5. Business ethics is included, as many economists and theologians, like the general public, have become critical of the ability of governments to manage economic activity in a fair and just fashion. There seems little point in criticisms of capitalism, when the alternative of government-run command economies has become so discredited, and even mixed economies have arguably had their day. Rather, there is an interest in how capitalism can be reformed from within, which has

resulted in a renewed discussion of issues of corporate governance. There has also been an interest in how those in business
can be persuaded to conduct their dealings in conformity with
some moral standard, whether defined through religion or
simply a respect for humanity.

IS THERE A PLACE FOR MORALITY IN ECONOMICS?

Economists today are seldom regarded as moralisers. Indeed
most of the profession would regard making such judgements
as unscientific, and beyond the remit of their subject. Economists may have high moral values, but that is regarded as a
matter for their personal, rather than their professional, lives.
Yet the pre-classical economists did not divorce economics from
moral questions, and the Scholastic philosophers, whose contributions will be discussed in Chapter 3, treated both together.
Even Adam Smith regarded himself as a moral philosopher as
much as a political economist.[2] Smith's first major work was
his *Theory of Moral Sentiments*,[3] the ideas from which were to
influence his writing in *The Wealth of Nations*.[4] By the nineteenth century, following the work of David Ricardo, economics had become separated from its ethical roots, with enquiry
centred on the mechanics of price and wage determination
rather than issues such as the 'just' price or 'fair' wages.[5] Personal value judgements were increasingly regarded as non-
scientific, as economics moved from being normative to being
positive, one central concern being to explain how markets
actually worked, not how they *should* work. A good theory was
one that was logically consistent and which stood up to empirical testing, not a theory that was built from 'sound' moral
foundations.

[2] Denis P. O'Brien, *The Classical Economists*, Clarendon Press, Oxford, 1975,
p. 24.
[3] Adam Smith, *The Theory of Moral Sentiments*, Clarendon Press, Oxford, 1976.
Edition edited by D.D. Raphael and A.L. Macfie.
[4] Adam Smith, *An Inquiry into the Nature and Causes of Wealth of Nations*,
Clarendon Press, Oxford, 1976. Edition edited by R.H. Campbell and
A.K. Skinner.
[5] Ingrid H. Rima, *Development of Economic Analysis*, Irwin, Homewood, Illinois, 1991, pp. 137–67.

Yet recent decades have seen a reassertion of normative economics, especially with the emergence of managerial economics as a sub-discipline in its own right.[6] Its focus is on how scarce resources should be managed, using economics, especially the techniques of neo-classical analysis, as a tool, but with the objectives determined by management independently of economic considerations. Although managerial economics texts make little or no reference to ethical issues, it should be feasible to postulate exogenous moral objectives for management, and to construct an economic system to meet these objectives. General equilibrium models where all variables are endogenously determined by economic forces look suspect from an ethical perspective, as this suggests the economics drives the ethics rather than the other way round. Marxist models are suspect for the same reason, as beliefs are accorded no dignity in their own right, human behaviour being solely economically determined.

Leading thinkers on methodological issues have adopted definitions of economics that put the subject in a wider perspective, and ultimately raise moral and religious issues. Vilfredo Pareto pointed out that political economy did not have to take morality into account, but an economist who extolled a particular practical measure should consider the moral as well as the economic consequences.[7] Real men included not only *homo oeconomicus*, but also *homo ethicus* and *homo religiosus*. It is legitimate to separate economic effects from ethical and religious questions; indeed for Pareto this is how art became science, as there are certain uniform laws that men appeared to conform to in their economic dealings, which were distinct from moral and religious laws. However, the economist who, in commending a law, considered only the economic effects was, in Pareto's view, not much of a theorist. When science becomes advanced, then not only are the different parts of a

[6] The approach and scope of managerial economics are discussed in the introductions to most of the major texts in the field. See for example Edwin Mansfield, *Managerial Economics: Theory, Applications and Cases*, 3rd ed., Norton, New York, 1995, pp. 4–7 or Mark Hirschey, James Pappas and David Whigham, *Managerial Economics*, Dryden Press, London, 1993, pp. 3–5 and 16–18.
[7] Vilfredo Pareto, *Manual of Political Economy*, Macmillan, London, 1971, p. 13. Translated by Ann Schwier from the French edition published by Librairie Droz, Geneva, 1927.

phenomenon separated, but they are subsequently put together in a synthesis.[8] Hence the economic, ethical and religious consequences have all to be taken into account.

John Neville Keynes, father of John Maynard Keynes, and a notable contributor to methodological debate, sought to distinguish between the positive science which seeks to discover economic laws and the ethics of political economy which seeks to determine economic ideals.[9] He believed it was possible to study economic laws without passing ethical judgements; indeed, like Pareto, he thought they should be separated. Neville Keynes rejected the approach of German economists such as Adolph Wagner who believed that economic and ethical problems should be treated together. Wagner and the German school asserted that the British classical tradition had become amoral. For them positive economic theorising could not be distinguished from economics as a practical science which proposed measures with ethical consequences for society.[10] Although not many contemporary economists would agree with this proposition, there is still the issue of how economists choose which problems to investigate and theorise about. The theory itself may be positive, but the economist's own choice of subject matter may be determined by his or her ethical values. This is part of the distinction which John Neville Keynes made, one which is certainly valid, and which has implications for the freedom of economists to choose the area they work in within their own discipline.

THE MOTIVATION OF *HOMO OECONOMICUS*

Joan Robinson identified the pre-requisites for an economic system as 'a set of *rules*, an *ideology* to justify them, and a *conscience* in the individual which makes him strive to carry them out.'[11] This neatly encapsulates the conditioners of human behaviour in a workable economy. Humans need rules or laws

[8] Ibid., p. 15.
[9] John Neville Keynes, *The Scope and Method of Political Economy*, 4th ed., Macmillan, London, 1917, pp. 37–46. (1st ed., 1891)
[10] Adolph Wagner, 'The present state of political economy', *Quarterly Journal of Economics*, Vol. 1, No. 1, 1886, pp. 113–33.
[11] Joan Robinson, *Economic Philosophy*, C.A. Watts, London, 1962, p. 13.

if order is to prevail, as economies can usually be observed to function most effectively in stable conditions. The absence of rules increases uncertainty which results in higher transactions costs. Markets work best if there are regulations which ensure buyers meet their payments obligations, and sellers actually provide the goods and service they claim to be able to provide. Markets, in other words, need a legal framework in which to operate effectively, as indeed do command economies. This legal framework includes moral law. Meeting payments obligations can be a matter of honour, and providing goods to the quality specified can be a matter of trust. In both cases a legal backup to ensure a moral order may be necessary given the inevitability of human moral failure. Rules can come from natural law, but they can equally well be derived from religious laws, the written and oral *Torah* for Jews, the Old Testament and the Gospels for Christians and the Islamic *Shariah* law for Muslims.

Robinson sees humans as being ideologically motivated.[12] Ideology is no longer fashionable, as with the ending of the Cold War, the demise of communism and the eclipse of socialism, at least in its traditional form, there is supposedly only capitalism left. Joan Robinson herself was a socialist, and at various times was an enthusiastic supporter of Stalin and Mao, but her inclusion of ideology in the definition of an economic system is important. There is a market ideology, the justification for the system being that although each participant pursues their own self-interest, there is what Adam Smith suggested was an 'invisible hand' that brings about a socially advantageous outcome. Many, of course, disagree with this proposition, but there is little doubt that only those who believe in what they are doing will make a success of it. Command economies worked as long as those involved believed in them, but when they ceased believing the economies collapsed. It is generally those who believe in markets who do best out of market systems, and those who don't who do worst.

Ideology may motivate, and result in economically efficient outcomes, while at the same time constraining self-interested behaviour. However, particular ideologies are not necessarily moral in the sense of respecting essential human dignity, as was

[12] Mark Blaug, *The Methodology of Economics*, Cambridge University Press, 1980, p. 122.

evident in the cases of communist and fascist ideologies. Robinson stresses that conscience also has a part to play in an economic system, which suggests an ethical dimension to the evaluation of both economic behaviour and economic outcomes. Robinson sees ethics as unrelated to reason, but rather a consequence of upbringing. Even those who rebel against the moral standards of previous generations, like Joan Robinson herself, are influenced by the ideas they rebel against.[13]

Having a conscience is not only morally desirable, but may also be sound business sense. A reading of business history shows that companies run by a management with a moral conscience and an awareness of social responsibilities have usually fared well, while those preoccupied only with material rewards for their management and shareholders have seldom been able to sustain their business in the long term. This is not to suggest that high material reward is wrong, but rather what matters is the satisfaction from providing the best possible products and services for customers, and the company having the trust and respect of its own employees. Meeting these two criteria should enhance rewards, not reduce them.

Mark Blaug described Joan Robinson's *Economic Philosophy* as 'a puzzling little book that depicts economics as partly a scientific study and partly a vehicle for propagating ideology.'[14] Taken as a whole there is much in the book which many can disagree with, and viewed thirty years later the ideology depicted seems rather obsolete, as it is the economists with whom Joan Robinson disagreed whose thinking has prevailed. Nevertheless there are some interesting observations in the book about economics in relation to moral and metaphysical questions. Robinson sees 'the solutions offered by economists as no less delusory than those of the theologians they displaced.'[15] However she retains the hope that economics can advance towards science, and that enlightenment is not useless. According to Robinson, economists if they read their own doctrines correctly, should foster an ideology based on more than mere monetary values.

---

[13] Joan Robinson, *Economic Philosophy*, p. 12. Robinson was the daughter of a Christian socialist, General Maurice.
[14] Mark Blaug, *Methodology of Economics*, p. 122.
[15] Joan Robinson, *Economic Philosophy*, p. 146.

NEEDS, WANTS AND SCARCITY

There many definitions of economics, but one of the most widely quoted is that by Lionel Robbins, author of *An Essay on the Nature and Significance of Economic Science*. This was a controversial work which stated that economics was a positive science, and that propositions with ethical content had no place in economics. Lionel Robbins defined economics as: 'the science which studies human behaviour as a relationship between ends and scarce means which have alternative ends.'[16]

Is economics an art, or a science as Robbins asserts, or perhaps trying to become a science as Robinson suggests? Many universities still designate their economics degrees as bachelors or masters of arts rather than of science. This implies a view of economics as an art involving judgement, which in turn brings in a moral dimension. This is not simply a matter of the division between mathematical and econometric approaches to economics on the one hand and institutional approaches, involving qualitative evaluation, on the other. Economic models may be mathematically rigorous, but there will always be judgements to be made about the sensitivity of the results to the assumptions, and whether the actions assumed to be taken by the economic agents is moral. Econometric findings can be tested for their statistical significance, a purely scientific matter, but moral judgements may be made when the results are interpreted and their implications for economic policy worked out. This is where experience comes in, and where the moral attitudes of those involved in the evaluation becomes an issue.

According to Robbins economics is said to be the science of scarcity, which can be interpreted as the difference between what people would like to consume, and the actual quantities of goods produced. For some, however, scarcity is a result of human greed which arises from immoral desires.[17] There is ample abundance of production, the problem is that people

---

[16] Lionel Robbins, *An Essay on the Nature and Significance of Economic Science*, 2nd ed., Macmillan, London, 1935, pp. 16–17.

[17] Donald Hay, Review of Bob Goudzwaard and Harry de Lange, *Beyond Poverty and Affluence: Towards a Global Economy of Care*, Erdmans, Grand Rapids, Michigan and World Council of Churches, Geneva, 1995, in *Association of Christian Economists Journal*, No. 20, 1995, p. 45.

want more and more. Some ecologists and environmentalists take the view that the need is to constrain consumption through regulation rather than augment production. Most economists, however, view scarcity as a challenge rather than a problem.[18] They argue that environmentalists and ecologists do not appreciate that the role of the price system is to ration, and that constraint on consumption is involved in the price system itself. At the same time if production grows through price incentives there will be the resources to tackle the problems of the environment and pollution. In this view economic growth results in fewer moral dilemmas, not more.

Robbins also stresses the notion that resources can be used for competing ends. This refers to what is produced, and how it gets allocated. The emphasis could be on the production of military equipment rather than provision of health care, housing, education or consumer goods. There are always trade-offs, often with ethical implications. The question of who gets what is also controversial, and can be regarded as a moral issue. Market systems often result in considerable inequalities in income and wealth. Many feel that it is important that the basic needs of everyone are satisfied, so that all humans can live with some degree of dignity.[19] However, most religious teaching does not stress equity, but rather the satisfaction of basic needs through a 'just' system of distribution, with arguments amongst religious scholars about how justice should be interpreted.

Homo œconomicus, economic man, is often regarded as a maximiser of personal income or wealth. Economic behaviour is often thought of as resting on Jeremy Bentham's utilitarian calculus, the aim being to maximise utility or satisfaction and to minimise pain or disutility. Bentham, who lived in the second half of the eighteenth century and the early decades of the nineteenth century (1748–1832), was a philosopher and economist, and his concept of utilitarianism was to have a great influence on the later classical economists, notably John

[18] A detailed critique of Lionel Robbins' methodology and his view of scarcity is provided by Denis P. O'Brien, *Lionel Robbins*, Macmillan, London, 1988, pp. 23–40.
[19] For a lucid discussion of distributional issues from the point of view of applied ethics see Peter Singer, *Practical Ethics*, Cambridge University Press, 1993, pp. 218–46.

Stuart Mill in the nineteenth century.[20] While Adam Smith was a moral philosopher as well as an economist, John Stuart Mill was not, and it can be argued that utilitarianism took the morals out of economics, or at least led economics to develop as a field of enquiry quite distinct from moral philosophy.[21] This is not to suggest that Mill himself was unconcerned with moral questions, but he stressed economic outcomes. In other words his interest was in how much was produced, rather than the ethics of how goods were produced, and on satisfaction in consumption.[22] Economics was seen by some as solely materialistic, and economic behaviour as *amoral* if not *immoral*, that is, it was seen to be at best unconcerned with morals if not actually dissolute or failing to comply with any moral standards.

This is a misleading view of economics, however, as economists are concerned with much more than mere consumption, and academic economists at least cannot be accused of being excessively materialistic given university salary levels. Utility or satisfaction was always about more than consumption, as it was and is quite possible to derive utility from helping others, through altruistic behaviour, and not merely selfish behaviour. Material goods themselves may be simply a means to utility or satisfaction, and not the end. Through people's earnings, or even through inheritance, they gain control over resources. Arguably, what matters is how the resources are used, not simply the quantity possessed. People have responsibility, or stewardship, for the resources they control. These can be used for socially desirable purposes, or in a wasteful and selfish way. There may be some who derive utility or satisfaction from waste, but as wasted resources quickly yield no further utility, it could be argued that this is neither maximising nor rational behaviour.

[20] For a modern view of Jeremy Bentham's economic writings see Terence W. Hutchinson, *The Uses and Abuses of Economics: Contentious Essays on History and Method*, Routledge, London, 1994, pp. 27–49.
[21] An interesting critique of John Stuart Mill's philosophy of economics is provided by Daniel M. Hausman, *Essays on Philosophy and Economic Methodology*, Cambridge University Press, 1992, pp. 33–53. Some historians of economic thought, notably Roger Backhouse, believe that Hausman tries to read too much into his interpretation.
[22] Mill was concerned about wage levels, income distribution and business organisation, but in his writing these were dealt with through economic analysis, rather than through a moral assessment of rights and wrongs.

Economics addresses many social concerns. Many economists are concerned with issues of income and wealth distribution, and have developed various ways of comparing income distribution in different societies. Welfare economics is the branch of economics which attempts to analyse how income can be distributed so that those who enjoy the largest shares do not gain at the expense of the less well off. It attempts, in some versions, to include social welfare, and not simply the welfare of individuals.

Furthermore, the concerns of ecologists and environmentalists can be analysed with the help of economics, and environmental economics is a rapidly growing branch of the subject. Projects are worth undertaking if the net benefits exceed the net costs, where both benefits and costs themselves include not only market-tested valuations but also externalities. Market valuations themselves may require correction by the use of shadow prices.

These examples, the economics of altruism, welfare economics and environmental economics, illustrate how versatile the subject has become. Economic analysis contains many important tools and involves the use of powerful techniques which can make a real difference in perceiving and potentially solving many of the major social challenges. There is a moral purpose in much of positive economics, and simply equating its utilitarian foundations with selfish individualism is mischievous, if not downright misleading.

ETHICAL IMPLICATIONS OF CONTEMPORARY METHODOLOGICAL DEBATE

A recent book edited by Roger Backhouse contains contributions by Terence Hutchinson, Alexander Rosenberg and Kevin Hoover which question the aims and objectives of economists and economics, in particular the relevance of modern theorising for economic policy.[23] As economics has developed as a discipline, research has become directed at serving the interests

---

[23] Roger E. Backhouse, (ed.), *New Directions in Economic Methodology*, Routledge, London, 1994.

of the subject itself rather than any wider aim.[24] Perhaps this is inevitable as a subject becomes mature and, indeed, given the large size of the community of academic economists, simply serving the interests of such a group can give a meaning and purpose to the lives of economists. Yet the issue of excluding the wider society of non-economists raises moral and ethical issues, although these are not discussed in the Backhouse volume, as the contributors confine their attention to issues of methodology.[25] If, however, prediction is impossible in economics as McCloskey asserts,[26] then it can be argued that economics has become a policy irrelevant subject.[27]

Rosenberg, in his contribution to the Backhouse volume, considers the cognitive status of economics. He sees it as subject to the same conceptual pigeonholing as geometry, which is certainly not a subject involving ethics.

> Just as geometers in the nineteenth century explored the ramifications of varying the strongest assumptions of Euclidean geometry, economists have devoted great energies to varying equally crucial assumptions about the number of agents, their expectations, returns to scale and divisibilities, and determining whether a consistent economy – a market clearing equilibrium – will still result, will be stable and will be unique. Their interests in this formal result are quite independent of, indeed are in spite of, the fact that its assumptions about production, distribution and information are manifestly false.[28]

Yet this statement shows that it is more difficult for economists than mathematicians to escape from ethics. Economic models must ultimately relate in some sense to the real world, as the

[24] For a broader consideration of these issues see Terence W. Hutchinson, *Changing Aims in Economics*, Blackwell, Oxford, 1992, pp. 15–29.

[25] Elsewhere Hutchinson refers to the need for economics to be 'a more honest science' in terms of its contribution to policy making. See Terence W. Hutchinson, *The Uses and Abuses of Economics*, p. 256.

[26] D.N. McCloskey, *The Rhetoric of Economics*, University of Wisconsin Press, 1985, p. 15.

[27] Terence W. Hutchinson, 'Ends and means in the methodology of economics', in Backhouse, *New Directions*, p. 29.

[28] Alexander Rosenberg, 'What is the cognitive status of economic theory', in Backhouse, *New Directions*, p. 229.

aim of abstraction is to at least explain if not predict. As real world transactions involve ethical issues, so must those in economic models even if they are subsumed under transactions costs or the expectations of economic agents. Furthermore, where assumptions are manifestly false this falsity raises moral issues, especially if the models used are supposed to explain economic processes. Such models can deceive, and those who build them are at best being only partially truthful, especially if they believe the assumptions are wrong, but do not emphasise their concerns. Economists are often reluctant to discuss *ceteris paribus* qualifications, but this may be necessary in the interests of intellectual honesty.[29] There may even be a temptation to lie, especially if the researcher has spent much time and effort in developing a model, and there are pressures to publish before a fuller investigation can be made.

Issues of belief, doubt and truth in relation to economic method are considered by Kevin Hoover in his contribution to the volume edited by Backhouse.[30] His discussion draws on the ideas of Charles Peirce, the American philosopher who is credited with introducing the concept of pragmatism.[31] Inquiry for Peirce, and Hoover, aims at establishing peace of mind as a firm basis for action. It is about reducing the element of surprise, and overcoming the doubt and hesitancy which thwart action.

It is Peirce's view that to function effectively people need beliefs, a central human predicament being how to obtain stable beliefs. Beliefs can be fixed by governments or churches or similar social institutions exercising their authority, but some ideas inevitably escape regulation, and may ultimately destabilise authority. Beliefs can also be fixed by an *a priori* method, that is by what is agreeable to reason. Economic theories are established in this way, Peirce viewing economics as a branch of the philosophy of common sense. The *a priori* method has its

---

[29] Daniel M. Hausman, *Essays*, p. 101.
[30] Kevin D. Hoover, 'Pragmatism, pragmaticism and economic method', in Backhouse, *New Directions*, pp. 286–315.
[31] There are many edited editions of the work of Charles Peirce. One of the most widely used is E.C. Moore, *Charles S. Peirce: the Essential Writings*, Harper and Row, New York, 1972. The most authoritative source is A.W. Burks, C. Hartshorne and P. Weiss, *Collected Papers of Charles Sanders Peirce*, Vols. 1–8, Belknap Press, Cambridge, Massachusetts, 1931–58.

limitations, as fashions of opinions change, undermining any stability. Nevertheless the *a priori* method is a way of progressing, and it should only be abandoned when confronted with a problem which cannot be solved through our thinking. It is in these circumstances that people may seek a constraint which is external to themselves, such as the authority of the state or organised religion.[32] Peirce himself came from a Unitarian background, but he later joined the Trinitarian Episcopal Church.[33]

The difficulty of escaping into pure positivism is compounded when the language and terminology which economists use is value laden. These issues are considered in Roger Backhouse's volume by Willie Henderson who considers metaphor in economics[34] and Vivienne Brown who looks at the economy as text using the tools of linguistic analysis.[35] Metaphor involves the transference of the meaning of one word or phrase to another, an example in economics being the equating of investment in education with the creation of human capital. Such terms are value laden, and have moral and ethical implications. The notion that human capital can be created by outside intervention has implications for human autonomy. Individuals may choose to pursue a particular course of study out of a desire to enlighten themselves, and see education as an end in itself. Once provision is tailored to the dictates of manpower planning, in an effort to boost national competitiveness or some other elusive goal, which the individuals concerned may not care about or regard as important, then ethical dilemmas inevitably arise.

Language can have religious significance. Indeed, texts such as the Bible and the *Koran* are seen as divinely inspired, the Word of God. Particular translations may be regarded with special reverence, such as that of the King James authorised version of the Bible which played a special role in the religious life of the English-speaking world. In economics, as in other disciplines, students are taught the language of the subject, and

[32] Kevin D. Hoover, 'Pragmatism, pragmaticism and economic method,' in Backhouse, *New Directions*, p. 298.
[33] Ibid., p. 312, footnote 14.
[34] Willie Henderson, 'Metaphor and economics', in Backhouse, *New Directions*, pp. 343–67.
[35] Vivienne Brown, 'The economy as text', in Backhouse, *New Directions*, pp. 368–82.

are introduced to its literature. In economics, as with other technical disciplines, books and articles are not usually read for their literary merit, but rather for the ideas they convey. The authors are demoted from the position of being the originator and guarantor of a unique textual meaning to being scriptors, where the reader rather than the author ascribes the meaning to the text. There is no reverence for text in economics, the aim of authors being to communicate, and for readers to understand, which implies at least a clarity of objectives. The moral constraint is for authors not to deceive, and for readers not to misinterpret, especially if the ideas are to be conveyed to other parties.

Yet the terminology of economics itself is far from being unambiguous. Vivienne Brown cites the example of the interpretation of the term 'competition', which can be applied to the competitive equilibrium of Walras based on exogenous prices, the dynamic competitive process of Hayek where the emphasis is on the informational and incentive role of prices, and the competitive creative destruction of Schumpeter where firms compete over prices and market share.[36] In each of these cases the nature of the competitive process is quite different, which illustrates how competition has no unique meaning.[37] Misinterpretation in such circumstances is quite probable, and those applying the ideas of Walras, Hayek or Schumpeter may unwittingly deceive.

A deconstructionist approach can, of course, be taken to economics, to borrow a term from literary criticism, where a particular ideological schema is applied to 'discover' what are the underlying values implicit in the text. This is often done in the interests of purity, but the problem remains that deconstructionism is itself extremely vulnerable since there is no way it can be protected from the application of its own technique to itself.

If ambiguity is to be avoided an obvious way forward is

---

[36] Ibid., p. 373.
[37] Some of the discussion of the different meanings of competition in the 1930s in the context of debate on the theories of the firm is potentially misleading. See Denis P. O'Brien, 'Research programmes in competitive structure', *Journal of Economic Studies*, Vol. 10, No. 4, pp. 29–51, Reprinted in Denis. P. O'Brien, *Methodology, Money and the Firm*, Vol. 1, Edward Elgar, Aldershot, 1994, pp. 277–99.

through mathematical model building where textual ambiguities are eliminated. Yet one consequence is that much of the richness of understanding economic processes, such as competition, is lost. Text may involve shades of meaning, and good economic writing can have nuances which cannot be conveyed through algebra. It does, however, open up moral pitfalls over interpretation, which a more rigorous approach avoids, although the simplification process involved in the mathematical modelling of economic phenomenon poses its own moral dilemmas regarding selection and exclusion. As the assumptions made in mathematical model building still contain implicit values this does not represent an escape route from the difficulties with text.

ETHICAL ECONOMICS AS A SPECIALISM

Although it is possible to argue that ethical concerns are embodied in much economic research, and that economists are just as much moral beings as those in other disciplines, ethical enquiry is starting to emerge as a sub-discipline in its own right. There are few courses on economics and ethics in relation to the increasing popularity of business ethics, but there is a growing body of research on the borders of economics as a discipline and moral philosophy.

Early work specifically on economics and ethics was undertaken by J.A. Hobson, a largely neglected economist who was much influenced by the Christian socialist movement and the ideas of R.H. Tawney.[38] Hobson's approach was more humanist than Christian, and he attempted to derive a human standard of value, which he saw as preferable to a monetary standard.[39] Although this endeavour was arguably misguided, in his later work he discussed economic and ethical values, including the ethics of property, harmony and discord in economic life and the ethics of bargaining.[40]

---

[38] J.A. Hobson, *Work and Wealth: A Human Valuation*, Macmillan, New York, 1921.
[39] Ibid., pp. 1–18.
[40] J.A. Hobson, *Wealth and Life: A Study in Values*, Macmillan, London, 1929, pp. 112–213.

Notable recent contributors in the field of economics and ethics include Ellen Frankel Paul,[41] Amartya Sen,[42] Kurt Rothschild,[43] Gay Meeks[44] and Alan Lewis and Karl-Eric Warneryd.[45] A comprehensive review of much of the literature was undertaken by Daniel Hausman and Michael McPherson, who cited almost 350 books and articles which were, at least in part, concerned with the interaction between economics and ethics.[46]

Hausman and McPherson discuss the proposition that economics determines the means and ethics the ends.[47] Many economists see their subject as providing tools of analysis, and themselves as in varying degrees technicians, but with some very powerful instruments at their disposal. These include the techniques of welfare economics, the theory of public choice, the economics of altruism and concepts such as utility. Economics is more than a mere bag of tools however, as economists have provided theories that have helped sharpen the thinking of moral philosophers. Notable contributions include

[41] E.F. Paul, J. Paul and F.D. Miller (eds), *Ethics and Economics*, Blackwell, Oxford, 1985. The most original contribution is perhaps that by Dan Usher, 'The value of life for decision making in the public sector', pp. 168–91.

[42] Amartya Sen, *On Ethics and Economics*, Blackwell, Oxford, 1987. The discussion of the consequences of freedom is especially interesting, pp. 58–89.

[43] Kurt W. Rothschild, *Ethics and Economic Theory*, Edward Elgar, Aldershot, Hampshire, 1993.

[44] Gay Meeks, (ed.), *Thoughtful Economic Man: Essays on Rationality, Moral Rules and Benevolence*, Cambridge University Press, 1991. Tony Cramp's essay is perhaps the most interesting from a moral standpoint: 'Pleasures, prices and principles', pp. 50–73.

[45] Alan Lewis and Karl-Eric Warneryd, (eds), *Ethics and Economic Affairs*, Routledge, London, 1994. Despite the title, many of the contributions to this volume are in the field of business ethics. However, there are interesting chapters by Peter Söderbaum, 'Ethics, ideological commitment and social change: institutionalism as an alternative to neo-classical theory', pp. 233–50; Benedetto Gui, 'Interpersonal relations: a disregarded theme in the debate on ethics and economics', pp. 251–63; Josef Wieland, 'Economy and ethics in functionally differentiated societies: history and present problems', pp. 264–85, and Monroe Burk, 'Ideology and morality in economic theory', pp. 313–34.

[46] Daniel M. Hausman and Michael S. McPherson, 'Taking ethics seriously: economics and contemporary moral philosophy', *Journal of Economic Literature*, Vol. 31, No. 2, 1993, pp. 671–731.

[47] Daniel M. Hausman and Michael S. McPherson, op.cit., p. 672.

game theory, Kenneth Arrow's impossibility theorem[48] and Amartya Sen's liberal paradox theory.[49] The last two are concerned with aggregating the interests, preferences and judgements of different individuals or groups to determine public choices, which ultimately involves moral issues. When economists acknowledge the importance of moral philosophy, it does not mean all the traffic has to be one way.

Hausman and McPherson question whether 'economically useful virtues can be sustained by rational self interest, or if the success of economies depends crucially upon non-self interested moral commitments.'[50] Defining rationality as self-interest would appear to both legitimise and foster such behaviour, and there is some evidence from experimental economics to suggest that economics and business students are less cooperative than others. The Australian economist, William Oliver Coleman, sees rationalism as much more than self-interest. Rather it reflects a pensive, meditative predisposition, where people look to their own minds rather than the wider world.[51] It could even be regarded as introspective, but that is not to suggest it is unethical. In contrast anti-rationalists see the human mind as a heap of contradictions, to use the phrase coined by the eighteenth-century philosopher David Hume. The solution to this for the anti-rationalists is to look outward, and adopt an empirical rather than a theoretical approach to explain the complexities of economic life. For the anti-rationalists the ethical questions arise in the selection of what to study, and in the value system used to interpret the wealth of often contradictory information available.

Problems arise not when economics extends knowledge, but when it restricts it. Those involved in welfare economics are often socially motivated and well-intentioned, but factoring normative questions into mere equity and efficiency trade-offs

---

[48] Kenneth Arrow, 'Extended sympathy and the possibility of social choice', *Philosophia*, Vol. 7, No. 2, 1978, pp. 223–37.

[49] Amartya Sen, 'Liberty and social choice', *Journal of Philosophy*, Vol. 80, No. 1, pp. 5–28.

[50] Daniel M. Hausman and Michael S. McPherson, 'Taking ethics seriously', p. 673.

[51] William Oliver Coleman, *Rationalism and Anti-Rationalism in the Origins of Economics: The Philosophical Roots of 18th Century Economic Thought*, Edward Elgar, Aldershot, Hampshire, 1995, pp. 4–8.

may result in other moral questions being overlooked. Some of those with few possessions, such as monks, may have arrived at their position by choice, and may not want to 'benefit' from an income redistribution from those who are materially better off, but perhaps spiritually worse off. Hausman and McPherson cite the case of a starving person who begs for money to make a sacrifice to God. In these circumstances gifts will not make the beggar better off, at least in a material sense. Donors may take the view that such preferences are based on false beliefs, and should not be satisfied, but this involves making a moral judgement.[52]

The same could be said to apply to the drug addict who wants money to satisfy his or her habit. Redistribution through social security or income support to such people may be seen to condone an illegal activity, but the decision to withhold payments, or to make them conditional on attendance at a drug rehabilitation clinic, is to try to impose one set of ethical values on another person, and deny their autonomy of choice. There is the more general issue of how far social policy should be responsive to individual preferences. Satisfying anti-social or sadistic preferences is highly questionable, but if preferences are to be 'laundered' by those in authority to remove their more disagreeable features, then some reference must be made to higher moral values. One answer to this question is provided by John Rawls in his *Theory of Justice*. Rawls argues that while well-being can be identified with the satisfaction of rational preferences a theory of justice cannot simply be based on preferences. Rather, Rawls identifies instead 'primary social goods' such as education or a living income, to which everyone can agree as a basic entitlement.[53] Individuals may want more than this, but there is no social obligation to satisfy such wants.[54]

The theory of contracts is a useful starting point for viewing the role of moral commitments, especially in fields such as

[52] Hausman and McPherson, 'Taking ethics seriously', p. 690.
[53] John Rawls, *A Theory of Justice*, Harvard University Press, Cambridge, Massachusetts, 1971, p. 92.
[54] For a discussion of economic rights see Asbjørn Eide, 'The right to an adequate standard of living including the right to food', in Asbjørn Eide, Catarina Krause and Allan Rosas, (eds), *Economic, Social and Cultural Rights*, Martinus Nijhoff, Dordrecht, 1995, pp. 89–106.

employment. If employees merely work in accordance with the letter of their contracts, 'a work to rule', organisations will seldom function very effectively. Effort levels may not simply be governed by what is formally required, but by what Akerlof refers to as an exchange of 'gifts' between employer and employee.[55] A fair day's work for a fair day's pay involves the worker putting in an effort above that which can be enforced in exchange for a rate of pay above the market rate. This implies a level of trust between workers and employers, in the absence of formal mechanisms to monitor performance. Given the costs and difficulties in information gathering, an organisation in which there is trust between employees and employers, and a moral commitment by both parties, will fare much better than one in which such a commitment is absent.

Similar gains can be realised through honesty, which reduces transactions costs as the need for legal contracting and policing is reduced. Melvin Reder, when discussing the economics of honesty, argues that social investment in religious education in schools and churches may increase economic efficiency as well as serving a moral purpose.[56] Although Amartya Sen would not agree with this proposition, he does argue that moral codes of behaviour can play a part in achieving economic success. Trust, co-ordination and co-operation can be seen as essential prerequisites for capitalism to work, as much as competition. Sen cites the Japanese case, and stresses that capitalism's need for motivational structures is much more complex than simple profit maximising models might suggest.[57] Sen even sees Mafia involvement in business as a way of making pre-capitalist structures work, given the bonds of loyalty and trust within if not between 'families' of organised criminals. This issue is developed further by John Flemming where he sees the Mafia capitalism of Eastern Europe as a reflection of the lack of trust and social cohesion in post-communist

[55] George Akerlof, 'Gift exchange and efficiency wage theory: four views', *American Economic Review*, Vol. 74, No. 2, 1984, pp. 307–19.
[56] Melvin Reder, 'The place of ethics in the theory of production', in Michael Boskin, (ed.), *Economics and Human Welfare: Essays in Honour of Tibor Skitovsky*, Academic Press, New York, 1979, pp. 133–46.
[57] Amartya Sen, 'Moral codes and economic success', in Samuel Brittan and Alan Hamlin, (eds), *Market Capitalism*, pp. 23–34.

society.[58] This is deplored by Flemming, rather than being condoned. In fairness to Sen, however, it has to be stressed that he views Mafia success as reflecting social deficiencies which need to be rectified. Essentially the message is that by studying Mafia organisation it is possible to identify where to start. It can be argued, however, that the emergence of a new Mafia in Eastern Europe reflects not an absence of trust and social cohesion, but rather the lack of a definition of property rights and security of property.

What can be concluded is that ethical economics as a subdiscipline is resulting in more attention being paid to the institutional complexities which play a role in determining economic behaviour. Institutional economics has, of course, a long tradition as being part of the broad church of economic inquiry, drawing originally on German economics in the nineteenth century, but owing much to the efforts of Wesley Mitchell in the early years of the twentieth century and contemporary economists such as John Adams. Recently rediscovered documents reveal the breadth of Mitchell's thinking. In a critique of modern civilisation Mitchell states that 'We boast of progress but lack the insight to see that the term means nothing because we have not thought for what destination we are bound.'[59]

John Adams sees society as an amalgam of institutions – churches, governments, families, banks and codes of law – the 'matrix of culture and the institutional structures that provide a context for personal behaviour.'[60] If church affiliation is indeed a determinant of economic behaviour, this is perhaps an apt starting point for an investigation of comparative religious perspectives on economics.[61]

---

[58] John Flemming, 'The ethics of unemployment and Mafia capitalism', in Samuel Brittan and Alan Hamlin, (eds), *Market Capitalism and Moral Values*, Edward Elgar, Aldershot, 1995, pp. 45–56.

[59] Wesley C. Mitchell, 'The Criticism of Modern Civilisation', *Journal of Economic Issues*, Vol. 29, No. 3, 1995, p. 669. Hand-written copy of Mitchell's introduction to the programme for the Kosmos Club for 1909–10 edited by Malcolm Rutherford.

[60] John Adams, 'Economy as instituted process: change, transformation and progress', *Journal of Economic Issues*, Vol. 28, No. 2, 1994, pp. 332–3.

[61] John Adam's views on the role of religion were very similar to those of Adam Smith. For a critique of the latter see Warren J. Samuels, *The Classical Theory of Economic Policy*, World Publishing, Cleveland, Ohio, 1966, p. 34.

2 Judaism

Judaism, as the oldest of the three major world religions originating in the Middle East, is the natural starting point for this investigation. Over 3000 years of Jewish history have provided a rich tradition of spiritual thinking and moral law on all aspects of human existence including the economic dimension. Christianity builds on the Old Testament teachings, and Muslims also recognise the prophets of the land of Israel, and take the teachings of Moses and Abraham (Ibrahim in Arabic) as precursors to the teaching of the prophet Mohammed. It seems appropriate, therefore, for an investigation into comparative religious writings on economic issues to begin at this common entry point.

The debate about whether the Jews are a nation, an ethnic people or a religious group has implications for the way in which the economic teaching of Judaism is interpreted.[1] To a considerable extent the Old Testament represents the history of the Jewish people in the land of Israel. The *Torah*, although sometimes referred to loosely as the entire Old Testament, or even the entire Jewish religious writings, is essentially the five books of Moses, which were received through divine revelation in Sinai. These books constitute the core of Jewish law, including the economic laws which adherents to Judaism are expected to practise in their daily lives.

This chapter starts by reviewing the laws governing economic relations in the *Torah*, focusing in particular on the ten commandments and the teachings in Deuteronomy and Leviticus. Then different areas of economic life are considered: notably the creation, ownership and distribution of wealth; the laws on usury and their implications for banking and finance; markets and good trading practices and the role of government in regulating economic activity. When examining these issues the emphasis is not only on the divine revelation in the *Torah*, but also how this has been interpreted by Rabbinical scholars throughout the Jewish world, especially since the industrial revolution in Europe.

---

[1] Jacob Neusner, *Judaism and its Social Metaphors: Israel in the History of Jewish Thought*, Cambridge University Press, 1989, pp. 8–18.

Judaism is not a religion fossilised in Old Testament law and teachings, but rather a living and developing faith which has been remarkably adaptable to the changing circumstances in which Jews have found themselves. It provides its own unique view of the world, including a distinct position on economic matters. In this context it is relevant to consider the workings of the modern economy of Israel. To what extent have modern Israeli governments simply followed secularist economic policies, or has the fact that the country is a professedly Jewish state influenced the direction of the economy? There is also the issue of how practising Jews of the *diaspora* are to conduct their everyday business. What rules should govern their transactions with their *gentile* neighbours, and how are they as minorities to fit in to economies which are either secular or influenced by other religious traditions? Reference will be made to recent studies by economists and theologians which re-examine Jewish law from the perspective of modern economics and political economy.

JEWISH LAW AND ECONOMICS

As the revelation of the *Torah* relates to a people, the children of Israel, and provides the basis for the laws of the land of Israel, it is especially interesting to consider its implications for both the economic behaviour of individuals and Jewish businesses at the microeconomic level, as well as for government policy in Israel. This concern extends to states with substantial Jewish minorities or where Jews occupy positions of economic power at the macro level. In the case of the latter there is the question of whether this will involve a conflict between individual religious conscience and public responsibilities to both Jews and *gentiles*. *Yahweh*'s followers, God's chosen people, initially lived in an Egypt where the majority worshipped other deities. Subsequently, when the Jews were delivered to the land of Israel by Moses, they had peoples with other sets of beliefs as their neighbours. Hence the issue of how to conduct business with *gentiles* is as old as Judaism itself, and the *Torah* provides explicit guidance on this. It is clear that the Jewish tribes of ancient Israel traded extensively with their neighbours, especially the Phoenicians, who were the most dynamic trading people of the region. The latter may, in Jewish eyes, have worshipped false idols, but this was no bar to normal commercial relations.

Jews must practise Jewish law as set out in the *Torah*, the Pentateuch, consisting of the books of Genesis, Exodus, Leviticus, Numbers and Deuteronomy. After the destruction of the temple, and the final collapse of the Jewish monarchy, Judaism became increasingly the religion of the book, the source of inspiration for Jews in their long exile. That is not to say the religion was fossilised, as Rabbinical interpretation has always been important, and in many respects became increasingly so as the Rabbis lead the spiritual life of the people in the lands of the *diaspora* through the many sufferings and persecutions. Jewish law, the *Halakhah*, is not systematic despite being derived from the *Torah*, as different views are possible. One issue is what weight to give to each opinion, the opinions of better-known and respected Rabbis being treated more seriously than those of the lesser-known, and majority views being generally accepted rather than those of a minority. Economic life changed through the ages, and each country presented a different set of opportunities depending on the material circumstances. The *Torah* had to be rediscovered in the light of these challenges, as indeed did other Jewish traditions, including those of the 'oral *Torah*', which was eventually written down by the patriarch Yehuda ha-Nisi as the *Mishnah* (Hebrew for repetition or learning) and the *Talmud*, the Babylonian and Jerusalem commentaries on the *Mishnah*.[2]

All this may seem complicated, and indeed it is, as the Babylonian *Talmud* or *haggadah* consists of 6000 folio pages commenting on virtually every single aspect of life, including the economic.[3] This however represents the authoritative source for the teaching and religious laws for Jewish orthodoxy, the concern not being dogmas or tests of faith, as there is little disagreement over such matters in orthodox Judaism, but rather with 'right living' under the *Torah*, including making sure economic actions conform to the religious law. Study of the *Talmud* is necessary because of the complexities of economic life, as it provides guidance to the *Halakhah*, literally the way to be taken.

[2] Isidore Epstein, *Judaism*, Penguin Books, London, 1990, pp. 121–31.
[3] Hans Küng, *Judaism*, Crossroad, New York, 1992.

At the core of Judaic law is the decalogue, the ten commandments. Three of these are concerned specifically with economic matters, the commandments not to labour on the Sabbath, not to steal and not to covet a neighbour's possessions (Exodus, 20:8–11, 15, 17). The commandment to keep the Sabbath holy is spelt out in some detail:

> Remember the Sabbath day by keeping it holy. Six days you shall labour and do all your work, but the seventh day is a Sabbath to the Lord your God. On it you shall not do any work, neither your son or daughter, nor your manservant or maidservant, nor your animals, nor the alien within your gates. For in six days the Lord made the heavens and the earth, the sea, and all that is in them, but he rested on the seventh day. Therefore the Lord blessed the Sabbath day and made it holy.[4]

Many Christian as well as Jewish writers interpret this commandment literally, and economists interested in the teachings of Judaism often take it as their starting point. Meir Tamari, for example, perhaps the most lucid Jewish writer on the implications of Judaism for economic activity, stresses the limitations imposed by time.[5]

As well as the need to abstain from work on the fifty-two Sabbaths each year, there are also eight major Jewish festivals, the week of mourning for close relatives who have died, and the mandatory week after his wedding when the bridegroom is not permitted to work. There is also the obligation on Jews to spend as much time as possible on the study of the *Torah,*

---

[4] All biblical quotations in this chapter and the next are from the New International Version, originally published in the United States by the International Bible Society in 1973. The scripture was used for the Student Bible produced by the Zondervan Publishing House of Grand Rapids, Michigan in 1986, and adapted and republished for the international market under the title the NIV Insight Bible by Hodder and Stoughton of London in 1992. This version was chosen because of its international popularity, especially amongst University staff and their students, and the accuracy of the text. Some Jewish readers may be unhappy with quotations taken from a Christian text for this chapter on Judaism, but this was done in order to ensure consistency with the quotations in the next chapter from the New Testament.

[5] Meir Tamari, *With All Your Possessions: Jewish Ethics and Economic Life*, The Free Press, Macmillan, New York, 1987, pp. 25ff.

although as Tamari points out, this has been interpreted in the *Mishnah* to mean that people should not work excessively in pursuit of material rewards at the expense of their spiritual obligations. On the other hand, there is also the implication that religious devotion should not be at the expense of earning a living, as without material provision spiritual activity cannot continue.[6]

The commandment prohibiting stealing is not contentious on moral grounds, indeed there is no major religion which sanctions such behaviour, but the economic and social implications of this prohibition are worth stressing. Jewish religious law was designed to ensure the affairs of ancient Israel were conducted in an orderly manner, and that anarchy did not prevail. A prohibition on theft meant that property rights had to be respected, arguably including those of the twelve tribes of Israel as much as rights over personal possessions.[7] The extent of ownership rights can be debated however, as neither individual nor tribal rights are absolute. Meir Tamari points out that the prohibition against stealing was not merely on social grounds, but because the Divine is the source of all wealth, and the ultimate owner of property. Respect for this property is therefore a religious obligation, and not just a social duty.[8]

The penalty for theft in the Jewish penal code is the return of the stolen property plus a fine equal to the value of the property, rather than imprisonment or physical punishment, which can include amputation in the case of Islamic law. The law provides for the punishment in relation to the crime against man. The retribution for the sin against the Deity is another matter, for which the criminal will also be called to account, but that is not a matter for the courts of man to decide, but rather the Deity himself.

The commandment not to covet a neighbour's possessions is concerned both with economic behaviour and attitudes to property. This final commandment goes well beyond prohibiting theft, by making envy, the thought as well as the deed, a

---

[6] Ibid., p. 27.

[7] James D. Martin, 'Israel as a tribal society', in R.E. Clements, (ed.) *The World of Ancient Israel: Sociological, Anthropological and Political Perspective*, Cambridge University Press, 1989, pp. 95–117.

[8] Meir Tamari, *All Your Possessions*, p. 39.

sin. In this the *Torah* goes much further than other religious law into the economic sphere, as material longings are often relative rather than absolute, that is they relate to what others already have and which those without aspire to possess. The theories of consumer behaviour in modern macroeconomics include, for example, Dusenberry's relative income hypothesis, which states that consumption is related to that of the peer group, which may be comprised of neighbours, business associates or others.[9] The higher the income of the peer group, the greater the consumption level, a type of 'keeping up with the Joneses' hypothesis, which much empirical evidence seems to support. Does this conflict with the commandment not to covet a neighbour's income? Clearly, as with most law, religious or secular, different interpretations are possible. If to covet refers to the wish to have the possessions which actually belong to the neighbour, then this could represent a wish to steal, even though theft may not actually occur. Alternatively, it may refer to the desire to have possessions which are the same as the neighbours', in which case the commandment is implying that it is the material desires which result from envy which are sinful, a much broader issue.

WEALTH AND POSSESSIONS

The *Torah* does not state that there is any sin in the possession of material goods, indeed they are seen as a blessing. God designated a geographic area for the Jews to live in, the land of Israel, which was flowing with milk and honey, not an austere barren desert region. Much of the Old Testament can almost be read as a celebration of the abundance which the Divine has provided for His followers. Economics may stress the concept of limited resources, but scarcity is not something which usually comes to mind when reading the Bible, despite the efforts of some economists to interpret Old Testament teaching as a solution to the scarcity problem.[10]

[9] James S. Dusenberry, *Income, Saving and the Theory of Consumer Behaviour*, Harvard University Press, Cambridge, Massachusetts, 1949.
[10] Barry Gordon, *The Economic Problem in Biblical and Patristic Thought*, E.J. Brill, Leiden, 1989, pp. 1–5.

Although there are references in the *Talmud* to the virtues of poverty, this is viewed as outside the norm. As Meir Tamari asserts:

> By and large, there are no vows of poverty in Judaism as a means of achieving a Divinely blessed state of affairs. There are no accusing fingers pointing at those engaged in normal economic activities and the earning of material goods . . . Mainstream Judaism saw man's material welfare as a reward from Heaven, a gift from the Deity, and therefore as something not intrinsically bad, but rather to be valued and prized.[11]

It is seen as legitimate to pray for prosperity; indeed, on the holiest day of the Jewish year, *Yom Kippur*, the book of *parnasah*, a collection of writings concerning economic and material welfare, is opened. After the atonement service, a special prayer is offered, asking for the coming year to be one of abundance, so that Jews will not have to be dependent on others for their livelihood. This tradition has been handed down from the time of the ancient Temple in Jerusalem.

That is not to say that there was abundance for everyone in ancient Israel, as the land contained beggars as well as the rich, slaves as well as kings, nobles and those who humbly toiled. Ancient Israel was not an egalitarian society, and there were clearly considerable differences in income and wealth. This is not viewed as an unjust state of affairs, but rather as a natural outcome of the way the society was structured, and perhaps even arguably a recognition that, because people's talents and abilities differed, so their material rewards differed. There is no virtue in poverty in Judaism, indeed it is to be avoided as it involves unnecessary suffering. That is not to say that the poor are to blame for their own fate; often it results from unfortunate circumstances which could not be helped, including bad health or accidents. Indeed there is a recognition that those who have enjoyed the bounty of the earth, perhaps through exercising their God given talents, have a duty to help the poor and needy. The Jewish societies of ancient Israel were tribal in nature, and there was an obligation to help all members of the tribe. This tradition of care for all those within the group has continued in some closely-knit Jewish

---

[11] Tamari, *All Your Possessions*, p. 30.

communities to this day, and even when there are disagreements and major differences of opinion within the group, a basic solidarity remains.

There is provision in the *Torah* for addressing the inequalities which inevitably exist in any economy. This is not so much a matter of redistribution, but rather one of creating a level playing field for each generation so that material advantages acquired through one generation's acquisition of wealth are not handed down. In the *Torah* there is much discussion of land rights, land and labour being the crucial factors of production in ancient Israel rather than capital. As the ultimate owner of land is God, humans do not have the right to sell it permanently, or indeed to acquire a freehold through purchase. In Leviticus the implications of the year of Jubilee for land are spelt out: 'Consecrate the fiftieth year and proclaim liberty throughout the land to all its inhabitants. It shall be a jubilee for you; each one of you is to return to his family property and each to his own clan.'[12] This would seem to imply that all slaves are to be freed, and that those who have leased or purchased land should hand it back to the original owner. The book of Leviticus teaches that the allocation of tribal land is made by God, and must be respected. Tribal society had little 'natural' material inequality, but through people using their talents this would inevitably arise as some would be more economically successful than others. Land could be purchased, but the right of ownership expired at the next Jubilee, and the number of years left for harvesting crops could be reflected in the purchase price. It would be interesting to see evidence on how this worked in practice.

There was, in other words, nothing wrong in market transactions in land, but these should not result in the tribal order which had been determined by God being changed. Market processes should not determine land distribution in the long run, as this might make accumulated wealth the master rather than God. It is recognised that circumstances may arise where someone facing financial difficulties may want to sell the right to their property until the next Jubilee. In such cases relatives have the right to come and redeem what has been sold. If the seller finds his financial position has improved, he has the

[12] Leviticus, 25:10.

right to purchase the property back at a price which reflects the number of harvests up to the next Jubilee.[13]

Some question how effective these provisions are in alleviating hardship. Even if the Hebrew verses are translated to imply that the relative had the duty, and not merely the right, to purchase back the land sold by his impoverished kinsman, it is evident that it is only relatives who can afford the redemption price who are obliged to make the repurchase. The hardship facing a poor kinsman with poor relatives is not aided.[14] Arguably what is really at stake is the honour of the tribe, which justifies the rights of repurchase, although, in the longer term, in the year of the Jubilee tribal rights will be restored in any case.

The position regarding houses in a walled city is regarded as different from that of open land, perhaps because cities are regarded as works of man, but the countryside as a work of God. Houses can be sold subject to the seller retaining a right of redemption for up to a year after the transaction. If this is not exercised the sale becomes permanent, and the house can be passed on by the buyer to his descendants. In the case of such urban property there will be no return to the original owner in the year of the Jubilee,[15] which could imply greater disparities in wealth and property in cities than in rural areas.

There is support for the poor in the *Torah* through the laws governing agricultural production and good farming practice. The position is set out in Leviticus:

> When you reap the harvest of your land, do not reap to the very edges of your field or gather the gleanings of your harvest. Do not go over your vineyard a second time or pick up the grapes that have fallen. Leave them for the poor and the alien.[16]

This implies that there are poor and landless in the land of Israel whom those fortunate enough to have land should make some provision for. In Deuteronomy the need to set aside one tenth of all produce for the poor and the needy is spelt out:

---

[13] Leviticus, 25:28.
[14] Eryl W. Davies, 'Land: its rights and privileges', in R.E. Clements, (ed.), *The World of Ancient Israel*, pp. 360–1.
[15] Leviticus, 25:30.
[16] Leviticus, 19:9–10.

> When you have finished setting aside a tenth of all your produce in the third year, the year of the tithe, you shall give it to the Levite, the alien, the fatherless and the widow, so that they may eat in your towns and be satisfied.[17]

The rules governing such offerings are specified in great detail in the *Mishanic* laws on agriculture in the *Tractate Peah*.[18] Similar provisions are made for the support of the priests through setting aside part of the harvest.[19] In both cases redistribution is involved, either on the basis of a tithe system, which represents a tax in kind, or through leaving output which can only be exploited through additional effort. One implication of the latter is that subsistence is available for the needy, but only if they work for it, an interesting solution for handling welfare. Another implication may be that the cultivator's time might be better spent in worship or studying the *Torah*, rather than exploiting the last grain of the harvest. The over-harvesting of production should be avoided, especially if this is only the result of material greed and at the expense of the poor.

Although the children of Israel were led by Moses into a land of abundance, for which they should be thankful, there are concerns expressed in the Old Testament that the newly rich will forget the fact that it is God who has brought them their wealth.

> Otherwise, when you eat and are satisfied, when you build fine houses and settle down, and when your herds and flocks grow large and your silver and gold increase and all you have has multiplied, then your heart will become proud and you will forget the Lord your God who brought you out of the land of slavery.[20]

There is almost a nostalgia for the simplicity of the desert, and a recognition that wealth and possessions can bring complacency, and encourage people to forget their origins and their debt to God. One danger is that the accumulation of material

[17] Deuteronomy, 26:12.
[18] Roger Brooks, *Support for the Poor in the Mishanic Law of Agriculture*, Brown Judaic Study, number 43, Scholars Press, Chico, California, 1983, pp. 17–39.
[19] Alan Peck, *The Priestly Gift in Mishnah*, Brown Judaic Study, number 20, Scholars Press, Chico, California, 1981, pp. 1–28.
[20] Deuteronomy, 8:12–14.

riches become the driving force in society, and create a distraction from the worship of God.

Meir Tamari points out how the Hebrew concept of modesty, *tzniyut*, not only implies not wearing revealing clothing but also refers to the moderation to be shown in the consumption of food and the acquisition of excessive personal belongings. Ostentatious and luxurious living are not regarded as desirable ends, not only because of the social jealousy that may result, but because such lifestyles are thought to be inappropriate for devout Jews. Rabbis and religious Jew have restrained their consumption expenditure over the centuries, and possessed relatively simple furniture, modest houses and inexpensive clothing. Maimonides, the name used to refer to the influential Rabbi Moshe ben Maimon, who lived in twelfth-century Egypt, codified into law the position on eating for scholars of the *Torah*. Such religious scholars were proscribed from participating in public feasting; they should eat normal meals at home, the only exception being meals associated with a religious precept, such as their own marriage.[21] Meir Tamiri cites regulations stipulating modesty in consumption from Jewish communities in the Rhineland of the thirteenth century, Castile in the fifteenth century and Poland from the mid-sixteenth century.[22] Tamiri also cites the examples of the *Admor* (spiritual leader) of Gur in modern Israel, who encouraged his followers to move from Jerusalem where property prices were high to modest residential areas of Ashdod and Hatzor. Many of the religious *kibbutzim* on the West Bank have spartan dwellings and their inhabitants consume rather basic communal meals.

MONEY, BANKING AND INTEREST

Jews have been involved in moneylending and moneychanging over the centuries in Europe, North Africa and the Middle East. From the early days of banking in Lombardy to the international financial centres of the late twentieth century, many of the leading bankers and financiers have been Jewish. Dealing

---

[21] Tamari, *All Your Possessions*, pp. 56–7.
[22] Ibid., pp. 57–8.

in usury, which was proscribed for medieval Christians, and is still proscribed for Muslims, was seen as legitimate for Jews. How were such dealings justified, and what is the position of the *Torah* and other Jewish writings on these issues?

There are several verses dealing with interest in Leviticus and Deuteronomy. The poor in particular should be exempted from interest obligations according to Leviticus: 'If one of your countrymen becomes poor and is unable to support himself among you, help him . . . Do not take interest of any kind from him . . . You must not lend him money at interest or sell him food at a profit.'[23] This could be interpreted to mean that interest transactions are not themselves prohibited in normal circumstances, but when fellow countrymen are in financial difficulties, they are not to be exploited by such payments being demanded. Deuteronomy appears to go further, however, and it is the verses in this book that were the basis for the medieval Christian view of interest as being undesirable: 'Do not charge your brother interest, whether on money or food or anything else that may earn interest.'[24] As this follows verses prohibiting prostitution and dealing with personal hygiene, it could be inferred that interest transactions are classified with unclean matters. Yet the following verse can be interpreted as stating that interest transactions are permissible with non-Jews: 'You may charge a foreigner interest, but not a brother Israelite, so that the Lord your God may bless you in everything you put your hand to in the land you are entering to possess.'[25]

These verses were used to justify Jewish involvement in moneylending and banking in Europe from medieval times onwards, especially as many were prohibited from owning land, and prevented from earning a livelihood by other means because of legislation or customs that discriminated against non-Christians.

Deuteronomy not only deals with the issue of interest, but also with the collateral which is often required by lenders when loans are made. Limits are placed on the type of collateral which it is legitimate to accept. A worker's livelihood should not be endangered by the potential seizure of any security offered in

---

[23] Leviticus, 25:35–38.
[24] Deuteronomy, 19:19.
[25] Deuteronomy, 19:20.

return for a loan: 'Do not take a pair of millstones – not even the upper one – as security for a debt, because that would be taking a man's livelihood as security.'[26]

The manner in which a debtor with a secured loan is treated is also a matter of concern, as is the financial state of the debtor.

> When you make a loan of any kind to your neighbour, do not go into his house to get what he is offering as a pledge. Stay outside and let the man to whom you are making the loan bring the pledge out to you. If the man is poor, do not go to sleep with his pledge in your possession.[27]

There is nothing wrong with accepting collateral, but the dignity of those who mortgage their property in this way must be respected, and the poor should not be exploited.

Whether such restrictions also apply to loans to *gentiles* has been an issue of debate amongst Rabbinical scholars. Some, notably Maimonides, have interpreted the law not to lend at interest to Jews as an obligation to charge interest to *gentiles* by interpreting the Hebrew *tashikh* as meaning 'you shall' rather than 'you may'.[28] As Maimonides became almost a law maker, because of the respect for his philosophical works and his commentaries on the *Mishnah*, this position on interest became respectable throughout the medieval Jewish world. Some commentators have suggested that charging interest to *gentiles* in Europe from the thirteenth century onwards ensured that relations with Christians were kept on a business footing, while those with fellow Jews were more friendly and intimate, being based on exchanging favours and close mutual trust. This reinforced the bonds within the Jewish community, and prevented assimilation with the majority Christian population.[29]

As the Jews throughout medieval Europe were usually prevented from owning land and suffered discrimination in employment, often being refused membership of the guilds of craftsmen and traders, their scope for earning a livelihood was

---

[26] Deuteronomy, 24:6.
[27] Deuteronomy, 24:10–13.
[28] Tamari, *All Your Possessions*, p. 180.
[29] Léon Poliakov, *Jewish Bankers and the Holy See: From the Thirteenth to the Seventeenth Century*, Routledge and Kegan Paul, London, 1977, p. 16.

restricted. Moneylending and moneychanging were occupations which were open to Jews, however, especially as many Christians felt dealing in interest was unholy, a position much debated in the church following the work of Thomas Aquinas.[30] There were circumstances under which Christians could deal with credit, for example in the conduct of trade, although simply dealing in money itself was more doubtful, and banking was seen as morally suspect.[31] Even more restrictive conditions applied in North Africa and the Middle East, as Muslims were prohibited from dealing in *riba*, which can be interpreted as applying to all forms of interest, an issue discussed in Chapter 4. In the Muslim world there was, however, less anti-Jewish discrimination, and an absence of the anti-Semitism which manifested itself in repeated persecutions throughout the countries of Christendom.

Léon Poliakov saw the Jews as having a competitive advantage in moneylending, banking and finance in medieval Europe, not merely because Christians withdrew from activities such as pawnbroking, but also because they were not subject to restitution by the ecclesiastical authorities. Like Christians they were obliged to pay taxes, but Poliakov in his research into Italian legal records on commerce and taxation could only find one instance, in Pisa in 1317, where a Jewish moneylender was obliged to make a payment to an ecclesiastical tribunal.[32] Furthermore, because of the limited range of employment opportunities open to Jews, they had a strong motivation to acquire financial skills and expertise, which were passed on from generation to generation. The fact that Jewish moneylenders maintained close contact with their fellow Jewish moneylenders, and provided each other with interest free loans, meant that they had additional financial resources which could be called upon if necessary. There evolved what could almost be regarded as an informal Jewish inter-bank market based on trust between co-religionists.

Moneychanging and credit for international commerce was

---

[30] George O'Brien, *An Essay on Mediaeval Economic Teaching*, Augustus M. Kelly Publishers, New York, 1967, p. 194.
[31] Barry Gordon, *Economic Analysis Before Adam Smith*, Macmillan, London, 1975, p. 170.
[32] Léon Poliakov, *Jewish Bankers*, p. 51.

facilitated by the fact that the Jewish community in one state maintained frequent, usually friendly, contacts with Jews in other European countries, and the same contacts also existed across North Africa and the Middle East. As a consequence they were in a good position to arrange export and import finance and the exchange of currencies. They had better channels of information than any of their Christian or Muslim rivals, and thus an advantage in terms of the economics of search.

One major advantage of moneylending and moneychanging as an occupation was that it was less time consuming than hard labour in agriculture or in craft activities in the medieval world. This allowed more time for religious observance and the study of the *Torah*. Money was not seen as a barren commodity,[33] indeed Yitschak Abarbanel, the financier and Rabbinical scholar in the Spain of Ferdinand and Isabella, saw no distinction between making a profit out of money and getting a return from dealing in commodities such as wine or corn.[34] The attitudes in the Jewish *diaspora* towards money and finance were essentially pragmatic, to some extent of necessity, at a time when religious dogma was dominant amongst Christians and Muslims over these issues.

MARKETS, FAIR TRADING AND GOVERNMENT REGULATION

In the *Torah* markets are viewed as a natural part of economic life. The benefits of a market system are not extolled, but neither is there any inherent wrong in market transactions. Buying and selling are simply seen as normal everyday activities, with transactions permitted in durable and non-durable commodities, housing and land. Dealings in the latter are subject to the provisions of the Jubilee, but apart from this there are no limits on what private property may be traded. There is a recognition that markets can be abused however,

---

[33] In contrast to the view of Thomas Aquinas, who, while recognising that money could serve as a medium of exchange and a unit of account, believed that money was barren and without value. See Barry Gordon, *Economic Analysis*, pp. 159–65.

[34] Tamari, *All Your Possessions*, p. 181.

and in particular that one party may exploit another, perhaps by having greater buying or selling power, or simply having better access to information. For example 'If you sell land to one of your countrymen or buy from him, do not take advantage of each other.'[35] The emphasis is on fair trading, and on honesty in all dealings: 'Do not use dishonest standards when measuring length, weight or quantity. Use honest scales and honest weights, an honest *ephah* (a dry measure) and an honest *hin* (a liquid measure).'[36] Deception is regarded as a likely temptation to be avoided at all costs, as high ethical standards should be maintained in business transactions.

Market intervention by the authorities can be justifiable, including price regulation. Tamari cites the case where, in the last days of the second Temple in ancient Israel, women were required to offer a pigeon for each birth or miscarriage they had as part of the rites of purification. This was causing the price of pigeons to rise, so that the poor could no longer afford them. Rabbi Shimon ben Gamiel announced that henceforth each woman would only be obliged to offer one pigeon, and as a result the price immediately fell.[37] There is a notion of a just price in Judaism, the concept of *ona'ah*, which seems to imply not only an honest price, but a price which is fair in the sense of not being exploitative. *Ona'ah* only applies to transactions between Jews however. Honesty is required in all dealings with *gentiles*, but there is no specific restraint required if the Jewish partner is in a superior bargaining position to protect the financial position of a non-Jew.[38] This question of economic discrimination in dealings between Jews and non-Jews is a sensitive issue, but it arises not only with respect to the notion of a just price in Judaism, but also in interest dealings as already mentioned.

Such discrimination by Jews in their economic dealings has to be seen in the context of tribal societies where each tribe protected its own members. In commercial life this can be interpreted in terms of mutual financial help in times of need, a kind of insurance underwriting for members only. There is

---

[35] Leviticus, 25:14.
[36] Leviticus, 19:35–36.
[37] Tamari, *All Your Possessions*, p. 93.
[38] Ibid., p. 96.

also the matter of the moral standing of the Jew in his own community which would be undermined if he disregarded the law in the *Torah*. A *gentile* cannot be bound in the same way by Jewish law, and therefore is inevitably viewed by Jews in different terms to fellow believers.

Nowhere in the *Torah* is unrestricted competition seen as a virtue. Indeed, there is support for restrictive trade agreements in the *Talmud*. Artisans and merchants can reach agreements to restrict competition by establishing entry barriers, fix prices and determine the quantity of goods produced. Such agreements can be recognised under Jewish law provided all the parties agree, and this can be interpreted as applying to guilds of craftsmen and traders, and in the modern world, cartels and labour unions.[39] The authority for this comes from Deuteronomy: 'Do not move your neighbour's boundary stone set up by your predecessors in the inheritance you receive in the land the Lord your God is giving you to possess.'[40] Tamari points out that this refers to the concept of *hasagat g'vul*, which was distinguished from theft by rabbinical scholars. It is taken to mean encroachment on each other's livelihood.[41] Traders, craftsmen and workers should have their livelihoods protected, if necessary, by restrictive agreements. The emphasis is on economic security and respect for the work and the position of others. In such circumstances economic change and occupational mobility can still arise through new opportunities, but not by taking away a fellow Jew's existing opportunities to earn a living.

As the land of ancient Israel was a tribal society of small communities, the question arises of how the economic laws in the *Torah* are to be applied in the modern nation state, and what the regulatory role of government should be. There would appear to be some scepticism expressed in the book of Samuel regarding the position of rulers: '(The king) will take the best of your fields and vineyards and olive groves and give them to his attendants. He will take a tenth of your grain and of your vintage and give it to his officials and attendants.'[42] The fear

---

[39] Ibid., p. 107.
[40] Deuteronomy, 19:14.
[41] Tamari, *All Your Possessions*, p. 108.
[42] I Samuel, 8:14–15.

seems to be that rulers simply tax income and expropriate wealth from their subjects, and provide little in return. Nevertheless, in spite of the arguments of Samuel, the peoples of ancient Israel still wanted a king, presumably for protection, and the book makes clear that God has no objection in principle to there being a king.[43]

Tamari interprets *Halakhic* sources[44] as implying that Jews, regardless of where they reside must obey the law of the land, *dina d'malkhuta*, even if the authorities are *gentile*.[45] This includes an obligation to pay taxes levied by a non-Jewish ruler. Often in medieval Europe and the Ottoman Empire, the Jewish community authorities would organise the collection of the taxes and hand over the proceeds as a lump sum, even where the taxes were arbitrary and confiscatory, a kind of fine imposed on Jews for the right to live in *gentile* societies. The main concern of the Jewish authorities was to protect their community, and if this involved paying taxes to *gentile* rulers, then this would be done.

The main principle of Jewish taxation is that there should be some relationship between payment and benefit.[46] Tamari suggests that the reasoning behind this utility concept was the notion that to derive a benefit from another person's money without his or her consent is theft.[47] This obviously has major implications for progressive taxation involving redistribution, although in a democracy it can be argued that tax payers have given their consent through their votes. Even if the government imposing the redistributive taxes does not consist of the party or parties which the Jewish electorate have voted for, by participating in the elections, they have given recognition to the system, and accorded legitimacy to the government's fiscal policy. Under an autocratic regime the utility principle applies, however, with the payment of taxation in return for protection in medieval Europe and the Ottoman Empire. The

[43] I Samuel, 8:22.
[44] Teachings derived directly from scripture, see Isidore Epstein, *Judaism*, p. 115.
[45] Tamari, *All Your Possessions*, pp. 215–16.
[46] For an account for the history of western economic thinking on the benefit approach to taxation see Richard Musgrave, *The Theory of Public Finance*, McGraw Hill Kogakusha, New York and Tokyo, 1959, pp. 61–89.
[47] Tamari, *All Your Possessions*, p. 219.

Roman Catholic and Orthodox rulers of medieval Europe did
not always carry out their part of the bargain, as the persecutions
in Spain and the pogroms of Poland and Russia demonstrated.
This was one reason why European Jews were influenced by
Luther, who argued that a ruler should be a secular Prince
accountable to the people and protecting them from the religious authorities of the church in Rome.

THE THEORY OF PRICES IN *TALMUDIC* LITERATURE

Ephraim Kleiman of the Hebrew University adopts a rather
different approach from that of Tamari.[48] Kleiman's work is
arguably more incisive, although he covers much less ground
than Tamari in terms of economics. Nevertheless, Kleiman
is not only a good analytical economist, but he also has an
excellent knowledge of *Talmudic* literature and is able to
appraise its contribution to economics in the light of the
economic system of antiquity. He provides the reader with a
properly referenced view of what the *Talmud* actually says on
economic matters, but at the same time is realistic about its
limitations when viewed from the perspective of modern economic theory. The *Talmud* provides some interesting insights
into the economic thinking of the time, which is worthy of
investigation as it anticipates some of the subsequent developments in value theory. There are both parallels and contrasts
with the economic thinking of the early Christian fathers, and
indeed there appears to have been some debate between them
and the Rabbinical scholars in Palestine at the time the Jerusalem *Talmud* was written.[49] The level of economic analysis by
Jewish writers around AD 200 was certainly sophisticated for
the age, although Kleiman does not suggest that the economics
of the *Talmud* should be substituted for modern theory, or that
it should be applied in Israel or anywhere else.[50]

---

[48] Ephraim Kleiman, ' "Just price" in *Talmudic* literature', *History of Political
Economy*, Vol. 19, No. 1, 1987, pp. 23–45.
[49] Ibid., p. 43.
[50] A detailed economic analysis of the *Talmudic* literature has been carried
out by Roman A. Ohrenstein. For summary details see Roman A. Ohrenstein,
'Economic analysis in *Talmudic* literature: some ancient studies of value',

The most useful contribution of *Talmudic* literature appears to be to the concept of a just price. Price regulation has already been referred to in the previous section, but Ephraim Kleiman's treatment is considered here, as he relates it to the history of economic thought, and not the working of actual economies as Tamari attempts to do. Kleiman, like Tamari, sees the *Talmudic* concept of the just price as coming from the teaching in Leviticus regarding fraudulent dealings, although he has also clearly read the Christian Scholastic literature on this topic. Kleiman explores the circumstances in which it is legitimate to revoke a deal which is considered as unjust, and sees this as being defined functionally in terms of a market information search.[51] A day was seen as too long a period to be permitted to revoke a deal. The buyer or seller could be allowed a period of hours to ascertain that a just price was paid for a good, after which the deal was binding. The *Talmudic* literature is concerned with the rights of sellers, and underpayment by buyers, as deception can take place on both sides.[52] There are divergent opinions in the *Talmudic* literature on the merits of government intervention on price controls, but it is recognised that official prices are 'sticky' and that price cutting can 'ease the market'.[53] Indeed, Roman Ohrenstein points out how price competition could be used to expand the market, although non-price competition through product differentiation was also justified in the *Talmud*.[54]

The ethical objective of the *ona'ah* rules governing transactions in the *Talmud* was, according to Kleiman, to prevent inequality of information having consequences for income

American Journal of Economics and Sociology, Vol. 39, No. 1, January 1980, p. 22. The review here concentrates on the studies by Kleiman, whose writings overlap and confirm the work of Ohrenstein, largely because Kleiman is a mainstream economist, while Ohrenstein is more of a political economist concerned with broader sociological issues. Ohrenstein's distinctive analysis of self-interest in *Talmudic* literature and his work on money in the business cycle is considered later in this chapter.

[51] Ephraim Kleiman, 'Just price', p. 26.
[52] Ibid., pp. 28–9.
[53] Ibid., p. 35.
[54] Roman A. Ohrenstein, 'Economic thought in *Talmudic* literature in the light of modern economics', *American Journal of Economics and Sociology*, Vol. 27, No. 2, 1968, pp. 190–2.

distribution.[55] There was no attempt to question the pricing system itself, and there was no worry about the need to reconcile 'intrinsic' with exchange value,[56] an issue much debated by the Christian Scholastics, as will be seen in the next chapter.[57] There was, however, a notion of intrinsic value in Judaism, which had legal though not pricing implications, which will be discussed when the work of Neusner is considered in a later section.

Kleiman believes Spengler's assertion that the economic thoughts of the ancients could be described as *protoeconomics*, 'incomplete visions of imperfectly conceptualised worlds.'[58] For Kleiman this applies to the *Talmud* as much as other early literature on economic thought. Kleiman provides as an example of this the understanding of *Talmudic* writers of opportunity cost. They did not appreciate the concept fully in its modern economic sense, but they came close to this notion with the laws on material compensation for injury. Thus casting aspersions on a bride's virginity, which might be considered to reduce her value, involved compensating the bride's father, and not being permitted to divorce the woman in question.[59]

Kleiman shows how the *Talmudic* writers had a concept of human capital valuation. This applied, for example, to material compensation to a husband of a rape victim by the rapist, or to the husband of a pregnant woman who has miscarried as a result of a deliberate injury, in this case payable by the man causing the injury.[60] Someone who is blinded in one eye or loses a limb is to be valued as a slave in a market for purposes of compensation, the idea being to assess how much the person was worth before the injury, and how much afterwards.

[55] Kleiman, 'Just price', p. 39.
[56] Ibid., p. 41.
[57] See also Raymond de Roover, 'The concept of the just price', *Journal of Economic History*, Vol. 18, No. 4., 1958, pp. 418–34; John T. Noonan, *The Scholastic Analysis of Usury*, Harvard University Press, 1957, pp. 82–99; Stephen T. Worland, *Scholasticism and Welfare Economics*, University of Notre Dame Press, 1967, pp. 16–19 and 250–63; and George O'Brien, op.cit., pp. 102–20.
[58] J.J. Spengler, *Origins of Economic Thought and Justice*, Carbondale, Illinois, 1980, p. xii, cited in Kleiman, 'Just price', p. 40.
[59] Ephraim Kleiman, 'Opportunity cost, human capital and some related concepts in *Talmudic* literature', *History of Political Economy*, Vol. 19, No. 3, 1987, p. 262.
[60] Ibid., p. 263.

The economic result, according to Kleiman, was based on 'the decline in the income the individual might be expected to earn in the future.'[61] In fact the *Talmud* goes further, taking into account in the assessment of compensation for injury whether the victim will be able to consume at the same level as before, or at a reduced level due to the injury. In the latter case, less compensation is required. In the case of an injured slave, there is the issue of how much compensation is to be paid to the slave, and what proportion to the master.[62] In the case of a Hebrew slave in temporary bondage, this would be determined by the length of the anticipated period of continuing bondage after the injury in relation to the expected life span as an injured free man.[63] This introduction of the time element shows just how sophisticated the rules for compensation in the *Talmud* became.

Roman Ohrenstein shows how in *Talmudic* literature the concept of *s'kbar b'teilo* or lost time was very close to the modern economic notion of opportunity cost.[64] It would be morally wrong for a Rabbi, a religious teacher, to be paid for his work, as this would imply profiting from preaching and interpreting the word of God. This also applied to judges and religious scholars. In practice however, some reward was necessary, simply in order for the Rabbi to survive, and this could be provided under the concept of *s'kbar b'teilo*. When the Rabbi is preaching or working on the religious texts, he cannot be doing other work. Therefore he is entitled to compensation for the work given up, this obviously being dependent on the work he is capable of doing.[65] This concept of lost time also applied to compensation for cancelled contracts. If workers had already brought their tools along, and set aside a certain period for a particular task, then they would have to be compensated for the remuneration they might have obtained by working elsewhere,

---

[61] Ibid., p. 267.

[62] Slavery was taken for granted in the ancient world, but in literature on the history of western economic thought the notion of workers having a market value was also seen as a useful analytical device. For example, Richard Cantillon, the eighteenth-century economist, used the concept of slavery as a standard approach in his valuation of human life.

[63] Kleiman, 'Opportunity cost', pp. 273–4.

[64] Roman A. Ohrenstein, 'Economic thought', pp. 185–6.

[65] Ibid., pp. 187–8.

rather than simply in relation to the value of the cancelled contract. If the workers are content to take a leisurely rest, then only partial compensation is required.[66]

RESOURCE ALLOCATION IN A PERFECT STATIC ECONOMY

Modern economics has been defined as the study of how scarce resources are allocated. Economic agents are assumed to act rationally, in the sense of their objective being to maximise welfare, usually, although not necessarily, in a material sense.[67] Markets are one means of allocating resources, the alternative being a command economy, or what Jacob Neusner refers to as a distributive economy.[68] Perhaps the greatest debate among economists, and certainly political economists, has been on the relative merits of market versus command economies, with the advocates of each system (or compromise positions) having their victories during different time periods. Most modern economists take as their starting point Adam Smith in the eighteenth century, or, in some cases, the physiocrats in the seventeenth century, but there have been few attempts to consider how resources were allocated in ancient societies, including ancient Israel. Morris Silver is one of a select group of economists interested in this field of study,[69] his major contribution being to refute the view of Karl Polanyi,[70] the economic and social anthropologist, that markets became important only in the eighteenth and nineteenth centuries.

Jacob Neusner clarifies the position of the *Mishnah*, the oral *Torah*, on the role of markets and allocative issues more generally. The codes contained in the *Mishnah* apply the teaching

[66] Ibid., p. 189.
[67] Lionel Robbins, who did so much to further 'positive' economics in the mid-twentieth century, tried to separate economics from ethics. He was however very concerned with 'non-material' welfare. See Denis P. O'Brien, *Lionel Robbins*, Macmillan, London, 1988, p. 23.
[68] Jacob Neusner, *The Economics of the Mishnah*, University of Chicago Press, 1990, pp. 5–7.
[69] Morris Silver, *Economic Structures of the Ancient Near East*, Croom Helm, London, 1985, pp. 1–3.
[70] Karl Polanyi, *The Livelihood of Man*, edited by Harry W. Pearson, Academic Press, New York, 1981.

of the written *Torah*, through a series of terse pronouncements
and examples, to matters of everyday living in ancient Israel,
including economic life. To understand the significance of the
Mishnah, it has to be seen in the context of its authors' particular view of the world, and the position and purpose of man in
relation to God and society. A lengthy quotation from Neusner
sums up the essence of the *Mishnah*:

> It is that the Israelite world – Jews in Palestine/Israelites in
> the land of Israel – forms a world unto itself, a world order
> of enduring statis, in which no significant change will disturb
> the stable society. This world order, down below, attains
> that enduring, indeed eternal, statis because it serves to com-
> plement and complete the other world order, the one in
> heaven. In the complementary and wholeness attained
> through the union of two opposites – heaven and earth –
> on the sacred time of the Sabbath and in festivals, creation
> is renewed, and on that account, creation in all its complete-
> ness and perfection once more provokes in God the ben-
> ediction and sanctification of the Creator such as the original
> excellence of creation had elicited.[71]

The economic order is therefore permanent, and should
reflect the divine order. Imperfection occurs when it deviates
from this, and such imperfections should be weeded out at
times of renewal. Indeed, the restoration of a perfect order is
what renewal is about, despite the difficulties of man achieving
such a state. This approach to economics is clearly very different to modern economics, which few practising economists
would view as being divinely inspired, yet some of the language and symbolism – perfect markets, the concept of equilibrium, efficiency in transactions which implies perfect
knowledge – all perhaps unconsciously, could be viewed as a
striving for some heavenly ideal.

Given the dual vision in the *Torah*, the written scriptures, and
the interpretation in the *Mishnah*, economic policy in ancient
Israel had to be seen as an attempt to restore the equilibrium,
the perfect order. The purpose of civil penalties through monetary compensation was to bring the injured party back to his
prior condition. The balance had to be restored between those
who had unfairly profited from fraudulent transactions and

[71] Jacob Neusner, *The Economics of the Mishnah*, p. 141.

those who had suffered loss through deception. If the value of human capital was reduced through a criminal action, then it was important to try, as far as possible, to compensate for any depreciation.

It is against this background of the ancient land of Israel as the mirror of a heavenly order that earthly resource allocation must be viewed. Jacob Neusner stresses that the household is the basic economic unit in the *Mishnah*, in three senses. First the household is the basic unit for economic activity. Secondly it owns the land, the means of production, without which there could be no economic activity. Thirdly the household is the reference point for consumption. The household is defined to include all those living in a house, and not simply family members. It is the crucial economic actor, and there is no hierarchy of households, there being a social equality between the households. There are 'outsiders' living in the ancient land of Israel, but they are not governed by the economic laws in the *Mishnah*, either because they are not landowners, and therefore not guardians of the basic means of production allocated by God to man, or are *gentiles*, and therefore not subject to the laws designed for Jews.[72]

These laws could be taken as a justification for the economic discrimination between Jews and non-Jews referred to earlier. However, these outsider or 'excluded' groups included non-landowning Jews, working as landless labourers, craftsmen and those earning a livelihood from trade and investment. They were not of central concern to the authors of the *Mishnah*, as they did not control the basic God given resource, and therefore had not the same responsibilities. This is why the authors of the Babylonian *Talmud* paid relatively little attention to the *Mishnah*, which was regarded as relevant to the Jews in the land of ancient Israel, and not those in the *diaspora* in the Tigris–Euphrates valley.

EXCHANGE, EQUIVALENCE AND THE ROLE OF MONEY

Land ownership was stable in ancient Israel, reflecting the principles set out in Leviticus, and therefore markets had no

[72] Ibid., pp. 68–70.

role to play in the allocation of land in the long term, although, as already indicated, land could be alienated in the short term. The economy was self-sufficient, but the produce of the land was bought and sold internally through a market system under which households transacted with each other. There was a concept of a fair exchange of goods under the principle of equivalence; the market facilitated transactions, with money constituting an acceptable medium of exchange. The writers of the *Mishnah* were pragmatic, and observed how actual prices were determined in the market, which in turn reflected the value of goods or their underlying utility to the purchaser and the seller's willingness to engage in exchange. In this sense exchange is a matter of barter, but specie or commodity money could be, and usually was used, the price offered for a particular good reflecting what had been paid for that good in the past. If a seller raised a price to exploit a shortage, this would be regarded as socially unjust, as the notion of equivalence would be violated. This assumes value or utility is unchanging, and does not respond to economic circumstances. Price fluctuations or longer run inflation would be undesirable threats to the social order, and in the ideal static economy of the *Mishnah* such distorting tendencies should not arise. There is the notion that 'price tells all, but proves nothing',[73] which can be interpreted to mean that prices are indicative of economic conditions, but do not necessarily reflect the social value of the goods in question. In times of shortage there may be individuals with the resources to get what they want, and sellers willing to charge a high price. This does not make the transaction socially just, even if it is the economic reality.

For the authors of the *Mishnah* monetary transactions have an important advantage over barter; they can be undone. Once an exchange of commodities occurs, a transaction can be regarded as complete. An exchange of ownership has occurred, and the commodities can then be used or consumed. Money, however, can be repaid if the buyer feels he has been overcharged, or if he has been misled about the quality of the goods. There is a discussion in the *Mishnah* regarding overcharging, and the circumstances in which there is the right to

[73] Ibid., p. 77.

retract a purchase or sale. If the seller has received one sixth less than the 'normal' equivalence value or the buyer paid one sixth above, then either party has the right, but not the obligation, to revoke the transaction.[74] As the 'normal' value reflects what is considered socially just in static conditions, this sets a kind of ceiling and floor on price fluctuations for non-revocable transactions.

Roman Ohrenstein points out how the authors of the Babylonian *Talmud* recognised that the value of money, usually silver, could vary in relation to the value of agricultural commodities, reflecting relative shortages in commodity markets.[75] From this they went on to develop a theory of the business cycle, distinguishing between periods of prosperity when money was cheap and commodities were expensive and periods of recession when money was expensive and commodities were cheap. This is a demand-led theory, as commodities are expensive when business is brisk, reflecting higher levels of disposable income. The pressure of demand, in other words, results in inflation. In contrast, in a recession commodities may be cheap, but the population lacks the disposable income, the silver, to buy them. Hence prices fall, although this does not appear to stimulate demand through positive income effects.

One source of much confusion in the *Mishnah* is the notion that gold can be used to acquire silver, but silver does not acquire gold.[76] This may be interpreted pragmatically in the context of silver rather than gold being the more widely used means of exchange in the land of Israel as a result of its availability. A transaction could be annulled if the silver was reimbursed, but the repayment of gold could prove more difficult if it had been passed on. Furthermore, gold might be crafted into jewellery or other artefacts, but silver was more likely to be retained as coinage for future exchanges. This can be generalised into the notion that the more valuable commodity acquires the less valuable commodity, but not vice versa.[77] Value is, however, determined by relative scarcity, and the perceived

[74] Ibid., p. 78.
[75] Ohrenstein, 'Economic thought', pp. 194–5.
[76] Neusner, *Economics of the Mishnah*, p. 79.
[77] Ibid., p. 80.

worth of each commodity when transformed through manufacturing. Maintenance costs may also be a factor in value, perhaps implying a recognition of the notion of depreciation. The silver artefacts tarnish and have to be maintained through polishing, but those made of gold do not.

Neusner writes of the precious metal acquiring the less precious, whereas mere coin does not. From this he goes on to discuss the demonetization of money, in the sense that barter cannot easily be revoked, unlike 'mere' monetary transactions.[78] Neusner, therefore, equates barter with the determination of 'true' value, as compared with monetary value, but other writers, notably Ohrenstein, do not interpret the *Mishnah* in this way.[79] Equivalence is admittedly crucial for a just transaction, but this could be in coin. The problem with coin, as Ohrenstein and the writers of the *Mishnah* recognise, is the fluctuation in its value, the practical implication of which is that it should not be hoarded. Money is not regarded as a store of value in the *Mishnah*, but rather, as already indicated, as a means of exchange and a unit of account. This could be interpreted as a recognition of the significance of uncertainty, as an important feature of monetary assets is the absence of risk, which is violated under inflationary conditions.

SCARCITY, RATIONALITY AND ECONOMIC MOTIVATION

Wealth in the *Mishnah* is defined solely in terms of the ownership of land by Jews in the ancient land of Israel. Other assets, and land owned by *gentiles* is not counted as part of the stock of wealth, as the economy of the *Mishnah* is a closed system. It is wealth which was allocated by God to the Israelites through what Jacob Neusner calls 'the distributive system', a use of the term distributive which is different to that normally understood by economists. What Neusner means is a divine allocation, which should not be overturned by a market process.

---

[78] Ibid., p. 81.
[79] Ohrenstein, 'Economic thought', p. 196. A convincing case is argued that the ancient Jewish writers had identified a quantity theory of money, with a direct relationship between currency in circulation and prices.

However, land could be, and was, transferred between households on marriage through dowries, and it could also be transferred through judicial civil penalties as recompense for torts and damages.[80] There were strictly defined rules for legal compensation involving land in the *Mishnah*, illustrating how seriously the transfer of this basic resource and sole form of wealth was treated. Ultimately it was the fact that land had been allocated by God that brought it respect as the sole form of wealth. Trivial possessions accumulated by man were not viewed as wealth. As real wealth came from God it could not be accumulated in the economy of the *Mishnah*. It would be presumptuous, and an usurpation of God's role, for man to believe that he could create wealth.

Households, however, owned wealth, and the concept of private property was taken for granted by the writers of the *Mishnah*.[81] The owners had the right to use their property and exclude others from its use. The land was sanctified by the fact that the owners paid tithes to the temple authorities in recognition of their role in the worship of God. It was only legitimate to consume that agricultural produce which had been subject to tithes, and it was the responsibility of the landowners to ensure that this was the case. Hence, ownership implied duties as well as rights.

In the *Talmud* the concept of scarcity is recognised, although Israel was seen as a land of abundance as already indicated. Scarcity first arises in Genesis, as when Adam and Eve were expelled from the Garden of Eden, and they were forced to struggle for a living in the harsher conditions beyond.[82] Land, and hence wealth, was by its nature a limited resource, but the concept of scarcity applied to the produce from the land, rather than the land itself. For the framers of the *Mishnah*, scarcity represented heavenly judgement upon the condition of the land of the Jews, and to prevent scarcity it was necessary to please God.[83] This meant respecting and adhering to the law of God as set out in the dual *Torah*, but it did not mean that man should be fatalistic, and could take no action

---

[80] Neusner, *Economics of the Mishnah*, p. 97.
[81] Ibid., p. 98.
[82] Ohrenstein, 'Economic thought', pp. 192–3.
[83] Neusner, *The Economics of the Mishnah*, p. 140.

to overcome scarcity.[84] Rational measures to transport agricultural produce from areas of plenty to areas of scarcity would please God, and sensible provision for storage was seen as desirable. Barry Gordon, when discussing scarcity and work, interprets the teachings in Genesis as implying that: 'Humanity has a job to do . . . Man the worker is designed to cope with the burden of opportunity cost.'[85] Few Jewish scholars would argue with this interpretation. Work itself is seen as important in fulfilling the will of God, and not simply as a means of satisfying the needs of the worker as a consumer. Even before the Fall of man, work was a part of life in the Garden of Eden. Once expelled from the abundance of Eden, man's God-given ability to work and innovate could be utilised to overcome scarcity. The objective, however, was not material satisfaction, but rather pride in the labour itself, and the knowledge that it would be pleasing to God.

Scarcity which was due to poor systems of distribution is known as *Batzoret*. Man can work to overcome this, but crop failure due to climatic factors, *Kafna*, is a more fundamental problem which may eventually result in famine.[86] Prayer was the only solution in such circumstances. The authors of the *Mishnah* were in favour of pragmatism, and households had been given the means by God to help themselves and others. Man was empowered, and far from helpless.

Throughout the *Mishnah* it is assumed that man has the capacity to act rationally and economics involves part of that rational decision making. This issue is explored by Jacob Neusner in an important appendix to his work.[87] Economics can be defined as the theory of rational action with regard to scarcity, which, as is stated above, is recognised in the *Mishnah*. Neusner sees a two-directional reading in the *Mishnah*; not only is economics the theory of dealing with scarcity, but rational action to deal with scarcity is encompassed by economics. Economics is, in other words, more inclusive than modern definitions would suggest. For the writers of the

[84] For a discussion of scarcity in the Old Testament from a Christian perspective see Barry Gordon, *The Economic Problem*, pp. 1–10.
[85] Ibid., p. 3.
[86] Roman A. Ohrenstein, 'Economic thought', pp. 193–4.
[87] Neusner, *Economics of the Mishnah*, pp. 145–7.

Mishnah it involves any rational actions involving scarce resources, not all of which would be recognised in the modern
world as economics. Some of these matters might involve
the law, and matters of compensation. Others might involve
obedience to God, religious observance and the payment of
tithes. For the framers of the *Mishnah*, altruism can be rational.
Study of this can be enlightening for modern economists.

   Roman Ohrenstein considers the position of the *Talmudic*
Rabbis on the 'psychologizing of economic phenomena'.[88]
There was a recognition that man was motivated by avarice
and not simply altruism, and that virtue without vice would
necessarily be counter-productive. The forces of passion, ambition and greed should be seen as natural utilitarian vehicles
which keep society advancing, instruments which should be
harnessed rather than condemned. There are parallels with
Adam Smith's moral philosophy of the eighteenth century,
as *Talmudic* writers stressed that 'an operational balance exists which harmonises individual efforts with the interests of
society.'[89]

   Man is depicted as a basically selfish creature, whose economic actions are motivated by self-interest. The objective of
economic endeavour may be to enjoy the resultant material
rewards, but this is not to the exclusion of others, as man lives
in and relates to society, and the community at large can benefit
from individual efforts. How this happens is not spelt out in
the *Talmud.* There are no systematic mechanisms for redistribution, apart from that via the temple through tithes, but there
appears to be a social consensus, and an implicit natural economic order. Ultimately, man has a social responsibility, a feeling for his fellows,[90] and it is this individual conscience, and
duty to God that reconciles the private with the public interest
in most cases, rather than external coercion. There are, of
course, laws, as the *Torah* itself is about these and their interpretation, but they do not need to impinge too far into the
economic sphere and preclude individual initiative.

---

[88] Roman A. Ohrenstein, 'Economic self interest and social progress in
Talmudic literature: a further study of ancient economic thought and its
modern significance', *American Journal of Economics and Sociology*, Vol. 29, No.
1, 1970, p. 65.
[89] Ibid., p. 66.
[90] Ibid., p. 68.

IS THERE A DISTINCTLY JEWISH ECONOMIC SYSTEM?

The point of reference for answering this question is inevitably the work of Werner Sombart, a controversial German early twentieth-century economist.[91] Modern Jewish scholars, for reasons which are emotionally understandable, but also academically correct, reject Sombart's thesis. Jacob Neusner provides perhaps the most coherent critique.[92] Nevertheless, it is worth examining the work of Sombart, as it had a considerable impact both in its day and subsequently, because of the radical nature of the ideas expressed. Just as Max Weber had sought to explain the success of capitalism in terms of a Protestant ethic, a subject which will be returned to in the next chapter, Sombart attempted to explain the economic position of the Jews in Europe from the sixteenth century onwards in terms of a Jewish ethic. Sombart went well beyond Weber, entering the area of anthropology, with a chapter on Jewish characteristics which must be considered racialist in tone,[93] followed by a chapter on the 'race problem',[94] (in relation to Jews) that was to lay the basis for his own eventual support for the Nazis in the final part of his life.

The first part of the work by Sombart is an economic history of the Jews as a people during the period when capitalism was developing in Europe as a modern economic system. He seeks to define the role played by Jews in this process, moving from a predominance in commerce in cities such as Amsterdam, Hamburg, Paris and London, to being the financiers of capitalist expansion. Sombart provides evidence on the involvement of Jewish financiers in the building of the railways in Germany, and in north German gasworks, chemical plants, the

---

[91] Werner Sombart, *The Jews and Modern Capitalism*, Collier Books, New York, 1962. Translated by M. Epstein from the German original, *Die Juden und das Wirtschaftsleben*, Duncker und Humblot, Leipzig, 1911. Interest in the role of the Jews as capitalists was only one aspect of Sombart's work, *Der Moderne Kapitalismus* (Dritter Band, Munich, 1928) being perhaps his most important book. For a detailed critique of this see Wesley C. Mitchell, *The Backward Art of Spending Money and Other Essays*, Augustus M. Kelly, New York, 1937, pp. 258–78.

[92] Neusner, *Economics of the Mishnah*, pp. 2–4.

[93] Werner Sombart, *The Jews and Modern Capitalism*, pp. 263–98.

[94] Ibid., pp. 263–98.

textile industry and brewing.[95] Much of this is not controversial, although there must be some debate about whether private finance or the role of the state was the more crucial for German industrial development in the nineteenth century.[96]

More controversial, but of more interest for this study, is Sombart's examination of 'the peculiar socio-psychological and moral forces in the Jewish religious ethic and in Jewish patterns of life which fitted the Jews to promote this new set of economic relations.'[97] Sombart even believed that those parts of the Protestant religion which Weber identified as being of significance for the development of capitalism in fact came from Judaism. He considers Judaism as a rationalistic religion, devoid of mysticism, largely concerned with the observance of the law, which is seen almost in terms of a legal contract with God. Observance of the law brings rewards, which can be translated into capitalistic profit. Loyalty is to fellow Jews, not their Christian neighbours or Christian nation states. Hence Jews, according to Sombart, have no scruples in driving Christian traders out of business, by undercutting the prices set by the medieval guilds.[98] Sombart writes of the Jews having a 'double barrelled ethic', in the sense that their behaviour differed according to whether they were dealing with their fellow Jews or with non-Jews, a point picked up by commentators on Sombart's work.[99] It is suggested that Jews have no respect for national constraints on trade which seek to protect a country's tradesmen and workers. Rather, the Jew is most concerned about himself, his family and his fellow Jews, regardless of their nationality.[100]

Often, of course, Sombart is incorrect, not least in his inter-

---

[95] Ibid., pp. 115–17.
[96] W.O. Henderson, *The Rise of German Industrial Power, 1834–1914*, Temple Smith, London, 1975, pp. 71–9 and 123–9.
[97] Bert F. Hozelitz in his introduction to Sombart *The Jews and Modern Capitalism*, p. 11.
[98] Sombart, *Jews and Modern Capitalism*, pp. 139–54.
[99] Abram L. Harris, *Economics and Social Reform*, Harper and Brothers, New York, 1958, p. 282.
[100] The consequences of Sombart's view of the Jews as 'selfish' have been discussed by several writers. See for example Arthur Mitzman, *Sociology and Estrangement: Three Sociologists of Imperial Germany*. Transaction Books, New Brunswick, 1987, p. 204.

pretation of Judaism as being devoid of mysticism and basically rationalistic. His position is essentially anti-competitive, a
defence of restrictive practices and constraints on trade which
were developed into National Socialist corporatist economic
doctrines under Hitler. Sombart, in his study of the Jews and
modern capitalism, is more concerned, however, with the individual microeconomics picture than with the macroeconomics
of the nation state. He sees the stability of the Jewish family as
important for its economic success, and attributes this to Jewish rationalism which, according to him, sees the family like a
business.[101] Romanticism was not a distraction for Jews as it was
for Christians according to Sombart, rather the Jew was motivated by acquiring wealth, which was praised in the *Torah* as
an entitlement from God to the faithful, there being no ideal
and romantic vision of the virtues of poverty or simplicity in
life.[102] For Sombart this was eventually to be contrasted with the
Nazi romantic view of German folk traditions, and the virtue of
nationalism and a fatherland to which Jews could never belong.

SECULARIST INFLUENCES ON THE ECONOMY OF MODERN ISRAEL

Modern Israel was founded in 1948 as a Jewish state, and was
seen as a refuge for Jews throughout the world after the ter-
rible events leading to the Holocaust in Germany under the
Nazis. The role of the government of Israel was to ensure
protection for the Jewish people, which they had so clearly not
received in countries ruled by *gentiles*. The objective was to
provide a modern homeland in the area occupied by the
ancient tribes of Israel which they had been brought to by
Moses. The start can be traced back to 1878 with the first *Aliya*,
the founding by a small group of Jews from Jerusalem of the
agricultural settlement at Petah Tikva.[103] In 1882 refugees from
the pogroms in Russia arrived and were accommodated in
six new farm villages. Agriculture was seen as a viable activity,
especially as the swamp lands were drained, but the settlement

---

[101] Sombart, *Jews and Modern Capitalism*, pp. 221–6.
[102] Ibid., pp. 210–12.
[103] *Facts about Israel*, Ministry of Foreign Affairs, Jerusalem, 1979, pp. 40–1.

was inspired by religious zeal to return to the land into which Moses had led the twelve tribes of Israel. Modern Hebrew was adopted as the language of the new settlements, where Jews could live together in self-sufficiency rather than relying on communication and commerce with their *gentile* neighbours through the use of Arabic and other languages.

It was the *Hibbat Zion* (love of the land of Israel) movement associated with the settlements that was to prompt Theodore Hertzl to organise the First Zionist Congress in 1897 and found the World Zionist Movement, which was to campaign for the right of Jews to return to the land of Israel. In economic terms the so called 'productivisation' of occupations was stressed by the Zionists, the aim being to get away from the concentration on trading associated with the *diaspora*. The land of Israel was to be a 'normal' economy, where a full range of occupations would be open to Jews,[104] who would no longer be confined to what some saw as a kind of economic ghetto. The economic policies advocated by the Zionists have to be seen as a reaction against the economic conditions imposed on Jews in Europe, rather than being inspired by the law of the *Torah* and Jewish theology. Indeed, the small orthodox Jewish community in Israel prior to the arrival of the Zionists was largely urban, based in Jerusalem, and they spent much of their time in religious study and prayers. Their financial support came through charitable donations from Jewish communities outside Israel. This static Orthodox Jewish community was viewed with contempt by the new settlers for their lack of ambition and vision, and their continuing acceptance of dependence on outside funding.

Against this background it is scarcely surprising that, when the modern state of Israel was founded, the goal was to create an economy like those of the Western countries where the Zionists had mostly resided. Little attention was paid to the teaching of the *Torah* on economic issues, perhaps because the Lutheran separation of theology and the state had unconsciously influenced the founders of the Zionist movement. Theodore Hertzl and Chaim Weizmann were essentially political activists, who were concerned with the rights of Jews as a people, but not with Judaism as a religion. The debates about

[104] Yair Aharoni, *The Israeli Economy: Dreams and Realities*, Routledge, London, 1991, p. 55.

what the role of the state should be in economic activity were similar to those in the West, long before there was even an Israeli state. Chaim Weizmann took a leftist view like other European Jewish leaders, stressing the need for economic equality and social justice, and saw Jewish agricultural settlements on the *kibbutzim* communal model as an important means for achieving this ideal. In contrast, American Jewish leaders such as Judge Louis Brandeis stressed the role which foreign private investment could play in developing a free enterprise economy in the land of Israel.[105] None of this debate appears to have taken account of the position of the Jewish law on such matters and no attempt was made to seek the opinion of Rabbinical scholars.

In the early years of the state of Israel it was the European leftist view that most influenced economic policy, with a significant role seen for the state. David Ben-Gurion, the first Prime Minister of Israel, was concerned that the state should be sovereign, and resisted in particular any attempt by the voluntary organisations (the *Yishuv*), which had been so influential in the pre-state settlement period, to challenge government authority. Nevertheless, the government co-operated with organisations such as the *Histadrut*, the federation of trade unions, which continued to play a major economic role, and it supported the *moshavim* agricultural settlements, a looser form of co-operative arrangement for managing farming than the communal *kibbutzim*. The vision was to create a type of socialist paradise for the Jewish settlers, with the stress on organisation and institution building rather than encouraging the enterprise of the individual. The aim was co-operation, not competition, the model being what could be described as the central European corporatist social democratic ideal.

The *Histadrut* has played a very significant role in the economy of Israel both before and after independence for the new state. It was the major institution which represented Jewish economic interests in the pre-1948 period, not merely as a trade union for workers, but also as a body which catered for the needs of workers' families and as a pension fund for the retired. It was the pension contributions from the workers rather than their membership dues that gave the *Histadrut* enormous financial power. This was enhanced by substantial external financing from Jewish organisations in the United States before and after 1948 as, despite its socialist origins, American donors saw the *Histadrut* as an organisation that provided for the welfare of immigrants in the land of Israel.[106] This internal and external financing enabled the *Histadrut* to become the largest owner of productive assets in the new state, although 'there was to some extent a conflict between its ownership and management of industry and its role as a trade union promoting worker's rights. The resolution of such conflicts was entirely a pragmatic matter however, and there was no reference to the *Torah* or the position of associations of workers which was covered by the writings of Maimonides.[107]

Israel must be regarded as a state for the Jewish people rather than for Judaism as a religion. The laws are largely secular rather than derived from the *Torah*, and although it has been regarded by neighbouring Arab states as a Zionist entity, the stance of David Ben-Gurion towards the Jewish Agency was a disappointment to many veteran Zionists. The government did not even recognise the Jewish Agency, which has done so much to support the new state, as the sole representative of *diaspora* Jewry or even accord it special status, although it was exempted from certain taxes, and treated like a registered charity.[108] Ben-Gurion was critical of those who professed to be Zionists after the creation of the new state, but who had not actually immigrated to Israel themselves. Yet most of those who did migrate were far from being ardent Zionists, and were not especially religious. Many had come fleeing from the persecution in Europe. Often they would have preferred to have gone to the United States, but were denied work permits and even entry visas. The *sephardim*, those who came to Israel from North Africa, usually migrated for economic motives, as they hoped for a better standard of living. A high proportion of the *sephardim* were admittedly more regular in their religious observance than the majority of Europe's largely secular Jews, but it was rarely their religious fervour which prompted their migration.

[106] Alex Rubner, *The Economy of Israel: A Critical Account of the first Ten Years*, Frank Cass, London, 1960, pp. 40–7.
[107] Tamari, *All Your Possessions*, pp. 149–52.
[108] Alex Rubner, *Economy of Israel*, p. 5.

MANIFESTOS OF THE RELIGIOUS PARTIES IN ISRAEL

Against this background it is hardly surprising that religious parties receive so little popular support in Israel, although this may seem contradictory in what is supposed to be the world's only Jewish state. Most voters either support the Labour Party, which was in the European social democratic tradition, or *Likud*, a coalition of nationalist and economically conservative forces. The two main religious parties are *Mafdal*, the National Religious Party, and *Aguda*, the *Torah* Religious Party. *Mafdal* consists of two groups, *Mizrachi*, a Zionist organisation committed to the vision of a Jewish state based on religious law, and *Hapoel Hamizrachi*, the smaller group representing the minority religious *kibbutz* movement.[109] Within *Mafdal* the *Mizrachi* group stress the importance of applying religious law on matters of a personal nature such as birth, death, marriage and divorce, but on economic issues they favour a type of liberal capitalism. In contrast, *Hapoel Hamizrachi* favours moderate socialism, but is close to the *Mizrachi* position on personal issues.

Aguda is also a coalition of religious groupings, including the *Agudat Yisrael*, the association of Israel, and *Poalei Agudat Yisrael*, the workers' association of Israel. These groups originally opposed the establishment of a secular state, but have aligned themselves with Likud in the past, and now give the state lukewarm recognition. As the *Torah* Religious Party, *Aguda* remains committed to Orthodox Jewish law, stressing in particular the need to observe the Sabbath and other holy days. It has campaigned, with success, for all public transport to be banned on the Sabbath, including El-Al, the national airline, which is not permitted to fly on those days. It has also campaigned for the Law of Return, under which all Jews have the right to emigrate to Israel, to be interpreted more strictly, especially where *gentiles* have converted to Judaism, perhaps through marriage.

Although both the religious parties in Israel are small, they have exercised considerable influence on government, because of the proportional representation system.[110] This has resulted

---

[109] Henri Stellman, *The Israeli General Election: 23rd June 1992*, The Anglo-Israel Association, London, 1992, p. 16.
[110] Menachem Friedman, 'What are the ultra-Orthodox parties all about?', *MidEast Mirror*, 23 June 1992, p. 7.

in resentment from the more secularist Israelis, who feel uncomfortable with strict Sabbath observance, and object to the exemptions won from military service by some Orthodox sects, and the funding of religious schools. In the ultra Orthodox community young boys from the age of three enter a socialisation process. At 13 they enter a *yeshiva* high school where instead of vocational or conventional academic studies, the boys study the *Talmud* and its commentaries, before moving to a more intensive *yeshiva* from the age of 16 to 18. After that the men join a *kollel*, a salaried *yeshiva*, where they continue their religious studies, the religious parties having won state funding for these institutions.[111] At this stage the young men marry, and have large families, an average of six children, all of whom are supported by the state. This culture of dependence is resented by the secularists, who see the ultra-Orthodox taking so much from the state, but giving so little in financial terms, or even through their loyalty. For the religious parties and the ultra-Orthodox, such criticisms are irrelevant. Their support comes through prayer, their personal purity, and their devotion to religious study.

Both *Mafdal* and *Aguda* have been willing to support the economic policies of their senior coalition partners in return for financial support for their institutions, and concessions over matters such as observance of the Sabbath. They have shown little interest in the economic debates in the *Knesset*, the Israeli parliament, and appear rarely to voice their opinions on such issues in cabinet. There have been no demands, for example, for changes to monetary policy to abolish interest in dealings between Jews, even though this is covered by Jewish law. What happens in practice is that all banking transactions in Israel are governed by the principle of *heter iska*, whereby the parties enter a joint venture contract that converts a monetary transaction to a real transaction.[112] This means that *avak ribit*, rabbinical interest is avoided, but in practice *heter iska* merely formalises a situation which exists. Tamari states

---

[111] Ibid., p. 8.
[112] There are parallels between this practice and the medieval concept of *Damnum Emergens* which was initially a genuinely profit sharing arrangement, which permitted repayment of a sum greater than the original principal, but which became considerably more elastic over time.

this should not simply be regarded as a legal subterfuge, but in practice it appears to work in this way, as no attempt has been made to develop alternative financial instruments which would provide for profit and loss sharing as an alternative to interest.[113]

In modern Israel inflation has often been high, largely as a consequence of the level of defence expenditure by government in relation to receipts from taxation. Inflation can result in a redistribution of resources from lenders to borrowers as the real value of the debts is reduced. The money rate of interest will not necessarily compensate for rising prices. Not surprisingly, in view of the complexities which inflation gives rise to, there are different opinions in Jewish legal *Halakhic* sources regarding what action, if any, should be taken. A distinction is made between price changes brought about by domestic inflation and those resulting from the devaluation or depreciation of money itself as a store of value, but the religious parties in Israel do not appear to concern themselves with this. *Halakhically*, unless an agreement to the contrary exists, there is no need to make any allowance for the effect of anticipated or unanticipated inflation on the repayment of debt.[114] However, the parties to a loan may express the value of the debt in volume or weight terms with respect to a physical commodity, in which case inflation will have implications for the nominal amount of the loan which it is necessary to repay.

The religious parties in Israel have not made an issue of the high rate of inflation, or discussed its implications in relation to the *Halakhic* law. Both *Mafdal* and *Aguda* supported the efforts of *Likud* to reduce inflation, but *Mafdal* is more concerned with maintaining expenditure on religious settlements in the occupied territories than with the consequences of inflation for economic justice. Indeed, *Mafdal* has become increasingly involved in foreign affairs, and many of its supporters favour outright annexation of the West Bank of the Jordan[115] and are opposed to the peace process. The concern is more that of securing and safeguarding what are regarded

---

[113] Tamari, *All Your Possessions*, pp. 183–4.
[114] Ibid., p. 195.
[115] Henri Stellman, *Israeli General Election*, p. 17.

as Jewish lands rather than with the financial and legal consequences of these policies.

MODERN WESTERN JEWISH THINKING
ON ECONOMIC JUSTICE

The religious parties in Israel are by definition more concerned
with the application of *Halakhic* law in a particular state, rather
than with the development and adaptation of the law itself.
Some of their most influential members immigrated to Israel
from the United States because they rejected Western society
and wanted to return to the pure Jewish lifestyle which they
believed their ancestors enjoyed in the ancient land they were
led to by Moses. Other members have been preoccupied with
the need to take up residence in sites of religious significance
in Judea or Samaria or in Jerusalem itself. It could be argued
that this represents a form of escapism from what is perceived
to be a hostile *gentile* world, and to seek out the spiritual comfort and safety of a community of fellow believers. Not surprisingly there are few innovations in the religious thinking in
such communities, or attempts to address current global issues
from the perspective of the *Torah* or to develop the *Halakhic*
law. The orthodox Jews in Israel are often ultra-conservative,
inward-looking, and virtually trapped in their own view of
history.

For more reformist Jewish thinking on economics and other
matters, it is necessary to look to Jewish leaders in the United
States and other Western countries. At least some of the members of these communities are less concerned with the Jews as
a people, or the physical land of Israel, but rather with a deeper
spiritual landscape, and in particular with the meaning of
Judaism in the modern world. This has wide social and economic implications, which are recognised to encompass both
Jews and *gentiles.* Jonathan Sacks, the Chief Rabbi in the United
Kingdom, typifies this approach, with his concern for the way
in which British tax and benefits policy undermines family
values.[116] Such values were seen as particularly important in

---

[116] Paul Goodman, 'Brave new Britain's voice in the wilderness', *Sunday
Telegraph*, 5 March 1995, p. 15.

the Jewish community, but Sacks sees family disintegration as detrimental for all of society. There is dialogue with other religious leaders and theological scholars, including those from the major Christian traditions.

An interesting example of a similar dialogue on the other side of the Atlantic was the Jewish responses to the American Catholic Bishops' letter on *Economic Justice for All: Catholic Social Teaching and the United States Economy*. Pertinent and constructive responses came from Byron Sherwin, an ordained Rabbi and Professor of Jewish Philosophy at the Spertus College of Judaica in Chicago, Arnold Jacob Wolf, also a Rabbi in Chicago, Frida Furman of DePaul University and Leonard Fein, the American Jewish writer. It is obviously more appropriate to consider the contents of the Bishops' letter in the next chapter which is concerned with Christian views on economic issues, but the responses by these leading Jewish theologians will be considered here. Of particular interest is what Sherwin describes as the Jewish philosophy of poverty and the concept of economic justice.

First it is instructive to consider the views of reformist Rabbis as outlined by the American liberal Jewish writer, Frida Furman. She discusses the work and thinking of Stephen Wise (1874–1949), who was one of the leading Jewish reformers in the first half of the twentieth century in the United States. He supported the recognition and struggles of labour unions, racial equality and civil rights and women's suffrage, and campaigned actively against economic exploitation and political corruption.[117] Wise adapted Jewish religious practice to suit the custom in the United States, even to the extent of changing the Sabbath service to Sunday and dispensing with the readings from the *Torah*, a move he was later to regret after 42 years of ministry in New York. American Protestant thinking had a considerable influence on Wise, in particular the social gospel movement which Wise attempted to relate to the Hebrew prophets. He was particularly interested in the social implications of rapid industrialisation and concerned with the consequent

[117] Frida Kerner Furman, 'The prophetic tradition and social transformation', in Charles R. Strain, (ed.), *Prophetic Visions and Economic Realities: Protestants, Jews and Catholics Confront the Bishops' Letter on the Economy*, William B. Eerdmans Publishing, Grand Rapids, Michigan, 1989, p. 104.

economic exploitation. Wise stressed the ethical basis of
Judaism, being more concerned with moral issues than ritual
or *Torah* scholarship, yet he remained unquestionably rooted
in the Jewish religious and cultural tradition, and became even
more so towards the end of his life.

Rabbi Abraham Joshua Heschel (1907–72) was more of a
scholar than an activist, although towards the end of his life in
the 1960s he became involved in the movement against the
Vietnam War. Heschel wrote a widely read and discussed book
in English on the Hebrew prophets which stresses how their
message reveals God's care and will for humanity.[118] The
emphasis is on economic and social justice, and how God,
through the prophets, wants to be involved in the affairs of
humanity. As a consequence, men and women have a responsibility to act as God wishes, and indeed in his image, even
though human beings can never understand the essence of
God, as that is a matter of faith.

The progressive Jewish thinking of Wise and Heschel has
been taken forward in the last decade through writings in
Tikkun, an American Jewish journal founded in 1986, whose
title refers to the need to mend and transform the world. The
aim is not a Jewish world, as those in the reformist tradition
stress pluralism rather than conformity. Rather the message is
that Judaism has its own important contribution to make to
social ethics, and that this may have economic implications.
The stress is on 'functional autonomy' in the context of
'mutual responsibility', which means that individual freedom of
economic action is only permissible in the context of concern
for all others in the community, especially the disadvantaged.[119]
Halakhic norms are taken as a model for humanity, the ideal
not being the coercive centralist policy implementation associated with some forms of socialism, but rather a participatory
community of Jewish communities.

Byron Sherwin in his response to the American Catholic
Bishops' letter stresses the differences between Jewish and Christian approaches to poverty. For Jews, religious law is crucial,

---

[118] Abraham Joshua Heschel, *The Prophets*, Jewish Publication Society, Philadelphia, 1962.
[119] Arnold Jacob Wolf, 'The Bishops and the poor: a Jewish critique', in
Charles Strain, *Prophetic Visions*, p. 100.

the *Halakhah* is not merely a guide for living, it is how Jews are obliged to live, and how faith can be translated into deed. According to Sherwin, Christians are required to imitate the pattern of Christ's life, which is a matter of vocation. In contrast, Jews are impelled to act, and this duty implies actively helping the poor.[120] The Bishops' concern for the poor may be laudable, but for Sherwin, it is actions which matter and not just intent as he implies is often the case with Christians.

The Jewish theology of poverty is, according to Sherwin, in line with the Bishops' letter in seeing the plight of the poor as a calamity rather than a virtue, and a social misfortune rather than a divine punishment.[121] Sherwin sees the Bishops' letter as being more a messianic vision of economic justice than a practical programme for bringing this about. The call for full employment is unlikely to be realised, and will, Sherwin believes, be damaging, as it raises false hopes, and may result in the neglect of more attainable economic goals. Sherwin believes that the classical Jewish literature on economic justice is more realistic, as it recognises that needs are virtually limitless while resources are limited, the task being to establish priorities.

Sherwin states that Jewish sources deal distinctively with two important issues, the prevention of poverty, and the plight of those who once had an adequate income, but who have become poor. The implication of the first is that short-term measures to prevent people falling into poverty are preferable to long-term unemployment or social security benefits to those who are already, and perhaps have always been, poor. It is best to maintain the dignity of those who have suffered a temporary setback, rather than assist those who had little dignity in the first place. The poor should not be treated as a social group in need of permanent assistance, but rather as individuals who may need to be treated differently. Sherwin cites the Jerusalem *Talmud* as stating that:

If a person (who was rich) has become poor and requires public assistance, if he had been used to vessels of gold (to

---

[120] Byron Sherwin, 'The US Catholic Bishops' pastoral letter on the economy and Jewish tradition', in Strain, *Prophetic Visions*, pp. 83–4.
[121] Ibid., pp. 85–6.

eat and to drink from), then give him vessels of gold; if of silver, then give him vessels of silver.[122]

In other words, aid should be related to past status, which determines present need. Economic needs are not absolute, but depend on circumstances, and how these have changed over time.

THE CONTRIBUTION OF JUDAISM TO ECONOMICS

This survey of the Judaic writing and Jewish thinking on economic theory and policy illustrates the breadth of issues covered, and the penetrating nature of much of the analysis. Jacob Neusner's work on the *Mishnah* helps us to see the definition of modern economics from a very different and more encompassing perspective. The *Torah* or Christian Old Testament is the starting point, but for economic issues from the perspective of Judaism, the oral *Torah* is a crucial source, the latter being codified in the *Talmudic* writing beginning with the *Mishnah*. Meir Tamari has made a valuable contribution in trying to relate much of this to modern economics, and although Neusner argues persuasively that he takes quotations out of context, it is excessively restrictive to regard the economics of the *Mishnah* as only applicable to the closed society of ancient Israel. Ephraim Kleiman shows how *Talmudic* writings can shed new light on the concepts of a just price, opportunity cost and the valuation of human capital.

Sombart's controversial work on what he identifies as a distinctly Jewish economic system provides some insights into understanding Jewish economic survival in the *diaspora*, but is largely detached from the economic teachings of the *Torah*. This also appears to be the case with the economy of modern Israel, which in political terms regards itself as a Jewish state, but has a Western, essentially secular, economy. The religious parties have relatively little interest in economic policy in Israel, but are more concerned to recreate a closed and exclusive

---

[122] Ibid., p. 88. Original source, Maimonides, 'Laws regarding gifts to the poor', *Mishnah Torah – Book of Agriculture*, translated by Issac Klein, Yale University Press, 1979, p. 77.

society for their followers. Nevertheless, there is a logic and rationality in their position given the economics of the *Mishnah*, which is misunderstood both by more secularist Israelis and those in the *gentile* world beyond. Of greater interest, however, in that world beyond is whether modern Jewish writers can contribute to the debate on economic justice. Their responses to the American Catholic Bishops' pastoral letter shows that they can, and that there is much scope for inter-faith discourse on economic issues.

3 Christianity

Is there a distinctive Christian approach to economics? Can human behaviour in monetary transactions be consistent with Christian ethics? Is there a conflict between 'loving your neighbour' and the maximisation of personal gain in market dealings? Is an economic system involving private ownership and unregulated markets preferable from a Christian perspective to one with social ownership and resource allocation by government? What has Christian teaching to say on the distribution of income and the accumulation of wealth?

First in this chapter an examination is made of Biblical texts to see if any light can be shed upon these issues. Secondly, the position of the early Christian fathers is considered, particularly St Augustine, and the stance of the Scholastic philosophers is reviewed, notably Thomas Aquinas. Thirdly, the thinking associated with the Protestant reformation is outlined, including the views of Martin Luther and John Calvin. Fourthly, moving to the present century, the writings of modern Christian economists are reviewed, as well as the debates and controversies between contemporary theologians on economic questions. Finally, some conclusions are drawn concerning the nature of Christian economic values.

A BIBLICAL APPROACH TO ECONOMIC UNDERSTANDING

As with Judaism, the Bible is the ultimate source which determines Christian economic thinking. Christians share the inheritance of the Old Testament, and many writers on economic matters have drawn on the books of Genesis, Exodus, Isaiah, Leviticus, Ezekiel and Deuteronomy, as well as the Psalms. The New Testament, however, contains fresh insights on economic matters, especially the gospel of Luke, and to a lesser extent, Matthew and Mark, as well as the Acts of the Apostles in the sections dealing with early church history. St Paul in his letters to the Corinthians, Ephesians and Thessalonians displayed considerable understanding of how the economies of the Eastern

Mediterranean functioned, and his teaching covered issues such as work and remuneration and the obligations of the rich towards the poor. Revelations, the New Testament book of prophecy, although difficult to interpret with its spiritual vision, helps put the material world into perspective. This surely has implications for what the Christian believes the long-term objectives of economic development to be, with an emphasis on human enlightenment rather than mere material advance.

When considering the texts in the Bible which have possible relevance for Christian economic understanding, it is daunting to know where to start with such a rich source. As the teaching of the Old Testament was dealt with in the previous chapter on Judaism, the starting point in this chapter is the New Testament gospels. Clearly the Christian interpretation of the Old Testament may be different from that of the Jewish scholar, especially in view of the profound effect of the coming of Christ on the thinking of Christians. Such discussions are perhaps best left to theologians who are more qualified to write on these matters, but for a critique of Old Testament teaching from the point of view of a Christian economist the interested reader may find the relevant sections of Donald Hay's excellent book, *Economics Today: A Christian Critique*,[1] of value.

It should be noted that some Christian theological writers reject the notion of referring to biblical texts for detailed guidance on economic matters. Ronald Preston takes this view in his critique of R.H. Tawney's famous work on *Religion and the Rise of Capitalism*.[2] This rejection which is set out in Preston's *Religion and the Persistence of Capitalism*,[3] was further developed in his most recent work on *Religion and the Ambiguities of Capitalism*.[4] In this he criticises Hay's evangelical position in using the Bible literally, believing instead that the Bible: 'is for the regular nourishment of the spirit . . . (but) . . . is not a source for

---

[1] Donald Hay, *Economics Today: A Christian Critique*, Apollos, Inter-Varsity Press, Leicester, 1989.
[2] R.H. Tawney, *Religion and the Rise of Capitalism*, John Murray and Harcourt Brace, New York, 1926, and Penguin Books, London, 1938.
[3] Ronald H. Preston, *Religion and the Persistence of Capitalism*, SCM Press, London, 1979.
[4] Ronald H. Preston, *Religion and the Ambiguities of Capitalism*, SCM Press, London, 1991.

detailed rules of conduct.'[5] While accepting Preston's 'health warning', the Bible does seem the sensible place to start.

THE CHRISTIAN VIEW OF WEALTH

In his discussion of the New Testament, Donald Hay draws the reader's attention to the gospel of Luke, especially chapters 6, 12, 16 and 18. Chapter 6 gives an account of Christ's teaching on the position of the poor and the rich in the eyes of God: 'Blessed are you who are poor, for yours is the kingdom of God. Blessed are you who hunger now, for you will be satisfied,'[6] and further 'But woe to you who are rich, for you have already received your comfort.'[7] Christ is clearly concerned to stress the spiritual danger of earthly riches, but at the same time seems to imply that those who have suffered the injustice of poverty need not despair as they will receive a higher reward.

In Luke's gospel the message of Christ about the inadvisability of putting material possessions above all else is quite clear. It is set out in the parable of the rich fool in chapter 12: 'Watch out! Be on your guard against all kinds of greed; a man's life does not consist in the abundance of his possessions.'[8] The rich man who pulls down his smaller barns to build larger ones to store all his material goods has clearly adopted mistaken priorities.

> You fool! This very night your life will be demanded from you. Then who will get what you have prepared for yourself? This is how it will be with anyone who stores up things for himself but is not rich toward God.[9]

People should not worry about material possessions for their security, as they will be provided for by God who understands men's needs: 'Life is more than food, and the body more than

[5] Ibid, p. 103.
[6] Luke, 6:20–21. All quotations are from the New International Version of the Bible, Hodder and Stoughton, London, 1992.
[7] Luke, 6:24.
[8] Luke, 12:15.
[9] Luke, 12:20–21.

clothes,'[10] and 'For the pagan world runs after such things; and your Father knows that you need them.'[11]

This doctrine of providence is an important part of the Christian message. Faith in God must come first, the accumulation of goods for their own sake or indeed the worship of the material is explicitly condemned: 'No servant can serve two masters. Either he will hate the one and love the other, or he will be devoted to the one and despise the other. You cannot serve both God and Money'.[12] It should be noted that it is not the material goods which are condemned, nor indeed the rich themselves for possessing and using their wealth. It is rather the preoccupation with material wealth which is seen as wrong, especially if it distracts from the worship of God.

An important theme in Luke is the obligation of the rich towards the poor, as set out in the parable of Lazarus.[13] It was poor Lazarus who was received in heaven after his death. The rich neighbour, who had neglected Lazarus, was in anguish when he died for what he had failed to do during his life. There is a stress on giving as Donald Hay correctly asserts, as such generosity not only brings benefits to the poor but the rich can 'find freedom in giving.'[14] In Luke's gospel Christ shows his concern for the rich as well as the poor in his address to the Pharisee,[15] the tax collector and the rich ruler. When addressing the latter Christ's advice is: 'Sell everything you have and give to the poor, and you will have treasure in heaven,'[16] and also 'How hard it is for the rich to enter the kingdom of God! Indeed it is easier for a camel to go through the eye of a needle than for a rich man to enter the kingdom of God.'[17]

Many different interpretations are, of course, possible with respect to the Biblical texts on the position of the rich and poor. Christian theologians have debated these issues since the early days of the church. Economists, however, will note

[10] Luke, 12:23.
[11] Luke, 12:30.
[12] Luke, 16:13.
[13] Luke, 16:19–31.
[14] Donald Hay, *Economics Today*, p. 49.
[15] Member of a strict Jewish sect.
[16] Luke, 18:22.
[17] Luke, 18:24–25.

that questions of wealth distribution are not addressed in the teaching of Christ, and the New Testament is not prescriptive in these matters. There is no blueprint for an optimum distribution of material goods in earthly society, largely because material well-being is regarded as of very secondary importance in relation to spiritual fulfilment. Economics in the sense of the allocation of scarce resources is not to the fore in the New Testament, but nevertheless there is the assumption that the basic human needs of everyone should be satisfied, and it is the duty of all Christians, especially the rich, to ensure this happens.

Barry Gordon, whose work on biblical economic thought has already been referred to in the last chapter, draws attention to the passages in Luke's Gospel stressing the virtues of poverty.[18] In the early chapters of Luke, poverty is portrayed as a condition which will bring special care and favour from God. The Christian tradition of asceticism stems directly from the Gospels and the Epistle of James,[19] and this can be contrasted with the position of Judaism which sees no merit in poverty, indeed it is a misfortune to be avoided. Frederick Grant who wrote a useful account of the economic background to the Gospels in the 1920s stressed how 'pious' and 'poor' are made virtually synonymous in the Epistle of James.[20] There was a balance, a type of 'ethical dualism' between the poverty and afflictions of man's existence on earth and his rewards in Heaven.

The teaching in the Gospels is addressed to individuals rather than governments. The social, and indeed economic, obligations of individuals are spelt out, but the mechanisms by which, for example, basic human needs are to be fulfilled are not specified. As the teaching is supposed to have universal validity this is scarcely surprising, as clearly economic conditions vary between countries and over time. Christian socialists may argue that a minimum wage is necessary to ensure basic needs are satisfied, and this may well be appropriate for the European Union in the late twentieth century. Minimum wages are

[18] Barry Gordon, *The Economic Problem in Biblical and Patristic Thought*, E.J. Brill, Leiden, 1989, pp. 62–3.
[19] James, 1:9–11.
[20] Frederick C. Grant, *The Economic Background of the Gospels*, Oxford University Press, 1926, pp. 122–4.

a means, however, not an end. Christians on the right of the political spectrum may be equally concerned that the basic needs of all are met, but might assert that minimum wages discourage employment creation, hence denying the poor the dignity of work.

Similar differences may arise over methods of redistributing income such as progressive taxation. The New Testament does not stress material equality, as the much greater concern is the spiritual equality of all believers in the sight of God. The Gospels are realistic in addressing a world in which poverty and material inequality are present, as they have been throughout human history. Progressive taxation may well be an appropriate means of ensuring that the basic needs of the poor are met, and Christian socialists would certainly support secular governments which adopt such policies. On the other hand, Christians who favour market-based solutions, such as Christian Democrats, might argue that the basic needs of the poor would be better met through measures which encourage wealth creation. Freewill giving may be facilitated by wealth creation, whereas forced redistribution by a secular state may harm private investment and capital accumulation and undermine individual acts of charity.

There are no explicit criteria for the amount which the rich should give to the poor, although the issue is addressed in St Paul's letter to the Corinthians. In the churches of Macedonia, St Paul refers to church members' sacrifice and generosity: 'Out of their most severe trial, their overflowing joy and their extreme poverty welled up in rich generosity. For I testify they gave as much as they were able, and even beyond their ability.'[21] Giving should not, however, result in the donor being impoverished, as there is no merit in poverty for its own sake. Charitable donations should be, according to St Paul,

> according to what one has, not according to what he does not have. Our desire is not that others should be relieved while you are hard pressed, but that there might be equality. At the present time your plenty will supply what they need, so in turn their plenty will supply what you need.[22]

[21] 2 Corinthians, 8:2–3.
[22] 2 Corinthians, 8:12–14.

It is worth noting that St Paul states that there *might* be, rather than there *should* be equality. There is also the issue of whether St Paul is merely referring to material equality, or the equality of responsibilities in society. The Christian message is that those with command over material resources have responsibilities to those who are less well endowed, but that does not mean that they should surrender those resources in the interest of material equality. The emphasis is on community obligations and the sharing of resources, but not necessarily on common or collective ownership. There are parallels with the Old Testament teaching on community self-help, and St Paul in his letter to the Corinthians refers back to the teaching in Exodus.[23]

RESOURCE MANAGEMENT THROUGH CHRISTIAN STEWARDSHIP

Individuals should not simply seek wealth for its own sake. Neither should wealth be hoarded unproductively, as resources are to be used. The Christian position is clear from the parable of the ten minas as set out in the gospel of Luke. The servants who used the funds which their master had provided to make additional money are praised, whereas the servant who merely returned the money without gain is condemned.[24] Indeed the master asks:

> Why then didn't you not put my money on deposit, so that when I came back, I could have collected it with interest? Then he said to those standing by, 'Take his mina away from him and give it to the one who has ten minas. . . . I tell you that to everyone who has, more will be given; but as for the one who has nothing, even what he has will be taken away.[25]

It is worth noting how placing funds in a bank is not viewed as hoarding, the assumption being that the bank deploys its customers' deposits productively. This passage also seems to stress that interest receipts are a legitimate and welcome source

---

[23] 2 Corinthians, 8:15, where St Paul quotes from Exodus, 16:18.
[24] Luke, 19:22.
[25] Luke, 19:23–26.

of income. The stress on employing financial capital productively is repeated in the parable of the talents in Matthew,[26] so
there can be little doubt about the teachings of the gospels.

The parable of the ten minas is often used to illustrate the
importance of stewardship in the Christian message. People
are given control over resources by God, and have discretion
in how these resources are managed. Ultimately they will be
accountable for their actions, but it is up to each individual to
manage the resources under their stewardship to the best of
their abilities, and to make a positive return on investment.

People should plan ahead for their own futures, rather than
simply accepting fate. This message is spelt out in the parable
of the shrewd manager in Luke.[27] In this passage the manager
has been told that he is to lose his job, as he is accused of
wasting the possessions of his rich master. The manager knows
that as he is not strong enough to undertake manual work,
and ashamed to beg, his best course of action is to use his
current position to win favours from his master's debtors, so
that when he becomes unemployed, at least he will be welcome in their houses.

> So, he called in each one of his master's debtors. He asked
> the first, 'How much do you owe my master?'
> 'Eight hundred gallons of oil,' he replied.
> The manager told him, 'Take your bill, sit down quickly
> and make it four hundred.'
> Then he asked the second, 'And how much do you owe?'
> 'A thousand bushels of wheat,' he replied.
> He told him, 'Take your bill, and make it eight hundred.'
> The master commended the dishonest manager because
> he had acted shrewdly. For the people of the world are
> more shrewd in dealing with their own kind than are the
> people of the light.[28]

The implication is that the manager had acted correctly, making
the best of a bad situation, and safeguarding his own position,
while at the same time helping those in debt. The recommended changes to the debt instruments could be regarded as

[26] Matthew, 25:14–30.
[27] Luke, 16:1–13.
[28] Luke, 16:5–8.

dishonest instructions, but the only party to be disadvantaged is the rich master, who has perhaps acted unjustly in any case in sacking his manager. The master possibly recognises this himself, but the wider message is that those in business should use their skills, which in the case of managers, includes their ability to deal with people shrewdly.

ECONOMIC PERCEPTIONS OF EARLY CHRISTIAN SAINTS AND SCHOLARS

Throughout the history of the Christian church there have been many notable contributions by saints and scholars on economic matters. Saint Augustine (354–430) in his book on *The City of God*,[29] set out his belief that humans belong to two kingdoms, that of God and that of man. The former will endure for ever, whereas earthly dwelling in the kingdom of man is only temporary. The two kingdoms are interconnected, however, as it is man's behaviour on earth which will determine whether he enjoys everlasting life in the kingdom of God. Augustine was therefore concerned with the functioning of the kingdom of man, and how its economy should work. His writings encompass matters such as trade, profit and wealth, as well as the institutional arrangements for creating and distributing wealth. Augustine defends private ownership of property, but not luxurious living, which is viewed as inappropriate for Christians, as the temptations this brings might distract from religious observance.

In *The City of God* St Augustine stresses that position and power should be used to benefit the community rather than for personal gain:

> And, in active life, it is not the honours or power of this life we should covet, since all things under the sun are vanity, but we should aim at using our position and influence, if these have been honourably attained, for the welfare of those who are under us.[30]

---

[29] St Augustine, *The City of God*, T. and T. Clark, Edinburgh, 1878. Translated by Rev. Marcus Dods.

[30] Ibid., book 19, p. 329.

According to the well known international economist and historian of economic thought, Jacob Viner, who undertook some thorough research into the early Christian fathers,[31] their stance on wealth distribution was to condemn excess. Augustine saw almsgiving as highly desirable, but its function was not to eliminate poverty, but rather relieve extreme distress.

> The existence of poor and rich was in accordance with the wishes of God, so that each could provide the other with the opportunity for the exercise of the virtues appropriate to them, charity for the rich, patience and humility for the poor.[32]

The poor did not have rights or claims upon the rich, but the rich had a religious duty to make charitable donations. These were to be freewill offerings, there being no question of compulsion either by the state, or indeed by the church laying down a fixed formula. Augustine recognised, however, that riches could result in licentious living and excessive pride in possessions. If Christians were to differentiate themselves from pagans, they should resist the temptations that wealth brings. There was, however, no sin in wealth itself, it was its potential for misuse that was the problem. A restriction and reorientation of wants might be necessary for the rich, as their excessive consumption demands could not, and arguably should not, be met out of material growth.[33] Wealth brings responsibilities, both for wise stewardship, and for charitable deeds.

From St Augustine's treatment of property rights it is clear that the acquisition of property for productive purposes is seen as part of the natural order.[34] In other words, control over resources is needed by those engaged in production if their efforts are to be effective. The distribution of property is another matter however, related to the natural processes before the Fall of Man in Genesis. This distinction between production and distribution is important in St Augustine's writings, and Gordon draws parallels here with the nineteenth-century

[31] Jacob Viner, *Religious Thought and Economic Society*, Duke University Press, Durham, North Carolina, 1978, chapter one, pp. 9–45.
[32] Ibid., p. 21.
[33] Gordon, *Economic Analysis*, p. 104.
[34] Gordon, *Economic Problem*, p. 125.

economist, John Stuart Mill.[35] The natural order can be changed in order for production to increase, but those with the responsibility for the resources should ensure that the additional production helps the position of the poor and those without property.

St Augustine insisted that the rich should not use methods to acquire their wealth which involved the impoverishment of others. Honest labour is praised, not so much because of its contribution to economic productivity, but due to: 'its value in promoting moral discipline, its merit in agreeing with the express command of the Scriptures, and its importance as a protection against the moral hazards of idleness.'[36]

Slavery was prevalent at the time of St Augustine, as it had been for a millennium before, and indeed as it was to continue to exist for over a millennium after. As an institution involving private property, slavery was accepted, and the idea of freeing slaves was not seen as a priority for the church. It was recognised that there were good and bad slaves, just as there were good and bad masters. Slaves and masters were equal in the eyes of God, and slavery was merely seen as a material condition not affecting the spiritual quality of the slave. The abolition of slavery might bring economic chaos, which would damage both the Church and the community it sought to serve.

Commerce was treated by St Augustine and the other early Christian fathers with some disdain, as it was associated with fraud and greed. It could also turn men's minds away from seeking the true peace, which is only to be found in God.[37] Nevertheless, commerce was not condemned as such, but treated as part of the natural order. There was some reference to Old Testament teaching, but most of this concerned the temptations which the riches associated with the gains from trade brought, and not with the ethics of trading as such. There is relatively little written about trading in the Old Testament however, and even less in the New Testament, so the neglect of this field by the early Christian fathers was hardly surprising.

---

[35] Ibid.
[36] Jacob Viner, *Religious Thought*, pp. 31–32.
[37] George O'Brien, *An Essay on Mediaeval Economic Teaching*, Augustus M. Kelley, New York, 1967, p. 146.

Jacob Viner in his discussion of the early Christian fathers quotes Ecclesiasticus approvingly in support of trade.[38] This book is omitted entirely from the Protestant Old Testament canon, although twelve chapters are included in the New International Version of the Bible, from which the quotations in this chapter are taken. It is chapters 26–27 of Ecclesiasticus which deals with commerce, however, writings which Protestants neglect, and which are omitted even from the New International Version of the Bible. A central motive for Viner's work was to present a Catholic counterview to the work of historians such as Max Weber who wrote on *The Protestant Ethic and the Spirit of Capitalism*.[39] As the early Christians had much to say on economic matters, Viner's writing could be interpreted as refuting the view that it was the attitude of the church towards commerce in Roman Catholic societies that contributed to their economic backwardness.

SCHOLASTIC VIEWS ON VALUES AND PRICES

The greatest part of Viner's work on economics and religion focused on the Catholic moral theologians and philosophers from the Middle Ages to the sixteenth century. Foremost amongst these Church scholars in terms of economic writing were St Thomas Aquinas (1225–74) and Nicholas Oresme (1320–82). Aquinas' writings are extensive,[40] and touch on issues which have been central to economic debate over the centuries. The doctrine of the scale of values is perhaps the best starting point, the classic illustration being the 'water-diamond' paradox, with water clearly having a much greater value to man than diamonds, but the latter having a much higher market price. Modern economists explain this through

---

[38] Viner, *Religious Thought*, p. 36.

[39] Max Weber, *The Protestant Ethic and the Spirit of Capitalism*, 1905, English translation, Allen and Unwin and Scribners, London, 1930.

[40] Thomas Aquinas, *Summa Theologica*, Blackfriars in association with Eyre and Spottiswoode, London, and McGraw Hill, New York, 1975. Two volumes are of particular interest from an economic perspective, volume 34 on charity and volume 43 on temperance. Question 26 in volume 34 deals with the order of priority in charity, question 32 in the same volume concerns almsgiving. In volume 43 question 146 deals with abstinence and 147 with fasting.

the notion of scarcity, but for Aquinas the question was how a high price for goods in scarce supply could be morally justified. Aquinas was aware of the implications for income distribution, and Biblical teaching on wealth.

The doctrine of values is concerned with different scales, one scale for example applying to living creatures versus material objects, with a higher value assigned to living creatures regardless of their relative market price. Values in this scale are inherent in the creature or item, not in the human use value. Another scale differentiates between the value of an item to the community or society versus its value to an individual, the social value being of a higher order. It is, of course, possible to deal with the problem of the plurality of scales of value by regarding only one as ethical, and the others as sentimental, ontological or economic, as Viner suggests, with scarcity in relation to human demand presumably determining the economic value. For Christians the ethical scale is then given precedence over the other scales. The problem with this approach is that it is an admission that Christian values cannot be applied to the economic scale, and that Biblical teaching has no relevance for individual or social material choices. Modern neo-classical economics is supposedly 'value judgement' free, but does this also imply that it is unethical or merely amoral?

The theories of value of the Scholastics are certainty much richer than the narrow value concepts of contemporary economists, but they provide few answers to the wide ranging issues raised. The ethical and moral dimension is not incorporated into a value system for material goods, either in terms of the intrinsic values of the goods or their value to humans. It is only the latter which concerns modern economists, but if humans are regarded as being created in the image of God, a central tenet of Christian belief, then this may provide a way forward for the Christian economist.

As far as the Scholastics were concerned the notion of value is related to the concept of the just price. For Aquinas the price of a material good should reflect its use value.

> Again, the quality of a thing that comes into human use is measured by the price given for it, for which purpose money was invented . . . Therefore if either the price exceeds the

quality of the thing's worth, or, conversely, the thing exceeds the price, there is no longer the equality of justice; and consequently, to sell a thing for more than it is worth, or to buy it for less . . . is in itself unjust and unlawful.[41]

The Scholastics recognised that those selling a good were entitled to a return, and therefore a good could be sold at above its purchase price by a trader, provided the selling price reflected its worth to the final consumer. Aquinas was concerned with how markets operated, and justice in exchange. He recognised that the notion of equivalence, the exchange of like for like, would severely impede transactions, and that money was a legitimate means of exchange.

Transactions where one party was at a disadvantage are not explicitly condemned, as in any market the richer will inevitably have more purchasing power. Some types of transactions are, however, viewed as unjust or undesirable. Aquinas cites as an example of the former the case where a seller is forced to part with a good at a loss because they need the money to survive. This applies to those forced to pawn their possessions to meet necessary household expenses. In such circumstances a well intentioned buyer may be prepared to pay the seller more than the good is actually worth. The price should take account of the situation of the seller and not just the value of the good to the buyer. The just price may therefore be greater than the material price in a transaction involving Christians, with human circumstances included in the calculation.

Aquinas recognises that there is no fixed mathematical formula for price determination, and that prices may move to the advantage of the buyer or seller. So long as no deceit or dishonest dealing is involved, transactions involving a greater gain to one of the parties are quite legitimate under *civil* law. However, those who make a substantial gain at the expense of the other party ought, under *divine* law, to pay some compensation, especially if hardship results. In other words, equivalence of gain to all parties may be impossible given the workings of the market, but it would be unjust if a deal resulted

[41] *Summa Theologica*, cited in Ingrid Hahne Rima, *Development of Economic Analysis*, Irwin, Homewood Illinois, 1991, 5th ed., p. 15. The quotation is from question 77 in the *Summa*.

in one party being exploited by the other, even if this were unintentional.

Most writers agree that the concept of the just price had it origins in Roman law, which in turn is based on the notion from Aristotle that price is determined by estimation, a subjective human act.[42] It is, however, human need that determines the estimation, and Aquinas appeared to accept this position in his commentary on Aristotle.[43] In the debate about whether the just price was a subjective or objective concept, the Scholastic position appears to support the former proposition. There was also the debate about whether the just price should be determined by administrative means or through a market process.[44] As far as the Scholastics were concerned, there was no problem in prices being market determined, as this reflected the common estimate of what a good was worth.[45] The crucial issue was that the exchange should be voluntary; there should be no forced sales where a seller was driven, perhaps through financial circumstance, to accept a price below what the good would normally be worth if it was open to competitive bidding, or what could be obtained if the good was on the market for a longer period. The Scholastics favoured competition and condemned price discrimination, especially monopolistic practices, the evidence for this being carefully documented by the historian of early economic thought, Raymond de Roover.[46]

AQUINAS' POSITION ON USURY

The Scholastic theologians devoted much attention to the question of usury, which was regarded as a sin, although there was much debate on the issue, not least because the practice

[42] George O'Brien, *Mediaeval Economic Teaching*, pp. 104–5.
[43] John T. Noonan, *The Scholastic Analysis of Usury*, Harvard University Press, 1957, pp. 82–3.
[44] George O'Brien, *Mediaeval Economic Teaching*, pp. 106–7.
[45] Stephen Theodore Worland, *Scholasticism and Welfare Economics*, University of Notre Dame Press, 1967, pp. 16–17.
[46] Raymond de Roover, 'The concept of the just price: theory and economic policy', *Journal of Economic History*, Vol. 18, No. 4, 1958, pp. 418–38.
Raymond de Roover, 'Monopoly theory prior to Adam Smith: a revision', *Quarterly Journal of Economics*, Vol. 65, No. 4, 1951, pp. 492–524.

of charging high rates for lending was prevalent in the Middle Ages. Aquinas referred to the Old Testament teaching on money lending, especially Exodus chapter 22 verse 5 where usury is equated with extortion, but there was also reference to the New Testament, notably Luke's gospel: 'And if you lend to those from whom you expect payment, what credit is that to you? Even "sinners" lend to "sinners", expecting to be repaid in full.'[47] According to the Scholastics, this passage is not equating lending with charity, but rather saying that the lender should only receive the original sum as repayment.

Aquinas drew on the distinction in Roman law between fungible and non-fungible goods, which received some attention from twentieth-century economists, including Keynes and Schumpeter. A house, for example, is classified as a non-fungible good, as the transfer of possession and hence the right of use can be made without the transfer of ownership. Rent payments can compensate for the transfer, rather than an outright sale. As fungible goods are non-durable, and are consumed when used, they can only be obtained through purchase or gift. With foodstuffs, the transfer of possession to the final consumer implies the transfer of ownership. Money is regarded by the scholastics as a fungible good, as when it is borrowed it is not the same coin which is returned with repayment of the loan, as in the case of a house, but a different coin. Hence rent, or interest, cannot be paid on money, because of its fungible nature. Viner is very sceptical concerning this objection to usury by the Scholastics, not least because it derives from Roman secular law rather than from Biblical teaching.[48] Another historian of economic thought, Bernard Dempsey, takes a somewhat different point of view on the matter, as while admitting that Roman civil law was an important influence, mentions a number of Scholastic references to divine law.[49]

Money was regarded by the Scholastics as a medium of exchange, other uses such as lending being unnatural and improper.[50] There is the notion, which comes from Aristotle,

[47] Luke, 6:34–35.
[48] Viner, *Religious Thought*, p. 88.
[49] Bernard W. Dempsey, *Interest and Usury*, Dennis Dobson, London, 1948, pp. 115–16.
[50] Gordon, *Economic Analysis*, p. 160.

that each good or commodity, including money, should only have one use. Aquinas uses this 'proper use of money' argument in support of the case against usury. There is the view that exchange is productive and natural, whereas money lending involving usury is not.[51] Aquinas views investment as more acceptable than lending, as it does not involve a transfer of ownership.

> Unlike the lender of money (the investor) entrusts his money to a merchant or craftsman so as to form a kind of society, does not transfer the ownership of money to them, for it remains his, so that at his risk the merchant speculates with it, or the craftsman uses it for his craft, and consequently he may lawfully demand as something belonging to him, part of the profits derived from his money.[52]

It is, in other words, legitimate for the investor to obtain a reward for risk taking, but the moneylender faces no risk on his return, apart from the risk of payments default. If a borrower fails to repay due to difficult financial circumstances, then the lender should be charitable. If the default is due to fraudulent dealings, then this is a matter for God to judge, not the moneylender. Aquinas' distinction between a debtor who pays on time and one who falls into arrears can, however, have implications for interest.[53] At one point he asserts that those who pay on time should not be charged interest, but those who deliberately fail to repay should be liable to an interest penalty. This can be regarded as a type of charge to offset any gain they make on late repayment, this being a just practice under the principle of equivalence in exchange.

The French cleric Oresme extended Aquinas' arguments about the abuse of money through usury to the question of the debasement of coinage. In the Middle Ages it was common for princes to clip or debase coinage in order to raise money for their expenditures. This is analogous with modern governments printing money to finance expenditure which devalues the note issue. Oresme regarded such practices as

---

[51] O'Brien, *Mediaeval Economic Teaching*, pp. 178–9.
[52] *Summa Theologica*, cited in Viner, *Religious Thought*, p. 92. The quotation is from question 78 in the *Summa*.
[53] Noonan, *Scholastic Analysis*, pp. 117–18.

'monstrous and unnatural' according to Viner,[54] especially as the public are forced to use the debased coins, whereas at least with money lending, both parties agree to the deal. There is little biblical support for these ideas, however, even though Oresme became a Bishop, but there are certainly ethical arguments in favour, and perhaps economic arguments, not least Hume's law in the case of paper money where overprinting means that bad money drives out the good.

PROTESTANTISM AND CAPITALISM

The rise of capitalism has been linked to the Protestant reformation of the sixteenth and seventeenth centuries by many economic historians, particularly the development of commerce in the Netherlands and the industrial revolution in Britain. The ideas of Martin Luther have been influential in both Christian and secular economic thinking, although Max Weber's *The Protestant Ethic and the Spirit of Capitalism* is supposed to be more of a critique of the influence of John Calvin rather than Martin Luther.[55] That notwithstanding, it is possibly best to keep to the chronological order and deal with Luther first.

Although Luther himself did not formally set out the 'two kingdoms' doctrine separating the earthly kingdom from the kingdom of God, his treatise *On Secular Authority* was interpreted by many in this way.[56] Luther tried to show how Christians could cooperate with God's 'secular regiment', which was concerned not with people's faith but with their work. Luther

---

[54] Nicholas Oresme, *De Moneta and English Mint Documents* (English text by Charles Johnson. Referred to by Viner, *Religious Thought*, pp. 101–3).
[55] For a shortened English translation of some of Weber's critical writings see Stanislav Andreski, (ed.), *Max Weber on Capitalism, Bureaucracy and Religion*, George Allen and Unwin, London, 1983, pp. 111–25 especially. A sociological perspective on Weber's views on religion is provided by Arthur Mitzman, *The Iron Cage: An Historical Interpretation of Max Weber*, Transaction Books, New Brunswick, 1969, pp. 201–12.
[56] Martin Luther's works are available in English translation. For an introduction to the reformer's exegetical writings see Jaroslav Pelikan, *Luther's Works*, Concordia Publishing House, St Louis, 1959. This is a companion volume to the complete works, also published by Concordia.

was particularly critical of the view of the medieval church that life in the monastic orders was more holy than participation in a political and economic life. He believed that through secular callings and institutions, Christians could demonstrate their faith and love of their neighbours. Luther, therefore, urged Christians to participate fully in politics and economic activity, rather than trying to cut themselves off from the world through spiritual contemplation.[57] Witness to faith could be through work, and not merely through prayer. Christians should obey the secular law they lived under, but if the government was acting in a way that they thought was contrary to biblical teaching, they should not hesitate to speak out. Hence, Christians were encouraged to be critical and to question, rather than merely accepting the established social or economic order.

John Calvin also emphasised the importance of individual conscience, especially as man was created in the image of God, which meant everyone had the right to question authority.[58] People should be obedient to God, and observe the ten commandments of the Old Testament, the source of moral teaching. If they failed to live up to the Decalogue, and lapsed into sin, salvation was possible though Christ's grace, but the fear of both public penalties and hell itself should constrain the wicked who had not been saved. People were free agents however, liberated by the sacrifice of Christ, who had a choice between good and evil. They were not bound by a secular authority or even the church itself; what mattered was the individual's devotion to God, and the freedom to carry out good works in God's name.

Calvin's message was eagerly grasped in sixteenth-century Europe, especially by the urban middle classes who increasingly questioned the old feudal order. The French Protestant refugees who flocked to Geneva had little time for the authority of the Catholic church, and disliked both its hierarchical nature and the mixture of lay and clerical control. The extravagance of both the Catholic church and the French monarchy were criticised as being unchristian, the emphasis of

---

[57] Ulrich Duchrow, *Global Economy: A Confessional Issue for the Churches*, World Council of Churches Publications, Geneva, 1987, pp. 5–6. (Original German text 1986.)
[58] André Biéler, *La Pensée Economique et Sociale de Calvin*, Librairie de l'Université, Geneva, 1959, pp. 283–85.

Calvin being on self-denial, frugality, soberness, patience and restraint. The virtues of temperance in eating and drinking were strongly emphasised, virtues that were certainty absent from the French royal court and even the Catholic church hierarchy. Calvin urged moderation in consumption on his followers, however, and not total abstinence from alcohol, which some Presbyterian preachers, who profess to being Calvinists, advocate. The temptations of dancing and the theatre were to be avoided, especially the former which was suggestive of adultery. This was explicitly forbidden in the commandments. Card playing was regarded as a waste of time, but not prohibited.[59]

Perhaps surprisingly, in view of the assertions of Weber, there was little in Calvin's sermons depicting hard work as a Christian duty. In Calvin's commentary on Jesus with Mary and Martha the frenzied efforts of Martha on behalf of Jesus were rebuked, whereas Mary's willingness to sit and listen carefully to the teaching of Jesus is commended. Calvin saw much virtue in work, not as a means of accumulating wealth, but rather as a means of pleasing God.

> We know that people were created for the express purpose of being employed in labour of various kinds, and that no sacrifice is more pleasing to God, than when everyone applies diligently to one's own calling, and endeavours to live in such a manner as to contribute to the general advantage.[60]

It is wrong to suggest that Calvin believed salvation was possible through hard work alone. Calvin worked long hours himself, and was prolific in his writing, but the emphasis was on careful scholarship and moderation in work as in other activities. Individuals should make the best use of their abilities and be receptive to learning.

Business dealings were to be conducted in accordance with the ten commandments, with strict honesty in all transactions. Dealings which exploit the poor are condemned, as are sharp legal practices that deprive the poor or less knowledgeable of their property. Income disparities are considered normal, but

[59] Ronald H. Stone, 'The Reformed Economic Ethics of John Calvin', in Robert L. Stivers, (ed.), *Reformed Faith and Economics*, University Press of America, Lanham, New York and London, 1989, pp. 36–7.
[60] John Calvin, *Commentary on a Harmony of the Evangelists*, cited in Stivers, *Reformed Faith*, p. 37.

the richer have a duty to help the less well endowed, so that there is moderation in the distribution of wealth. Property ownership rights are respected but those who possess property have a duty to ensure it is used for the common good, and not merely individual self-indulgence. All individuals have a right to basic dignity, and Christians should lobby governments to ensure these rights are respected, and teach and preach this message.

One of the most radical of John Calvin's reinterpretations of the Old Testament related to usury. He believed that the passages in Deuteronomy (23:19–20) prohibiting usury between 'brothers' only applied to Hebrews, not to Christians, who were bound by the New Testament teaching on charity and justice.[61] This was clearly at variance with traditional Catholic teaching, and was much less ambiguous than Martin Luther's view that only high interest constituted usury. Natural reason was to be applied in the evaluation of usury, and not only the teaching of the scriptures. Nevertheless, the poor should not be shackled with interest burdens, and it was desirable that the borrower should profit from the loan as well as the lender. Rates of interest could be fixed by the state, indeed the clergy of Geneva fixed the rate at 5 per cent from 1543 till 1557, when it was subsequently raised to $6\frac{2}{3}$ per cent. Calvin had a positive view of the role of money, however, and this affected his teaching on interest. Money, like land or machinery, could be used to create wealth for the benefit of the Christian community. There was no need to be apologetic about lending, as the Catholic church had been in relation to the merchants of Lombardy. The Calvinist bankers in Geneva were free to develop their financial interests without any feelings of guilt, provided they observed the Christian teaching on justice to the poor and were totally honest in their dealings.

MODERN CHRISTIAN ECONOMISTS' VIEWS ON ECONOMICS

Recent years have witnessed a resurgence of interest in the relationship between economics as it is taught in Western

---

[61] Stivers, *Reformed Faith*, pp. 39–40.

universities and colleges and Christian teaching. This may reflect the growing popularity and influence of economics as a discipline and the enormous numbers now studying the subject, but it may also be a result of the questioning of the narrow assumptions of the subject regarding the behaviour of economic man. Interestingly, there are many more Christian theological writers on economic matters than there are economists writing from a specifically Christian perspective, which may say something about the moral state of the contemporary economics profession. As this is an economics study, it is appropriate to look first at what writings there are by economists, before considering the contributions from the theologians. The latter are perhaps more difficult for an economist to evaluate, not least because they have tended to draw on secular political economy and sociology rather than standard neo-classical economics. This may partly reflect the theologians' discomfort with the basic assumptions underlying economic modelling, but is also perhaps a result of their difficulty in grasping the technical complexities of the models economists use.

The Association of Christian Economists, which was founded in Oxford in 1979, and its American equivalent of the same name, have been important forums where many of the issues have been debated. One theme has been the Christian position on the working of the modern market economy, inspired in part by the profound economic changes brought about by the Thatcher government in the United Kingdom and the Reagan administration in the United States. John Sleeman anticipated some of the debate as early as 1976 in his book, *Economic Crisis: A Christian Perspective,*[62] which can be regarded as a prescriptive political economy critique. Sleeman notes that there is no clear position by the Christian churches on economic matters, largely because their congregations are unwilling to accept teaching in this domain, and the religious leaders are often deterred from making pronouncements by the complexity of economic issues. Sleeman states, however, that there can be a distinct Christian approach to economic debates, despite political differences within the Christian community, and between sincerely held beliefs in the economic policies

[62] John Sleeman, *Economic Crisis: A Christian Perspective*, SCM Press, London, 1976.

associated with both conservatism and socialism. He asserts that: 'Whatever their strongly held beliefs about the nature of society and the way in which it should be organised, Christians are under an obligation to hold their views under the judgement of the faith which they profess.'[63] Christians should respect the integrity, interests and views of others, espouse justice and goodness, and be willing to transcend their own personal interests.

> The distinctiveness of the Christian approach is thus one of attitude rather than of theory. It implies accepting people as people, whatever their circumstances, because it arises out of the belief that God so accepts them.[64]

In other words, there cannot be a Christian politics or economics in the same sense that there is a Marxist philosophy, but there is a distinct Christian approach.

Donald Hay is one of the most influential contemporary Christian economists. His approach in *Economics Today: A Christian Critique*,[65] is to start from Biblical foundations, beginning with the creation in Genesis, but stressing the fall and redemption. It is God's covenant with Noah which lays the basis for economic and social order in a community of the faithful, and indeed for Christians in their everyday economic dealings regardless of the community in which they happen to be living. Hay identifies three tasks for Christian economists, which he tries to address in his own work. First, it is necessary to identify from the Scriptures those standards which God requires of man. Secondly, there is a need for an accurate analysis of the economic and social situation where these principles should be applied. Thirdly, there is a need for Christians to examine themselves and their own motivations, to ensure that they meet the standards required.[66]

Hay, as a trained economist, is acutely aware of the shortcomings of economic methodology, but he does not advocate the abandonment of the conventional framework. He recognises the usefulness and achievements of neo-classical analysis,

---

[63] Ibid., p. 18.
[64] Ibid., p. 23.
[65] Hay, *Economics Today*.
[66] Ibid., p. 62.

and, like Sleeman, does not propose a Christian alternative to put in its place. Economics can never be entirely positive or value-free, however, and Christian values can provide a motivation for economic study, both in selecting the area for investigation and in the concepts that are used. There is a need to simplify the complex realities of the world into tractable models, which involves decisions about what to include and omit. Value judgements inevitably enter this process. Hay distinguishes between 'appraising' and 'characterising' value judgements, and stresses the usefulness of the former with its utilitarian assumptions in comparing efficiency indicators such as output per man. For the Christian economist, this is not the end of the story, however, as once the results are obtained, there is the moral issue of how they are to be used.

Caution and restraint are the hallmarks of Hay's approach. He recommends that any who reject the utilitarian approach to welfare economics should examine carefully the bases of the alternatives, as they are unlikely to be positive or value free either. Nevertheless, *if* the utilitarian framework is: '*untrue* in its claims about man in his social relationship and economic life, then the analysis will be seriously flawed. There is, therefore, a *prima facie* case for reconstituting economics within a Christian framework.'[67] Hay himself does not assert that the utilitarian framework is necessarily inappropriate for Christians. What is suggested, in careful wording, is that for the Christian, the Biblical teachings cannot be ignored, and need to be considered alongside the findings of any economic analysis. Economics is a tool, the scriptures are the guide to how to use the results.

Hay explores various economic policy debates from a Christian perspective, notably the role of the state in a capitalist market economy, planning in a socialist economy and macroeconomics management issues. It is evident that Hay is unsympathetic to both Marxist systems and unregulated free markets, and has a preference for the middle ground of the so-called 'soft left', but that is more a question of political choice rather than religious values, as Hay himself would be the first to admit. There is a predictable chapter on rich and poor nations touching on development issues, and a growth chapter concerned

---

[67] Ibid., p. 144.

with the environment and sustainable development. The problem with all this rather general material is that it is not clear exactly what the Christian perspective really is on these issues, or indeed if there can be a distinctly Christian critique as the title of Hay's book implies.

The deficiencies in the second half of Hay's book are to some extent remedied in the postscript where Hay draws a line of interpretation from Christian tradition to derived social principle to reality. The three elements of this reality are epistemological, ethical and prescriptive. Hay wisely avoids being prescriptive in the economic policy chapters, but recognises the centrality of ethics. He identifies a gap between the often harsh economic reality and the derived social principles, which, as a Christian, he attributes to the fallen nature of man. Hay is undoubtedly on a promising route in this regard, but he recognises how difficult any practical application would be. Hay's essential contribution is to suggest a Christian approach, but not to provide an operational model, which might be an impossible task. The incorporation of the ideas in the postscript to the earlier economic policy and issues discussion could be a fruitful exercise, although it could be interpreted rather negatively as a quest to identify the evil associated with the fallen nature of man, rather than the positive portrayal of the 'good news' of the salvation message which some Christians might prefer.

A CHRISTIAN ECONOMIST IN SUPPORT OF DEREGULATION

Brian Griffiths in his book on *The Creation of Wealth*[68] is specifically concerned with the reconciliation of Christian values with the institution of the market place. He recognises how many Christians, especially from the mid-nineteenth century, espoused socialism, and how in the twentieth century there has been much hostility voiced by Christian theologians and churchmen to the market economy. Griffiths extols the efficiency of the market system, pointing out its contribution to

[68] Brian Griffiths, *The Creation of Wealth*, Hodder and Stoughton, London, 1984.

wealth creation. It is not so much the chapter on the economic dimension of wealth creation that is of interest in his book, as much of the content is predictable, and, unfortunately, somewhat superficial. This material may be of some interest to historians of economic policy-making however, in view of Griffiths' financial and political influence.

It is the chapters on the theological and moral dimensions of wealth creation through market economies that deserve serious attention. Griffiths is no theologian, but his interpretation of the passages in Luke dealing with economic matters constitute a useful counter-argument to those who isolate particular parables and verses as support for their socialist agenda. Griffiths draws on the Old Testament to stress the message that man was created for work, not for leisure, indeed to share with God in this activity, while being at the same time accountable to God for the results.

> A businessman concerned with construction, manufacturing, agriculture, extraction or services is involved therefore in the complex task of fulfilling the creation mandate. Of course such a process may be open to abuse: monopoly, corruption, fraud, exploitation and pollution. But we should not judge the legitimacy of the process by its abuse . . . At heart the process of wealth creation stems from a fundamental human drive, the result of man being created in the image of God.[69]

Griffiths considers how the Christian concept of the Trinity relates to economic life, in particular the stress on the relationship between the Father, the Son and the Holy Ghost. Economic life, for Griffiths, is also about relationships, and men do not work in isolation, as Robinson Crusoe-type figures.

This notion is developed in Griffiths' consideration of what markets really represent when viewed from a Christian perspective:

> The act of employment is not just a legal transaction or some input into a production process; it becomes a personal relationship between two human beings and the work situation becomes a network of such relationships. The act of

[69] Ibid., p. 53.

selling is not just finding a point on a demand curve but a transaction between two people with a God given sense of absolute standards. The 'market' is not just some construct devised to solve the problem of price determination but a series of individual exchanges between people in which mutual trust is extended and accepted.[70]

Economic life is about order, not anarchy, with its emphasis on the plurality of relations. Marxism and fascism are one-dimensional with their stress on the role of the state, but the concept of the Trinity suggests that Christians should view all relations, including the economic, in multi-dimensional terms. *Homo oeconomicus* or economic man is often regarded as impersonal, his only characteristics being rational and maximising behaviour. For the Christian it is morality that gives personality, and it is this that transforms economic man into a human being in relationship with God through the community of the Trinity.

Griffiths asserts that a market economy cannot stand by itself, as it works in a cultural context, which requires the acceptance of certain values to give it legitimacy. These values, such as trust and honesty in dealings, are certainty compatible with Christian morality. Griffiths goes further however, and takes up the challenge of addressing what many believe are morally undesirable market motivations and outcomes from a Christian perspective. Griffiths recognises that self-interest is the main motivation for market behaviour, but does not see this as objectionable. He addresses the issue directly, and sees no need to be apologetic, or portray self-interest as a means to some morally desirable, community serving, end.

> Self-interest is usually taken to be synonymous with selfishness and the incarnation of selfishness is the economist's conception of economic man. But this is to misunderstand self-interest. . . . [As] Christians we can . . . argue that self-interest as a characteristic of human behaviour cannot be divorced from that self-respect of which our Lord spoke when he instructed us to love our neighbours as ourselves. What precisely is this self-love which Jesus takes for granted as a feature of human personality? Certainly it is not to indulge

[70] Ibid., p. 54.

and pander to our own ego. Nevertheless, it does imply our having a proper regard for our own welfare. Indeed, unless a person has self-respect in this sense, it is difficult to imagine that he could be of much use to his neighbour.[71]

It is pointless, according to Griffiths, to construct an economic system based on an unrealistic view of man's motivations, and for a government to attempt to manipulate the system in accordance with its perception of the common good.

Griffiths considers the nature and effects of competitive markets, in particular the merits of competition as a means of allocating scarce resources. He carefully distinguishes between the impersonal competition in economic models and the rivalry of the business world, seeing less harm in the former, indeed implicitly suggesting that competition is a better, or at least a more efficient means of allocating resources than through other methods, presumably involving the state. Nevertheless, Griffiths admits that competition is not a Christian ideal or aspiration, and in a perfect Christian world it would be redundant, not least because in such a situation there would be no scarcity. This raises the issue of whether scarcity reflects need or greed, but this is not pursued by Griffiths. For Griffiths, however, there is a moral case for a market economy, both in itself and as a necessary protection for the freedom and dignity of the individual. Respect for basic human dignity is certainly a Christian virtue, but Griffiths does not really prove that the market ensures this outcome. Ultimately, his argument for the market is a case for the second best, a better means than an allocation of resources by a secular authority, but a poor substitute for the ideal Christian world.

RECENT THEOLOGICAL PERSPECTIVES ON ECONOMICS

The most notable contributors to the writing by modern Christian theologians on economic issues must certainly include Philip Wogman of Wesley Theological Seminary in Washington, Douglas Meeks of Eden Theological Seminary in St Louis,

---

[71] Ibid., p. 68.

Missouri, John Atherton of Manchester Cathedral and University, Timothy Gorringe of St John's College Oxford and Michael Novak of the American Enterprise Institute in Washington. There are also a number of Christian evangelical studies concerned with economic questions, notably the book by John White, *Money Isn't God*,[72] and that by Bill Hybels, *Christians in the Marketplace*,[73] but the primary aim of these authors is to proselytise rather than contribute to academic debate. Hence these works are not considered here, but they are nevertheless 'good reads' that have influenced the lives of many practising Christians, and therefore deserve respect.

Philip Wogman's work is perhaps the best starting point, notably his book on *Christians and the Great Economic Debate*,[74] published in 1977, and his later work, *Economics and Ethics: A Christian Enquiry*,[75] published in 1986. Wogman has a deep understanding of political economy, and in particular the implications of different types of economic systems for wealth creation and distribution. He is not so much concerned with demonstrating the acceptability of any particular system from the Christian point of view, as with showing that ideology underlies and shapes economic thinking, and that economics and morality cannot be separated. In the chapter on moral foundations in his earlier book Wogman rejects the notion of Christian faith as 'other-worldly', separate from the material. Materialistic concerns do not detract from spiritual ones, as for Christians Jesus is also the creator of the material world. Yet, although Wogman rejects the dualistic notion of the material as evil and the spirituals as good, he recognises that there is a dualism between nature (the material) as an instrument and the spirit as the meaning. Nature refers to:

> The whole material realm which provides substance and foundation for the life of spirit. It gives something to work

[72] John White, *Money Isn't God: So Why is the Church Worshipping it?*, Inter-Varsity Press, Leicester, 1993, 1st ed., 1977.
[73] Bill Hybels, *Christians in the Marketplace: Making your Faith Work in the Secular World*, Hodder and Stoughton, London, 1993.
[74] J. Philip Wogman, *Christians and the Great Economic Debate*, SCM Press, London, 1977.
[75] J. Philip Wogman, *Economics and Ethics: A Christian Enquiry*, SCM Press, London, 1986.

with when interacting with fellow spirits. It gives God a vast, complex channel through which to communicate to humanity, and humanity a rich ground for creative expression.[76]

As economics involves the study of the human interactions within the material realm, it is of central concern to Christians and a legitimate area of inquiry for theologians.

Wogman notes how Christian teaching has emphasised the importance of the ordinary material necessities of life. Jesus had a role in feeding the hungry. Wogman refers to the last judgement in the gospel of Matthew where the decisive criterion of moral judgement is whether one has fed the hungry, given drink to the thirsty, clothed the naked and dealt hospitality with strangers, the sick and the imprisoned. While the production and consumption of material things is not what life is about, it is important to recognise that they are necessary conditions to what human life ultimately means. Without material needs being satisfied, humans cannot carry out God's mission and realise their spiritual potential. For this reason, the material means themselves must be created, protected and sustained.

A key task for Wogman when entering the great debate about comparative economic systems is to set out Christian criteria for the evaluation of each system. The five criteria include taking material well being seriously, measuring economic success in terms of its underpinning of mutual human love within the community, valuing each and every human being, recognising the basic equality of everyone, but also making realistic provision for the effects of human selfishness and sin. The question of what to do when a particular economic system satisfies some criteria but not others is not really addressed, but in his later book on *Economics and Ethics* Wogman recognises that there can be conflicts over priorities, even among Christians. The question then arises whether economic outcomes should be determined within a market system or by the state. As in the earlier volume, Wogman is careful not to come up with a simplistic ideologically biased answer, but rather considers a theological basis for determining social priorities.

Wogman questions whether Biblical passages such as the

[76] J. Philip Wogman, *Christians*, p. 45.

parable of the talents in Matthew should be applied to contemporary economic problems, as for him the passages were
never designed to have that type of use. Instead, Wogman identifies theological entry points for a Christian approach to economic matters. Six features of Christianity are singled out, two
relating to beliefs, and four to ethics and behaviour. The central beliefs are the physical existence of God's creation and the
priority of grace over works. The latter has crucial implications
for production and distribution, as Wogman makes very clear:

> If justice, ultimately, is only the proper rewarding of eco-
> nomic behaviour, then we have a clear paradigm for eco-
> nomic organisation. People should simply get what they
> 'deserve', nothing more and nothing less. But on the other
> hand if justice is patterned in accordance with the priority
> of grace, then economic goods should be produced and
> distributed in such a way as to enhance human well-being
> and self-acceptance and communal fellow feelings without
> asking first whether people have deserved what they receive.[77]

The four issues relating to Christian behaviour follow from
these beliefs, these being respect for both physical well-being
and social relationships, a sense of vocation, the responsibility
of stewardship, and the realistic recognition of original sin
with its implication that economic behaviour may be corrupted
by self-centredness.

Wogman sees considerable danger in the idolatry of materialism, in the abuse of property rights and in inflated theological images of both the achievements made possible by
capitalism on the one hand, and of socialist morality on the
other. Nevertheless, Wogman believes economic systems should
enable people to function as part of the community, although
he does not define how encompassing this should be, whether
it is the company, nation or entire world. Wogman takes the
middle, moderate, ground over most issues, as is evident in his
stress for a balance between security and incentive in economic life. Such views are eminently sensible, as is the recognition that because of human nature, security by itself can
never be enough.

Douglas Meeks' strikingly named book, *God the Economist: The*

---

[77] J. Philip Wogman, *Economics and Ethics*, p. 35.

Doctrine of God and Political Economy,[78] reaches new levels as far
as the Christian theological understanding of economics is
concerned. Although directed more at a theological readership, it deserves to be read widely by economists and political
economists, not least because it breaks new ground in terms
of the application of theology to the contemporary world.
Meeks' agenda is ambitious, but his arguments are persuasive throughout and have certainly influenced the thinking of
many in the church and beyond. His starting point is the reality of the separation of theology and economics, which was
evident even in nineteenth-century North America, and which
is even more the case today. Yet those professing the word of
God cannot fail to be aware that it is in economy, sexuality
and knowledge that idolatry takes place. As Meeks remarks,
'The ambiguity is that human beings cannot live without these
realities, but they can hardly live with them.'[79] The religious
vows of poverty, chastity and obedience are often seen to be in
conflict with economic motivations, and indeed are often perceived as a form of escapism from worldly material realities.
Yet at their best these vows, according to Meeks, can have a
humanising effect on economic activity, rather than being an
escape from it.

Meeks defines the doctrine of the church in terms of the
economy of God's household, the *oikonomia* of the creator's
realm. The church is: 'that place in history where God's interests for the world meet the interests of the world in the presence
and power of the Holy Spirit.'[80] As a consequence, Christian
churchmen cannot avoid being concerned with economic
matters, disconcerting as this may be when it means criticising
the economic behaviour of some in their own congregations
or the economic policies of governments or political parties
which many in these congregations may openly support.
For Meeks the problem is not so much any economic differences *between* different Christian denominations, which may
have been a fact of church life in the past. Rather the differences in economic views are *within* particular congregations

---

[78] M. Douglas Meeks, *God the Economist: The Doctrine of God and Political Economy,*
Fortress Press, Minneapolis, 1989.
[79] Ibid., p. 21.
[80] Ibid., p. 23.

and denominations which makes them much more difficult to handle.

Economic systems can be maintained either through acceptance or coercion, but the latter can scarcely be considered as just or legitimate. Acceptance is better ensured through some kind of faith which legitimises the system, whether it is faith in the efficiency of markets in themselves or in the system serving a divine purpose. Meeks recognises that economists are often unconcerned about the nature of the faith, as long as the system functions in delivering the goods, but Christians must have more specific concerns, based on their beliefs and values. What Meeks is concerned to do is to provide a Christian framework for bringing together God and the economy, providing a correlation or relationship between the two. This correlative relationship is described as *oikos*, meaning access to livelihood, a term not only of relevance to the functioning of early Christian communities but also the community of the modern church. Access to livelihood usually comes through market relationships, and Meeks views market economies as inevitable. He believes that markets should be confined to their rightful sphere, however, and that a 'market society' is undesirable, where market interactions are the only source of values. There are arguably some parallels here with the notion of different scales of values which received much attention from Scholastics like Aquinas.

Meeks identifies three ways of correlating God and the economy, the disclosive, the critical and the transformative. The disclosive involves consideration of the potential of religious symbols in explaining social and economic structures, which was, according to Meeks, the approach of Max Weber in *The Protestant Ethic and the Spirit of Capitalism.* It was not merely that Weber explained economic behaviour, but that the way people think about God is ultimately reflected in the way people think about their own behaviour and their institutions. In asserting this Meeks is arguably going beyond Max Weber. The critical approach starts from economic conditions in society, and believes that human views of God are a mere reflection of this, the implication being that perceptions change as economic conditions change. This notion of economic determinism, to which Karl Marx subscribed, is rejected by Meeks as unchristian, but it does explain the changing idolatry of people for new material goods. It is the transformative approach which Meeks sees as the most important, as this is associated with conversion through the power of the Holy Spirit. Ecumenical Christians should not merely reach out to their fellow believers, but to those who have not heard the message. In economic terms this translates into concern for those who are excluded from economic life, the unemployed and the exploited, who are outside the *oikos*. This does not merely mean caring for the poor and the economic losers as liberation theology advocates, but recognising that even the apparently successful may have been hurt by the economic structures created by man, and may need spiritual help.

CHRISTIANITY AND THE MARKET

Meeks discusses how, with the development of the theory of exchange by Adam Smith, an invisible hand replaced God, and the economic system was perceived to be self-regulating. Indeed, the concept of *oikos* became truncated to mean market rather than economy, and there was no need for any external intervention in price determination. The notion of earning a livelihood through a contribution to society was replaced by the more limited notion of exchanging goods and services in the market. Theologians went along with these developments, leaving the analysis of markets to the new economic scientists with their ever more complex techniques and models. The spiritual realm was felt to be the proper preserve of theologians, not the material world of commerce.

For most theologians the market in the nineteenth century was regarded as an alien environment, where impersonal forces caused much misery and destitution, and exploitation appeared to be the order of the day. Not surprisingly in such circumstances, theologians either ignored the market as an institution that was at least in some measure perceived to be unpure and potentially sinful, or they openly condemned market activity and sought other forms of managing economic activity. For many Christian theologians socialism seemed a preferable form of organisation with its emphasis on sharing and community obligations rather than self-seeking individualism. This line of thinking was especially prevalent in England, no doubt because of the excesses of industrial capitalism, and the low quality of life for the working classes which aroused the moral conscious-ness of at least some of the more socially concerned in the churches. The theologian F.D. Maurice was able to articulate many of these concerns in the early Victorian period, with the objective of both socialising the Church and Christianising socialism. It was left to R.H. Tawney well over half a century later to provide a more detailed Christian socialist critique of market outcomes, with his book on *Religion and the Rise of Capitalism*, which has already been referred to.

Markets and economic structures have changed consider-ably since Tawney's day. For this reason it is perhaps more instructive for those concerned with modern markets to exam-ine the views of the contemporary social theologian, John Atherton. Modern thinking on social ethics in Britain remains under the influence of the views handed down from Maurice and Tawney as is clear from the writings of R.H. Preston, notably *Church and Society in the Late Twentieth Century: The Economic and Political Task*,[81] perhaps his best work. Preston is acknowledged by Atherton as Britain's leading social ethicist. Although Pres-ton took an economics degree, it is clear from his writings that his chief interest, apart from theology, is politics rather than economics. Atherton classifies Preston as a liberal rather than a radical thinker like Maurice and Tawney, who does not con-demn the market, and indeed even regards it as a useful de-vice for allocating resources. For Preston, however, the market should be servant, not master, a liberal sentiment which Atherton applauds.

John Atherton's book on *Christianity and the Market*[82] repres-ents to some extent a response to the Thatcherite revolution in Britain in the 1980s, which through privatisation reduced the role of the state in the provision of goods and services, and tried to extend a form of market mechanism into public serv-ices such as health and education. As these changes affected the pastoral ministry of the Church, some response was needed. Much of that from the Church of England hierarchy was highly

[81] Ronald H. Preston, *Church and Society in the Late Twentieth Century*, SCM Press, London, 1983.
[82] John Atherton, *Christianity and the Market: Christian Social Thought for Our Times*, SPCK, London, 1992.

critical; the most vociferous criticism saw increasing inequalities and the injustice of poverty as the main outcome of the
policies. Atherton is aware of the depth of the challenge of the
changing economic circumstances for Christian social ethics
internationally with the demise of communism and the tri-
umph of market capitalism. In his book he reviews the main
responses to the market by Christian ethical thinkers, not only
those in the socialist and liberal traditions, but also those of
the old and new conservative right from Robert Malthus, the
clerical exponent of the economic consequences of population growth in the eighteenth century, to Brian Griffiths of the
new right.

After his review of the history of social thinking, largely
concentrating on the major British contributions of the last
200 years, John Atherton tries to develop his own position.
This involves a rather grudging acceptance of the market as
the least harmful alternative.

> In a period of rapid and extensive change, refusal to change
> to any significant degree is the way of eventual irrelevance.
> The future development of the market economy is no excep-
> tion. Facing the contemporary context will certainly require
> its reforming progression as a social market economy. . . .
> Yet because of the entrenched and pervasive nature of pov-
> erty and environment, they will continue to demonstrate the
> grave inadequacies of such progress. That is the nature of
> the task that constitutes the agenda for the development of
> Christian social thought.[83]

Atherton sees the market as a way of dealing with the untidi-
ness of reality, indeed he recognises it as the most efficient way
of allocating scarce resources. The emphasis is on distribution
rather than growth, however; the value of the market as a
means of creating wealth is not really recognised or addressed.
Instead, the discussion focuses on what the economists might
call market failures, the need for regulation to ensure that the
environment is not degraded and that the state provides a
safety net for the poor. The ethical dilemmas facing the more
affluent majority in a market economy are not really discussed.
There is an interesting chapter on the interaction between

---

[83] Ibid., p. 225.

Christian thinking and a largely autonomous market, and a brief reference to crisis theology and the theological realism of Reinhold Niebuhr.[84] In the end, however, it is a political middle way which is favoured by Atherton, a typical English compromise, with the approach to the market being almost apologetic, and yielding few new Christian insights on the nature of modern economies.

Timothy Gorringe's book on *Capital and the Kingdom: Theological Ethics and Economic Order* is, in some respects, a more challenging study.[85] His study is less about the economic alternatives facing modern Britain, but rather a theological perspective on the distribution of power in the global economy. Gorringe's thinking has undoubtedly been influenced by his experiences as a Christian with development challenges in India, although there is no reference to Hinduism or other religions. The theological discussion takes the society depicted in Deuteronomy as its starting point, but the framework of analysis, perhaps surprisingly, is Marxist. This is defended by stating that even though the communist system of the Eastern bloc countries is dead, Marxist analysis has great explanatory power which is more relevant than ever today given the global dominance of capitalism. Gorringe himself is no Marxist, however, as the vision he derives, largely from Old Testament teaching, is one of empowering people within a decentralised democratic system.

Although Gorringe looks to the authority of scripture, for him the Bible is no handbook of ethics, but rather a witness to God's activity in changing situations. Discovery of where God is acting now is seen to be at the heart of Christian ethics. For Gorringe it goes without saying that ethics presupposes community, although

> the tenacity of individualistic modes of thought should not be underestimated. There is an obvious sense in which an individual ethic, which did not recognise that I was my brother's keeper, would be a contradiction in terms.[86]

[84] Reinhold Niebuhr, *Christian Realism and Political Problems*, August M. Kelly, New York, 1953.
[85] Timothy J. Gorringe, *Capital and the Kingdom: Theological Ethics and Economic Order*, Orbis Books and SPCK, New York and London, 1994.
[86] Ibid., p. 26.

The community is defined not in terms of a nuclear family or a clan or even a nation, but the universal community of nations. Gorringe is scathing about the market, and sees it as a vehicle for exploitation:

> The market leaves us free to choose, but at the same time market forces are irresistible and those responsible for externalities take refuge behind the impersonality of the market. Masked behind this . . . is the domination which . . . [is] the essence of sin.[87]

Gorringe's model does not reject the market and the institutional framework that accompanies it, rather it is the behaviour and motivation of those who participate in market dealings that is the core of the problem:

> the new economic order must not be hampered by clichés of the struggles of the last century. There is nothing intrinsically wrong with enterprise, initiative and ownership. What is wrong is that these are harnessed to profit, power, self-aggrandisement and inequality.[88]

Economics has to be reconceived according to Gorringe, and freed from what he sees as its ridiculous positive laws. Rights and obligations will replace self-interest at the heart of the new system, with the emphasis on enabling and conserving. The economic system is to become part of the natural world, not a machine external to it which threatens its sustainability.

Almost alone amongst modern Christian theologians, Gorringe returns to the issue of usury, which is condemned, as he sees it as involving a redistribution of wealth from the poor to the rich. He sees money as an exchange of information, and has no objections to prices as market signals. What he objects to is the notion of material incentives in the market which create economic differentiation between people. Gorringe's ideas on taxation are quite startling, as he is against taxation on personal incomes, but instead urges taxation on land, citing Henry George with approval. Unlike George who proposed only a single tax to raise revenue, Gorringe favours taxes to stop pollution and on resource extraction in the interests of

[87] Ibid., p. 41.
[88] Ibid., p. 166.

conservation. Perhaps surprisingly in view of his overseas experience, Gorringe advocates taxes on imports and on international currency exchange. Such taxes would certainly impede international trade by introducing additional transactions costs, and slow economic growth, but given his concern with conservation, Gorringe may not object to this.

THE CHANGING NATURE OF CATHOLIC ECONOMIC DEBATE

The last three decades have witnessed a wide ranging debate over economic issues in the Roman Catholic church in the United States. This was partly prompted by the changing composition of the Catholic community within the United States, with more immigration of often poor Hispanics, but at the same time the increasing affluence in the traditional Catholic constituency of Irish, Italian and Polish Americans. There was also a consciousness of the liberation theology being expounded in Latin America, with positions which were often hostile to United States foreign policy, but which many American Catholics supported, like their Protestant and Jewish counterparts. At home there was an ever greater questioning in American society of traditional values, including those of the family, that encompassed the Catholic community as much as everyone else. In addition, with the Kennedy Presidency and the rise of Catholics to the highest levels in United States business, it was time to reinterpret the notion of the Protestant ethic in the spirit of capitalism as originally expounded by Weber. The United States was no longer a White Anglo-Saxon Protestant (WASP) society, but this did not appear to affect its economic dynamism or the process of wealth creation.

The highlights of the 1980s were undoubtedly the Pastoral Letter of the National Conference of Catholic Bishops, *Economic Justice for All*,[89] and the penetrating theological study by Michael Novak, *The Spirit of Demographic Capitalism*.[90] It would

---

[89] *Economic Justice for All: Pastoral Letter on Catholic Social Teaching and the US Economy*, National Conference of Catholic Bishops, Washington, 1986.
[90] Michael Novak, *The Spirit of Democratic Capitalism*, Madison Books, Lanham, Maryland and Institute of Economic Affairs London, 1982.

be mistaken to regard Novak's work in denominational terms, however, as the ideas have as much relevance for Protestants as Catholics, and indeed possibly Jews despite the numerous references to Matthew's Gospel and Paul's letter to the Corinthians. The objections to Novak have been more political than denominational, as his work is a defence of the market, and arguably of conservative Republican values.

The Bishops, in their pastoral letter, recognise the remarkable achievements of the United States economy, which has grown to provide unprecedented standards of living for most of its people, and given political freedom and economic opportunities for millions of immigrants, who continue to be drawn. The system emphasises economic freedom, but the market has rightly been limited, according to the Bishops, by fundamental human rights. The government has provided support for education, access to food, unemployment benefit, security in old age and protection of the environment, while labour unions have defended workers' rights. While acknowledging these successes, the Bishops identify the continuing challenges of living up internationally to American economic responsibilities as an economic giant and sustaining global ecosystems. There are also the domestic challenges of unemployment and the poverty of a minority of Americans despite the country's great wealth.

While European Catholic economic thinking has often been addressed to rural societies, despite the spread of manufacturing, the Bishops' letter is mostly addressed to urban industrial communities.

> Since the industrial revolution, people have had to define themselves and their work ever more narrowly to find a niche in the economy. The benefits of this are evident in the satisfaction many people derive from contributing their specialised skills to society. But the costs are social fragmentation, a decline in seeing how one's work serves the whole community, and an increased emphasis on personal goals and private interests.[91]

The Bishops stress their letter is not a blueprint for the American economy, nor does it embrace any particular school of

---

[91] *Economic Justice for All,* p. 11.

economic thought, as Catholics, like other Christians, differ
over such matters. Rather, the purpose is to consider what
the aims of economic life are, and what standards should be
adhered to in pursuing economic activity. The dignity of the
human person is seen as fundamental, but people are social as
well as sacred beings, and there must be some commitment to
the common good. The poor and vulnerable receive particular mention. Man's potential for sin is recognised, and those
who seek a substitute to God through security in material goods
risk these things becoming idolatry. The Bishops extend their
definition of idolatry to include power seeking for its own
sake, and the pursuit of pleasure or even popularity as an end.
Indifference is also condemned, indeed there are many facets
of American culture which a community of Jesus' disciples
must reject.

Much of the value from the Bishops' letter came from the
widespread debate about what it should contain and where
the stress should lie. Some commentators merely depicted it
as the work of the Democrat left at prayer, but that is unfair,
as the stress is on respect for basic human dignity, on which
there is political and economic consensus. Far from being a
weak statement of liberal values, it sets moral standards that
are extremely demanding. Furthermore, Catholics who are
usually depicted as being on the right of the political and
economic spectrum, such as Michael Novak, warmly welcomed
the document, as indeed did the evangelical Protestants and
Jews who participated in a conference on the Bishops' letter.[92]

The Bishops' letter aims to get a clear and simple message
across to a large number of people. In contrast, Michael Novak
was writing for an intellectual readership comprising social
scientists and theologians. His ideas have attracted much wider
attention, however, and demonstrate just how far American
Catholic theology has come from its European roots. Unlike
the Bishops, Novak is uncompromising in his use of language,
and almost invites controversy. His approach has opened a
debate, and taken the Christian understanding of capitalist
development and markets to new levels. For him, knowledge

---

[92] Charles R. Strain, (ed.) *Prophetic Visions and Economic Realities: Protestants,
Jews and Catholics Confront the Bishops' Letter on the Economy*, William B. Eerdmans
Publishing, Grand Rapids, Michigan, 1989.

of economics is crucial, and its neglect by theologians a major omission.

> Sophistication about history and politics avails little today, without sophistication about economics. Yet in no other sphere of life have the traditions of theology fallen further behind. For many centuries, of course, there was no science of economics and no sustained growth. So the lack was hardly felt. Today it is a scandal.[93]

The use of the word growth should be noted, for, like Griffiths, Novak is concerned with the creation of wealth under changing conditions, not with static redistribution. He does not take a cyclical view of economic history, as Gorringe at one point appears to do. Rather, his work is a celebration of wealth creation, a volume in praise of the market, rather than the reluctant acceptance of Atherton.

Novak, like the Bishops, points to the achievements of capitalism not merely in raising living standards but in creating opportunities and widening choice. He suggests Catholics should not be nostalgic for the medieval village as he himself once was, as such societies were static and stifling. Democratic capitalism for Novak is pluralistic with no unitary order, an analysis which is far removed from the notion of monopoly capital expounded by the American Marxist writers, Baran and Sweezy. Novak reaches a startling conclusion about the central core of capitalism.

> In a genuinely pluralistic society, there is no one sacred canopy. By *intention* there is not. At its spiritual core, there is an empty shrine. That shrine is left empty in the knowledge that no one word, image or symbol is worthy of what all seek there. Its emptiness, therefore, represents the transcendence which is approached by free consciences from a virtually infinite number of directions.[94]

It is this inner emptiness that is the strength of capitalism, as it does not attempt to impose a unitary vision as is the case in traditional and socialist societies. It allows space for diversity to flourish, for progress to continue, and for the free practice of

---

[93] Novak, *Democratic Capitalism*, p. 18.
[94] Ibid., p. 53.

religious expression. Because it does not impose rigid codes, capitalism is infinitely adaptable, it can allow for the unexpected, and permit creativity and innovation.

Both European Christian socialist positions[95] and those of the liberation theology of Latin America are rejected by Novak. He criticises not only the Catholic anti-capitalist tradition in Europe and the United States, but that of Juergen Moltmann,[96] who was concerned to refute the association between capitalism and Calvinism on which Max Weber's central thesis was based. The central tenets of the liberation theologists of Latin America, notably Juan Donoso Cortés[97] and José Miranda[98] are refuted in detail. Liberation theology rejects North American concepts of economic development, as it only serves to make the rich richer and the poor poorer. They are concerned to break what they see as the dependency of Latin America on the rich capitalist economies. Much of the analysis relies on concepts developed by political economists, and is often Marxist in tone, but the theological content attempts to reconcile this with Christian social values. Novak's rejection relies more on economic than religious arguments. He casts doubt on the empirical evidence of exploitation, and asserts that the economies of Latin America are largely traditionalist and feudalist in nature, and display few of the features of democratic capitalism.

Liberation theology has ceased to be the force it was when Novak's book was written, but not for the reasons that Novak asserts. Democratic capitalism has arguably started to emerge in Latin America, and economic performance has improved. Novak's critique is somewhat disappointing, as it is likely neither to satisfy economists, as ultimately for them the issues are empirical, and Novak is a theorist not an empiricist, nor will it satisfy many theologians, as he does not relate the theological elements of his case for democratic capitalism to the situation in Latin America, or indeed to his discussion of Christian

---

[95] For a discussion of the Catholic model of the corporate state see Abram L. Harris, *Economics and Social Reform*, Harper and Brothers, New York, 1958, pp. 308–45.
[96] Juergen Moltmann, *Theology of Hope*, Harper and Row, New York, 1967.
[97] Juan Donoso Cortés, *Essay on Catholicism, Liberation and Socialism*, Lippincott, New York, 1962.
[98] José Miranda, *Marx and the Bible*, Orbis Books, New York, 1974.

socialism in Europe. His theological critique of Marxism is devastating, but Marxist and traditionalist economic structures are not the only alternatives to democratic capitalism, although it is always open to debate just how far the boundaries of democratic capitalism extend. Novak subsumes social democratic mixed economies within this framework.

Novak tries to apply six theological doctrines to democratic capitalism: the trinity, the incarnation, competition (its use is explained below), original sin, the separation of realms and *caritas*, the compassion and sacrificial love of God as creator. The doctrine of the trinity involves community, and under this Novak discusses the relation of individual to the state, to a large extent restating and reinforcing the positions expounded earlier in his work. Under the heading of incarnation Novak reaches a more startling conclusion, that it is futile to seek a Christian economic utopia.

> The single greatest temptation for Christians is to imagine that the salvation won by Jesus has altered the human condition. Many attempt to judge the world by the standards of the gospels, as though the world were ready to live according to them. Sin is not so easily overcome. A political economy for sinners, even Christian sinners (however well intentioned), is consistent with the story of Jesus. A political economy based on love and justice is to be found beyond, never to be wholly incarnated within, human history. The incarnation obliges us to reduce our noblest expectations, so to love the world as to fit a political economy to it, nourishing all that is best in it.[99]

Competition at first sight might appear to sit oddly with the other five Christian doctrines discussed by Novak. To some extent those attracted to holy orders are of less competitive temperaments, and the Gospel of Matthew contrasts worldly success with the life of grace, by stating that the last shall be first and the first last.[100] Nevertheless, there is the inspirational 'onward Christian soldiers' which views daily life as a combat, and competition seems to make people strive to reach new heights of attainment and realise their human potential. Novak

[99] Novak, *Democratic Capitalism*, pp. 343–4.
[100] Matthew, 20:16.

does not see the spirit of competition as foreign to the Gospels, although he appeals more to natural law than the Gospel teaching itself.

The doctrine of the separation of the realms is to: 'give to Caesar what is Caesar's, and to God what is God's.'[101] Given this doctrine a Christian economy or a Christian economics is impossible, and the market should be open to all irrespective of religious belief. Novak sees economic life as non-exclusive, but that does not mean that Christians should not develop their own view of what constitutes desirable economic outcomes, and ethically acceptable policies to attain these objectives. Christianity is by nature tolerant, however, and others can apply their own views and ethical standards.

CHRISTIAN ECONOMIC VALUES

If a Christian economy is not possible, can Christian economic values be identified? This survey of both Christian economists and theologians concerned with economic matters shows that there is a complete range of views on what type of economic system is desirable, and indeed what the economic priorities should be. There is a strong Christian socialist tradition associated with Maurice and Tawney, but at the same time, as is evident from the work of Novak, theologians who are prepared to defend capitalism and the free market system. Others such as Wogman and Atherton attempt to review all the options from a theological standpoint, and then argue for the middle ground, a market system which is guided, and if necessary constrained, by laws and institutions through which Christian ethical standards could be applied. Atherton is not urging the creation of a Christian theocracy, however; no doubt he would be appalled by the concept. It is clear that he favours a liberal rather than an exclusive approach, although there remains the issue of how an ethically concerned government in a multi-faith society can reconcile Christian values with those of other religions, and indeed the values of those with no religious beliefs. As Novak rightly asserts this is not a problem with a wholly market economy, where there is no need for

---

[101] Matthew, 22:21.

prescription. The 'empty shrine' at the heart of democratic capitalism implies the individual has choices, the opportunity to live according to Christian ethics, but also the freedom to sin.

There are some on the fringes of liberation theology who have favoured Marxist solutions, but for the most part leftist Christian theologians such as Gorringe have preferred to keep to using a Marxist framework for the analysis of capitalism as a system, but they have not supported the adoption of Marxist policies. This is hardly surprising given the essentially materialistic nature of Marxism, which has economic rather than spiritual objectives. Weber as a historian is less concerned with religious values as an end, but rather examines whether religious beliefs have influenced capitalist development. Such an approach is essentially secularist.

Most theologians whose work is reviewed here have been preoccupied with broad issues of political economy, particularly the role of the state. The detailed economic analysis, and the methodology and assumptions of modern economic models have received much less attention. There has been no systematic attempt to discuss the merits of Keynesianism versus monetarism, or provide any Christian insight into the continuing macroeconomics controversies, although Atherton makes frequent reference to Keynes. Nor, with the possible exception of the field of economic development, are any of the subdisciplines of economics explored. Sleeman considers the ethics of a number of economic policy issues, but even the title of his book, *Economic Crisis: A Christian Perspective*, suggests a lack of perspective. The so called economic crisis of the mid-1970s, when his book was written, hardly constitutes a crisis in relation to the economic developments four decades before, or indeed to the decades since as far as many countries are concerned. Meeks goes further in exploring the assumptions around which markets operate, but in the end his book is also a theological perspective on political economy, as indeed its title makes clear, not an exposition of contemporary microeconomics.

The contributions of the trained economists who are committed Christians are in the end disappointing. Griffiths, although an economist, adopts an essentially political economy perspective. Hay goes furthest in grappling at the interface of theology and economic methodology, but his work raises more questions than it provides answers, although that is probably a good starting point. He deserves to be widely read. Viner is perhaps the most distinguished economist to make a substantial contribution in this field, but his uncompleted work was about the economic ideas of non-economists, and Viner himself tended to treat his endeavours in this field as an interesting sideline, a hobby, rather than a central part of his academic work. In the final analysis there appears, indeed, to be a separation of realms, as there are many first-class economists who are also committed Christians, but they do not choose to make their Christian beliefs explicit in their economic writings, or indeed to question the positive assumptions on which much of modern economic analysis is based. This may be explained by the fact that they recognise the need to keep economics in its place. The material is only one dimension of life, and economic analysis a mere tool. The problems arise when the analysis is used in areas where its application was never intended, such as child rearing, marriage and other areas involving the so called economics of the family. Rationality, maximisation and even the pursuit of individual gain have their place, but they are only one facet of human behaviour and experience. There are many other motivations, including for Christians the spiritual, which can be both inclusive and exclusive of utilitarian considerations.

4 Islam

Islam is the youngest of the great world religions, with a history extending back over 1400 years, most of which has been chronicled in detail. The early spread of Islam was accompanied by military, political and economic success, and submission by Muslims to Allah seemed to bring earthly as well as spiritual rewards. There did not appear to be any conflict between this most modern of religions and material prosperity. Furthermore, the spread of the new religion was accompanied by remarkable scientific advances, including the development of the modern system of numbering, and a cultural and artistic development that demonstrated that Islam had resulted in the emergence of a truly great civilisation.

Central to Islam is the concept of awareness, *al-wa'y*,[1] which implies that followers should constantly seek to educate themselves in its basic tenets, so that their knowledge can be applied for the benefit of society, including the economic order. All religions can be a way of life for their followers, but this usually applies to a minority of adherents. The demands of Islam, not least that to pray five times a day, results, however, in the religion affecting to an enormous degree the lives of believers, who are constantly being made aware of the basis of their faith. These demands, which consume much human energy, inevitably impinge to a great extent on economic activity. It is, in fact, difficult for Muslims to isolate the economic and the spiritual domain in their lives, as both are constantly alternating, with a daily as well as a weekly cycle.

There has been more written on Islamic economics in the last two decades than in the previous fourteen hundred years. The majority of Muslims today are aware of the basic tenets of Muslim teaching on economic matters, whereas there is much less awareness by most Christians and Jews of the positions of their own religions on economics. Indeed, the material and spiritual realms are viewed as separate and exclusive by many

[1] Mohamed Hilal, 'Ethical and social foundations of Islamic science and technology', in Klaus Gottstein, (ed.) *Islamic Cultural Identity and Scientific-Technological Development*, Nomos Verlagsgesellschaft, Baden Baden, 1986, p. 83.

115

in the Judaic Christian tradition, whereas for Muslims, conduct in economic affairs is seen as an integral part of religious observance. Many, indeed most, may not put their religious convictions into practice in the economic sphere, but there are few who challenge the basic tenets of these convictions, and even the less devout recognise that there is some substance in Islamic economics.

Why has there been so much interest in Islamic economics? What is the substantive core? How much comes from the *Koran* itself, and what are the economic principles embedded in the *Shariah* religious law? Economic and commercial conditions have clearly changed considerably since the time of the Prophet Mohammed, but part of the challenge for contemporary Islamic economists and *Shariah* scholars is to interpret Muslim belief in a modern context. There are inevitably different schools of thought, and disagreements, as is the case with all human endeavour, even when divinely inspired. Are there lessons from great Muslim philosophers and economists of the past such as Ibn Khaldûn for those involved in current scholarship?

In this chapter the tenets of Islamic economics will be reviewed, starting from the position as spelt out in the *Koran*. The evolution of Islamic economic thinking is traced, and the causes of the recent revival of interest in the subject are discussed. Although it is questions of finance which have received the most detailed treatment by contemporary economists, and the spread of Islamic banking is one of the most visible aspects of the Islamic economic revival, it is important to see the revival in a broader context. Islamic economics is often viewed from a political economy perspective as an alternative economic system to capitalism and communism. Most economies where Muslims live are classified as developing, or underdeveloped. The application of Islamic economic ideals is seen by many in Muslim countries as a way out of this underdevelopment, a means of restoring the success associated with the first century of Islamic civilisation. This is the vision of Islamists, those who want to see Muslim values respected in the political and economic sphere, so that their own lives can be governed by the *Shariah* law.

The term Islamist is used here and throughout, rather than Islamic fundamentalist, which has taken on a pejorative meaning in some Muslim countries and the West, as it is used as a label for those who support violent political action. Islamists constitute a much broader church, with an interest in economic as well as political questions, yet from a particular ethical and moral position.

SOURCES OF ISLAMIC ECONOMIC PHILOSOPHY

In order to understand the principles of Islamic economics and their significance for economic policy, it is important to know something about the sources. Western neo-classical economics makes little or no reference to biblical teaching, but the ultimate source of inspiration for Islamic economics is the holy *Koran*. The Prophet Mohammed as a leader and ruler was specifically concerned with economic justice and rights, and his experience as a trader meant he had a practical knowledge of commerce and the procedures involved in economic transactions. Hence the *Koran* is very explicit in its economic teaching, as is the *Hadith*, the sayings and the deeds of the Prophet Mohammed as recorded in the *Sunnah* holy writings. These represent another important source of authority for Muslims, especially for the majority *Sunni* sect, who dominate throughout the Islamic World with the exception of Iran.

There is much more space in the *Koran* devoted to economic matters than in the Bible. Over 1400 of the 6226 verses refer to economic issues, as the *Koran* provides a complete recipe for all aspects of life, material as well as spiritual. It is quite specific about the duties and obligations of believers, as well as their economic rights and entitlements. On inheritance, for example, it is stated:

A male shall inherit a portion equal to that of two females . . . for parents one sixth to each if the deceased left children . . . in what ye (the man) leaves (his wife's) share is a fourth if they die childless but if ye leave children, (your wife) gets an eighth after payment of legacies and debts.[2]

[2] Sûra 4:29. All quotations are from a translation of the *Koran* by Abdullah Yusuf Ali, *The Holy Koran: Text, Translation and Commentry*, That es-Salasil, Kuwait, 1988.

Under this formula a married man who leaves a widow, a son and a daughter, but whose parents are dead, will have his estate divided in the following manner.

Widow's share $= \frac{1}{8}$

Son's share $= (1 - \frac{1}{8}) \times \frac{2}{3} = \frac{7}{12}$

Daughter's share $= (1 - \frac{1}{8}) \times \frac{1}{3} = \frac{7}{24}$

This contrasts with the usual situation in the West where, in the absence of specific instructions in the will of the deceased, a widow inherits all of her husband's estate, which then gets passed on to each of the children, in equal proportions regardless of sex, on her death.

The Muslim inheritance laws, as with much of the guidance which is provided by the *Koran*, are enacted in the *Shariah*, the Islamic religious laws. These cover most aspects of economic activity and commercial life, as well as criminal justice and other matters.[3] In states such as Saudi Arabia and Iran, the *Shariah* law is the ultimate legal authority, but even in those states which have enacted Western commercial codes such as Egypt, Syria, Turkey and the Magreb countries, many believers still look to religious laws rather than the secular. These states have, in fact, incorporated Islamic inheritance laws into their legal systems, but not Muslim commercial codes. *Shariah* courts hear cases concerning commercial matters in the Gulf states and Iran, but even in the more secular countries in the Islamic World, with civil courts, many local businessmen prefer to have the religious authorities arbitrate in disputes between Muslims. In those states where there is no formal parallel *Shariah* court system, there is in practice an informal network, which looks after most everyday commercial affairs.

The other source of authority for commercial transactions in Muslim states is the *fiqh* which refers to Islamic jurisprudence. This is the science or philosophy of Muslim law, especially the necessary knowledge for its interpretation. The *fuqaha* are the jurists who give opinions on various legal issues in the light of the *Koran* and the *Sunnah*, and these opinions are

---

[3] For a discussion of the limits of the *Shariah* law in economics see Masudul Alam Choudhury and Uzir Abdul Malik, *The Foundations of Islamic Political Economy*, St Martins Press, New York, 1992, pp. 3–9.

included in the *fiqh*. On most fundamental matters there is a consensus amongst Muslim jurists which is referred to as *ijma*. As this has been reached by general agreement it is much respected. For many commercial and economic matters, especially those reflecting modern developments, it is the *ijtihād* which is important, the effort to derive judicial opinions.

Those most qualified to give such opinions are the *ulamā*, the religious scholars who are fully conversant with the *Koran* and the *Sunnah*. In the past such scholars tended to be often removed from the everyday realities of the commercial world, and had great religious knowledge, but little economic awareness. This is changing today as more widely educated and travelled Muslims are accepted into the *ulamā*, although amongst the highest Islamic legal authorities there remains more of an emphasis on scholarly work than on practical dealings.

THE *KORANIC* TEACHING ON COMMERCE

Economic activities have been classified as productive and unproductive by both Western classical and Islamic economists.[4] Adam Smith viewed manufacturing as productive, as it made a positive contribution to the wealth of nations, but trading and distribution were seen as unproductive as they did not add value. Islamic economists have always taken a rather different view, as trading is held to be as important as manufacturing. Without distribution and sales, production would be worthless. This is more in line with modern Western economic thinking that draws no distinction between the production of physical goods and services. What is classified as unproductive by Islamic economists is any task which requires no effort, yet is rewarded. It is those who work who will benefit: 'Those who patiently persevere will truly receive a reward without measure.'[5] Interest as a reward for deferring consumption is, for example, seen as unjust as the return comes from mere waiting, not from effort.

---

[4] For a parallel discussion of these issues in the context of Islamic models of economic development see Rodney Wilson, *Economic Development in the Middle East*, Routledge, London, 1995, pp. 105ff.
[5] Sûra 39:10.

There are many passages where trading is singled out for praise in the *Koran* as a worthy occupation. Exchange is viewed as mutually beneficial, and certainly preferable to keeping exclusive control over personal property: 'O ye who believe, eat not up your property among yourselves in vanities: but let there be amongst you traffic and trade by mutual goodwill.'[6] Another passage in the *Koran* speaks of the: 'Hope for a commerce that will never fail.'[7] Buying and selling can corrupt, however, and fraudulent and dishonest trading practices are explicitly condemned. Competition in the accumulation of material possessions is seen as especially harmful: 'The mutual rivalry for piling up the good things of this world diverts you from more serious things.'[8] In other words, material accumulation in order to show off to others, or even keep up with their consumption levels, can be a harmful distraction from more important spiritual concerns. As in the Bible, in the *Koran* the coveting of a neighbour's goods is regarded as undesirable: 'And in no wise covet those things in which God hath bestowed his gifts more freely on some of you than on others: to men is allocated what they earn and to women what they earn.'[9]

The prophet Mohammed himself had first hand experience of trading in camels following his marriage to Khadija. Later, as the ruler of Medina at the commercial heart of the Hijaz, he was frequently called upon to arbitrate in disputes between buyers and sellers. Disagreements over weights and measures were common, as were differences over exactly what bargain had been struck and the nature of the goods included. Honesty in trade is stressed in the *Koran*, and any attempt to deceive or cheat in transactions is condemned: 'Give full measure when ye measure, and weigh with a balance which is straight: that is the most fitting and the most advantageous in the final determination.'[10]

With agricultural products freshness was often an issue in a region with a hot summer climate and no technology to preserve fresh produce. Mohammed was concerned that proper

---

[6] Sûra 4:29.
[7] Sûra 35:29.
[8] Sûra 102:1.
[9] Sûra 4:32.
[10] Sûra 17:35.

contracts should be drawn up for trade, and that there should be transparency in all transactions and trading practices. People should not attempt to get involved in dealings in areas in which they have little knowledge: 'And pursue not that of which thou hast no knowledge; for every act of hearing or of seeing will be enquired into (on the day of reckoning).'[11]

Traders are respected as knowledgeable throughout the Muslim World, and they are seen as playing a key role in the dissemination of knowledge. Trade flourished during the early period of Islam in the Near and Middle East, including trade in luxury goods. The accumulation of capital was associated with trading, and those who prospered were praised; indeed, there was almost a celebration of the richness and diversity of the produce traded.[12] The emphasis was as much on the quality of the traded goods as the quantity. These attitudes owe much to traditional Islamic teaching and writings. However, such attitudes can be helpful for development in modern societies where the marketing matters as much as mere production.

The international advantage of Islamic economies arguably lies in efficient information transmission through a well developed trading system. This may act to the advantage of the Muslim World in coming decades, as links between smaller firms become more important and production is scaled down, with greater emphasis on flexibility and diversity. The obsession with large scale production under both the capitalist and the communist systems and the downgrading of mercantilism was ill-suited to Islamic societies. If the next stage of development is the emergence of a new form of mercantilism, the Islamic World will be in a much better relative position.

JUST REWARDS IN AN ISLAMIC ECONOMY

Western economists have always been deeply concerned with questions of income distribution both within and between nations, and modern welfare economics attempts to show how

[11] Sûra 17:36.
[12] Adam Mez, *The Renaissance of Islam*, Luzac and Co., London, 1937, pp. 470–84. This provides an illuminating discussion of trade in the ancient Near East under Islam.

a redistribution of income and wealth can bring about an improvement in utility or satisfaction for society as a whole. Islamic economists are also concerned with these issues, but their interest is not merely with the outcomes, but how material rewards can be justified. Merchants and traders, for example, earn their rewards through conveying information and taking risks. This is a justifiable reason for remuneration as it implies effort. Rewards on such a basis are always legitimate, whereas windfall gains as a result of gambling or the exploitation of others are viewed as unjust.

There are nine passages in the *Koran* that specifically deal with rewards. Muslims get their rewards from Allah both in their worldly life and in the hereafter, the latter being more important. All believers have a right to a basic entitlement during their lives, as without this, they would be unable to realise their human potential. The position is set out clearly in the *Koran*: 'It is God who has created you; further he has provided you with your sustenance.'[13] The amount of entitlement is not important, the emphasis being on needs rather than the situation of one Muslim relative to another: 'God may reward them according to the best of their deeds, and add even more for them out of his grace: for God doth provide for those whom he will without measure.'[14] There may be a minimum reward, but there is no maximum. In an economic policy context this could be interpreted as support for the notion of a minimum wage, so that all Muslims can live with dignity, but not for a programme of compulsory redistribution of income and wealth that takes from the rich to give to the poor. Such policies create resentments, and redistribution under duress from the secular authorities is regarded as undesirable in contrast to voluntary giving of alms which is viewed as part of a believer's duty in serving God. Riches bring responsibilities, including the responsibility to give:

> Your riches and your children may be but a trial: but in the presence of God is the highest reward. So fear God as much as ye can; listen and obey; and spend in charity for the benefit of your own soul and those saved from the covetousness

[13] Sûra 30:40.
[14] Sûra 24:38.

of their own souls . . . If you loan to God a beautiful loan, he will double it to your credit.[15]

The real reward of wealth is the ability to be generous. Wealth is only a means of serving God, not an end in itself.

Striving for material possessions may result in earthly rewards, but these are not important in the long run; indeed materialism may bring ruin: 'If any do wish for the transitory things of this life we readily grant them – such things as we will to such persons as we will . . . [but] . . . in the end we have provided hell for them.'[16] In contrast, those that strive in the service of God for a place in the hereafter will be blessed. It is not the material possessions which are condemned, however, what matters is how they were acquired. People should not become obsessed with the amounts of goods others have; God's bounty is for all believers, but not necessarily equally. What is important is that everyone should have sufficient, not that all believers should have the same:

> God has bestowed his gifts of sustenance more freely on some of you than on others: those more favoured are not going to throw back their gifts to those whom their right hands possess, so as to be equal in that respect.[17]

In other words, income and wealth distribution in this world are not important issues, as believers are promised so much more in the hereafter. It is submission to Allah during life on earth that brings fulfilment, but the fruits of this are enjoyed in the afterlife. Given such beliefs, concerns over worldly goods are inevitably secondary.

Private ownership of property is respected in Islam, indeed as already indicated, there are detailed rules governing its inheritance. The accumulation of property is not viewed as an end in itself or an incentive mechanism, rather private ownership is regarded as the natural state of affairs. Aggressive takeover activity is frowned upon in the Islamic world, as is any attempt to monopolise a market by driving competitors out of business. Believers should not deal with their fellow believers

[15] Sûra 64:15–17.
[16] Sûra 17:18.
[17] Sûra 16:71.

in such a manner. God is realistic about the aggressive nature of man, however, but although human conflict may be inevitable, it is important that this should not result in injustice. In the *Koran* there are several passages dealing with the distribution of the spoils of war: 'And know that out of all the booty that ye may acquire in war a fifth share is assigned to God, – and to the Apostle, and to near relatives, orphans, the needy and the wayfarer.'[18]

It can, of course, be debated whether this ruling should apply to price cutting wars between businesses, but the implied business ethics make some sense. In the *Koran* and other Islamic holy writings, there is always balance. The writings may be concerned with spiritual matters, but that does not mean they are out of touch with everyday economic realities.

THE PROHIBITION OF *RIBA*

One of the most well known *Koranic* injunctions in the economics sphere is the prohibition of *riba* or interest. This has been much debated in writings by Muslim economists, including the question of what is meant by *riba*, the alternatives to *riba* based finance and the implications for the relationship between Islamic and Western economies.

The definition of *riba* has itself been a contentious matter, complicated by the difficulty of the precise interpretation of meaning from classical Arabic, the language of the *Koran*, to English, the language of most Western economic writing and international commerce. Even the interpretation of classical Arabic in terms of modern colloquial Arabic used by bankers and businessmen can present problems, hence it is hardly surprising that much confusion and misunderstanding has arisen. *Riba* can be interpreted as the addition to a principal sum advanced through a loan, which accrues to the lender and is paid by the borrower. One *Shariah* court in the United Arab Emirates interpreted the addition as being compound interest, with the prohibition of *riba* not applying to simple interest. Most Islamic scholars reject this view, however, and see simple interest as an additional levy.

[18] Sûra 8:41.

There is general agreement that usury, meaning exploitive interest charged by a lender to a borrower, constitutes *riba*. Such exploitative practices are morally dubious, and the case for a prohibition on moral grounds appears convincing, especially if the lender is a wealthy individual or institution such as a bank, and the borrower is poor, and in need of funds. In such circumstances interest charges represent a redistributive flow from the poor to the rich, which can be regarded as regressive, a move worsening income and ultimately wealth inequalities. The *Koran* is explicit in condemning usury, which is compared unfavourably with rewards from desirable activities such as trade: 'They say that trade is like usury, but God hath permitted trade and forbidden usury.'[19] Debtors should be treated with leniency rather than exploited: 'If the debtor is in a difficulty, grant him time till it is easy for him to repay. If ye remit it by way of charity, that is best for you if ye only knew.'[20] In other words, debt rescheduling is desirable, and debt forgiveness especially worthy.

In developing countries, including the economies of the Islamic World, the charges levied by moneylenders are often regarded as usury. They advance funds to those who do not qualify for bank lending, either because they are perceived as too risky, or because the amounts required are small, and the transactions costs in processing the loan are large in relation to the potential returns. These can only be recovered by charging high rates to the borrower, either through interest, or some other means. Whether such charges are actually exploitative usury must be open to question, given that the borrower has no other access to funds. Islamic economists recognise that such charges have to be recouped if lending is to continue, the issue then being how the charges are calculated and levied.

The question of whether all interest constitutes *riba* is further complicated by the distinctions between real and nominal interest. Should interest charges be allowed to compensate for inflation? This would imply zero real interest, but a nominal interest rate equal to the rate of price increase. As inflation rates vary from month to month, this means frequent variations

[19] Sûra 2:275.
[20] Sûra 2:280.

in savings and lending rates if real interest is to be avoided. Yet such variations could be unfair, as not all savers and borrowers will be affected equally by inflation. If, for example, inflation reflects rising food prices, this may hurt the poor more. Yet as price indices include many non-food items which may be less prone to inflation, they may not adequately reflect the burden of inflation for those on low incomes.

The seasonal variations in the prices of fresh foodstuffs introduce additional difficulties. Are lending and borrowing rates to vary according to whether it is harvest or planting time? If so, then rates would presumably fall at harvest time when food is plentiful, but rise during planting when the last season's produce is running out. Yet in the rural communities of the Muslim countries it is during the planting season that farmers are seeking credit for seeds and fertilisers.

One of the injustices of interest transactions from the perspective of Islamic economics is the failure to distinguish between microeconomic and macroeconomic considerations. In Western economies interest is used as an instrument of monetary policy to control the level of aggregate economic activity. Interest rates are raised to curtail borrowing by consumers and investors to reduce short-term inflationary pressures. Rates of interest may also be raised when government deficits are increasing, in order to encourage the commercial banks and the public to purchase government securities. Such interest rate rises penalise existing borrowers whose loans are subject to variable interest, including those who have taken out long-term mortgages to purchase housing. Existing bond holders are also penalised, as the value of their securities falls reflecting its unattractiveness in comparison to the newer higher yielding government issues.

These macroeconomic developments are the responsibility of government, and have nothing to do with the borrowing by individuals and firms at the microeconomic level. The latter may suffer as a result of policies which they were not consulted about, and indeed often could not have anticipated when they entered their agreements to borrow. Islamic economics is therefore concerned to separate the microeconomic from the macroeconomic, but this does not mean it deals only with the former. Indeed in some respects the ideas of Keynesian macroeconomics are anticipated in the *Koran*. There is, for example, a realisation that hoarding is undesirable, as it removes funds from the circulation, reduces economic activity and causes suffering and hardship. 'And there are those who bury gold and silver and spend it not in the way of God: announce unto them a most grievous penalty.'[21] As *riba* encourages the abstinence from consumption and the removal of funds from circulation, it is seen as unjust and inappropriate.

In Western neo-classical economics interest is regarded as a reward for deferring consumption. Muslims, however, are not encouraged to hoard in a selfish fashion, but to spend and use the bounties which Allah has provided for the benefit of his followers: 'O ye who believe, spend out of the bounties we have provided for you.'[22] Believers are urged to be generous rather than miserly, and to share their earnings with the less fortunate: 'Give of the good things which ye have honourably earned, and of the fruits of the earth which we have produced. . . . And whatever ye spend in charity or devotion, be sure God knows it all.'[23] The faithful who are discrete in their giving are especially praised. 'If ye disclose acts of charity, even so it is well, but if ye conceal them, and make them reach those really in need, that is best for you.'[24]

Throughout the sections of the *Koran* dealing with *riba*, the contrast is made between the evil of seeking such rewards, and the blessings which will be bestowed upon those who give freely. The prohibition of *riba* should not be viewed negatively, as it is not just the lending for interest which will lead believers astray, but there is also the lost opportunity of almsgiving. It is this that represents the opportunity cost, as the generous rather than the miserly moneylenders reap the real rewards. 'The parable of those who spend their substance in the way of God is that of a grain of corn: it groweth seven ears, and each ear hath a hundred grains.'[25] Another verse contains a similar appealing message:

> And the likeness of those who spend their substance seeking to please God and to strengthen their souls is a garden

---

[21] Sûra 9:34.
[22] Sûra 2:254.
[23] Sûra 2:267.
[24] Sûra 2:271.
[25] Sûra 2:261.

high and fertile: heavy rain falls on it but makes it yield a double increase of harvest, and if it receives not heavy rain, light moisture sufficeth it. God seeth well whatever ye do.[26]

It is not the monetary value of the charity which matters, but the act of giving itself, and the spirit in which donations are made.

EARLY PIONEERS OF ISLAMIC ECONOMICS

Ibn Taimîyah, who lived in the late thirteenth and early fourteenth centuries, was one of the earliest Islamic scholars to write about economic issues. He was a scholar with many interests, from moral philosophy to science. His major economic writing was a treatise on the *Hisba*, the institutions governing economic activity.[27] This was concerned with how public life should be regulated so that a high degree of morality resulted, with society protected from bad workmanship, fraud, extortion and exploitation. The regulations were to be applied to a market economy, which was assumed to be the normal state of affairs, but Ibn Taimîyah recognised that market outcomes could be unjust.[28] What he provided were ethical guidelines for business and economic life, derived from *Koranic* teaching, with particular emphasis on correct weights and measures, honest trading, and the prohibition of hoarding which he identified as creating artificial scarcity and inflating prices.

A substantial contribution to the development of Islamic economic thought was made by the fourteenth century Islamic philosopher and historian, Ibn Khaldûn.[29] His economic

---

[26] Sûra 2:265.
[27] Ibn Taimîyah, *Public Duties in Islam: the Institution of the Hisba*, Islamic Foundation, Leicester, 1992, translated from the Arabic by Muhtar Holland.
[28] Abdul Azim Islahi, *Economic Concepts of Ibn Taimîyah*, Islamic Foundation, Leicester, 1988, pp. 75–106.
[29] Selections from the *Prolegomena* of Ibn Khaldûn have been translated into English by the economic historian, Charles Issawi, and organised by subject and topic. See Charles Issawi, *An Arab Philosopher of History*, John Murray, London, 1950. Chapter 3 concerns Ibn Khaldûn's economic writings, pp. 71–86. A complete translation of Ibn Khaldûn's *Prolegomena of History* into English in 3 volumes has been undertaken by Franz Rosenthal: Ibn Khaldûn *The Muqaddimah: An Introduction to History*, Princeton University Press, 1958.

writings are better known than those of Ibn Taimîyah and his influence on later Muslim scholars has been considerable, comparable to that of St Thomas Aquinas in the case of Christianity or Rabbi Moshe ben Maimon, Maimonides in the case of Judaism. Ibn Khaldûn's main aim was to explain rather than merely describe history, through the development of a science of culture which could be applied to both economic and political life. His approach was that of the social scientist, with the historical events treated as the data, the objective being to discover the general laws that lay behind the events, and ultimately determined them.

As Muhsin Mahdi points out, the crucial concept was that of *ibar* which in both Arabic and Hebrew means passing on, over, through or beyond, usually relating to a river crossing.[30] The notion of *ibar* was applied by Ibn Khaldûn in two senses. The first was the bridge or link between the external events of history and internal determinants of those events. The second was the bridge between the commonly accepted opinions about, and the true nature of, divine and natural beings. It is the bridge and the terrain around it which Ibn Khaldûn seeks to explore in his philosophical investigation. Culture is at the core, this being defined by the social interactions of men as natural beings. Islamic culture is in turn defined by the social interaction of Muslims, men who are prepared to submit themselves to the will of God. It is through such believers that the Divine enters culture and human history. To understand the work of the God, it is necessary to objectively study the actions of man, including economic transactions, to find the inner meaning.

Ibn Khaldûn was widely read, with an understanding of the Old Testament as well as the *Koran*, and a knowledge of Greek writers, particularly Aristotle, as well as earlier Muslim scholars. From his birthplace in Tunis, he had travelled to Granada and Cairo, and played a significant role in politics in both North Africa and Moorish Spain. It was from Aristotle that Ibn

---

An abridged English version was produced by N.J. Dawood for Princeton University Press, 1967. Chapter 5, pp. 297–333 provides a translation of much of the economics material.

[30] Muhsin Mahdi, *Ibn Khaldûn's Philosophy of History*, George Allen and Unwin, London, 1957, pp. 65–6.

Khaldûn developed his respect for historical facts, and the inductive methodology of trying to derive more general laws from empirical observation. As with Aristotle the question posed by Ibn Khaldûn was moral and ethical: what sort of income generating activity was it honourable and legitimate for men to undertake? The question was to be answered, however, by reasoned enquiry, rather than simply through dogma.

The politically oppressive regimes under which Ibn Khaldûn had to live did not encourage such enquiry. For this reason Ibn Khaldûn had to be careful in his use of language, as well as in his teaching, as he had already experienced imprisonment due to political involvement. Like European medieval Christian scholars, Ibn Khaldûn made little use of deductive logic, which may be explained by the fact that his methods of enquiry were derived from Aristotle rather than Plato. Aristotle's *Politics, the Nicomachaean Ethics,* had been translated into Arabic (*Kitâb al-siyâsa*) and Ibn Khaldûn's treatment is in the tradition of earlier Muslim scholars, notably Avicenna and Averroes.[31]

Ibn Khaldûn's view of economic life is closely connected with his ideas of political order and the role of the state. Indeed, he did not identify economics or politics as separate disciplines, such was his concern with the overriding science of culture.[32] Two different types of economy are contrasted, the primitive which consists of primary modes of production such as farming, animal husbandry and hunting, and the civilised which involves trade and industry.[33] Civilised economic activity is conducted in cities, where money is used for exchange, and elaborate arts and skills flourish. The most talented people are attracted to cities to work, and the more prosperous and attractive the city, the greater the talent attracted. The ruler guarantees security in the city, and an environment conducive to economic activity, with certain and consistent laws administered by an efficient bureaucracy. The ruler's spending provides the demand which keeps the artisans and traders in

[31] Ibid., p. 158.
[32] Joseph J. Spengler, 'Economic thought of Islam: Ibn Khaldûn', *Comparative Studies in Society and History,* Vol. 6, 1963–64, pp. 285–6.
[33] R. Maunier, 'Les idées économiques d'un philosophe arabe au XIV siècle, Ibn Khaldûn', *Revue d'Histoire Économique et Sociale,* Vol. 6, 1913, pp. 409ff.

business. In contrast, in primitive rural areas, security cannot be guaranteed, and economic activity is more precarious.

Under strong state protection, specialisation and division of labour are possible, as artisans will know that they will be paid, and that the traders can meet their demands.[34] Exchange is facilitated by state bureaucrats carrying out regular checks of weights and measures, and commercial laws are applied in a rigorous but fair fashion. Demand generated by the state as it commissions building programmes and public works tends to raise the price level, but moderate inflation is seen as a stimulus to economic activity, as those outside the city are attracted by the increasing money wages. Furthermore, the price of luxury goods may rise by more than necessities, such as basic food-stuffs, with increasing prosperity, and this increasing price differential encourages further artistic effort in the production of high quality goods and even greater specialism.[35] Ibn Khaldûn may have lived six centuries before the concept of the income elasticity of demand was derived, and macroeconomic theories of inflation devised, but his sophisticated economic analysis, based on his observations in Tunis, Granada and Cairo, anticipates the development of such concepts.

The prosperity of the city is self-sustaining, as long as the ruler and those around him are not divided, and the bureaucracy remains free from corruption. Ibn Khaldûn develops a theory of the business cycle, however, where the ruler and the bureaucracy become corrupted by the material prosperity of the city. Taxes are raised, often in an arbitrary manner, to finance the luxury consumption of the ruler and the court circle. It is these taxes, and the increasingly unfair nature of the economic system, which drives the most talented away to work in other cities, while those who remain are no longer strongly motivated to strive for the common good. As a consequence, the city and its civilisation go into decline, and are perhaps overrun by invaders, either from the primitive countryside, or from other stronger cities where the rulers have a stronger moral sense of purpose.[36]

[34] Dieter Weiss, 'Ibn Khaldûn on economic transformation', *International Journal of Middle Eastern Studies*, Vol. 27, 1995, pp. 29–37.
[35] Muhsin Mahdi, *Ibn Khaldûn's Philosophy*, p. 218; Charles Issawi, *Arab Philosopher*, pp. 74–5.
[36] Muhsin Mahdi, *Ibn Khaldûn's Philosophy*, pp. 219–20.

MODERN MUSLIM APPROACHES TO ECONOMICS

Two modern approaches to Islamic economics can be distinguished, the political economy avenue and the conventional economic avenue, with both avenues pointing in a moral direction. It would be misleading to view the two approaches as being in competition with each other or mutually exclusive. Indeed, in some respects they complement each other, although their advocates naturally have their differences, and approach Islamic economics from very different perspectives.

Often the political economy approach is almost polemic, urging that policy makers follow a particular line because it is morally right, almost regardless of the economic arguments, or indeed the economic costs. Economic theory is then adapted to fit the moral arguments, rather than any moral compromises being made, as it is the morality which is of paramount importance. This approach is interdisciplinary in the sense that economics is regarded as part of moral philosophy, even if those involved are working in a particular specialised area.

Advocates of this approach have attempted to construct a completely Islamic economic paradigm from first principles, drawing on the writings of early Islamic economic thinkers such as Zaid bin Ali and Abu Yusuf in the eighth century and later scholars such as Abu Ubaid, Ibn Khaldûn and Jamaluddin Al-Afghani.[37] Some followers of this approach ignore or even reject the conventional Western neo-classical literature and instead build up models which tend to be historical and legalistic in nature, with some parallels in institutional economics. Bani Sadr, the Iranian writer, and for a short time, President of the Islamic Republic, adopts such an approach. His writings are reviewed in the next section. The Muslim brotherhood in Egypt adopted a similar approach, being both anti-Western, seeking an end to the exploitation of Muslim resources by the West, and a revived Islamic order of prosperity that would bring strength and restored dignity to Muslims. Their thinking was arguably more political than economic, leading exponents

---

[37] Muhammad Abdul Mannan, *Islamic Economics: Theory and Practice*, Hodder and Stoughton and the Islamic Academy, Cambridge, 1986, pp. 22–4.

including Hasan Al-Bannā, Sayyid Qutb and Khālid Muhammad Khālid in the first half of this century.[38]

The second, more conventional, approach taken by many modern Islamic economists, perhaps the majority, draws on the writings of earlier Muslim scholars, but at the same time recognises the value of the tools and methods of Western economists. This approach is more in the mainstream of modern economics, at least with regard to method and style, but is nevertheless distinct in starting from different axioms.[39] Some Islamic economists are even more mainstream in approach, accepting the basic premises of Western theories, but modifying certain assumptions to make them acceptable to Muslims. For those who follow this approach, the task is to validate what is acceptable in classical and neo-classical theory, and weed out and suggest alternatives for what is not.

The advocates of this second approach are usually conventionally trained economists, often with higher degrees from Western universities, who have been prompted to rethink their approach to economics to take account of their own deeply held personal convictions as practising Muslims. This group of writers includes many economists from Pakistan, notably Sayed Naqvi, Muhammad Sidiqqi, Umer Chapra, Kurshid Ahmed and Fahim Khan,[40] and a number of Bangladesh economists. It was partly the consideration of the economic prospects of Pakistan and Bangladesh as distinctly Muslim states in the Indian subcontinent that resulted in these economists exploring the ideas of an Islamic economic and financial system. To some extent the idea of what constituted an Islamic economy was linked to that of the national development of largely Muslim states. These scholars are economists first and foremost, inspired by an Islamic ideal, with a knowledge of *Shariah* law, but with limited legal expertise.

[38] Kenneth Cragg, *Counsels in Contemporary Islam*, Edinburgh University Press, 1965, pp. 117–18.

[39] Masudul Alam Choudbury, *The Principles of Islamic Political Economy*, Macmillan, London, 1992, pp. 9–40.

[40] Fahim Khan typifies this approach, as he takes Keynesian and neo-classical macroeconomic and finance theory and adapts them from an Islamic perspective. See his *Essays in Islamic Economics*, Islamic Foundation, Leicester, 1995.

Perhaps the most distinguished advocate of this approach is Sayed Naqvi, who sees Islamic economics as the study of the behaviour of 'representative' Muslims, and a derivation of an economic system that meets their needs as identified through their observed actions.[41] The advantage of this definition is that it stresses the need for empirical observation, and puts Islamic economics on the same scientific footing as conventional economics, using well tried and tested methodologies. The alternative is to have economists acting as theologians, which they are ill-equipped to be, making their own interpretations of the *Koran* and the *Shariah*, and potentially imposing these on Muslims in the name of religion. Naqvi goes further, emphasising the need to free Muslims from anachronistic ideas, traditions and institutions, including those influenced by the great Muslim jurists. In other words, empiricism is to replace dogma, much as Ibn Khaldûn argued six centuries earlier.

An Islamic economic system is, in other words, man-made, just like any other, the difference being it reflects the economic choices of Muslims. There is no Divine guarantee of its success, or even survival, that being the challenge for the Muslims themselves. All Muslims can pray to Allah for guidance in their own actions, including economists and jurists. This is different however from seeking Divine approval to dictate to others, which contradicts the spirit of Islam. The individual Muslim is economically and socially constrained by his own conscience, and his responsibilities to the Muslim community, but other human agents should not seek to curtail his liberty.

Naqvi sees the four foundations of Islamic ethics as unity (*Tawhid*), equilibrium (*Al Adl wal Ihsan*), free will (*Ikhtiy'ar*), and responsibility (*Fardh*).[42] From these axioms Naqvi considers the rules of economic behaviour in Muslim societies, which may, or may not, function according to these principles. This gives the economist a yardstick to use when observing

---

[41] Sayed Nawab Haider Naqvi, *Islam, Economics and Society*, Kegan Paul International, London, 1994, pp. xix–xx. One of Naqvi's earlier works where he was developing his ideas was *Economics and Ethics: An Islamic Synthesis*, Islamic Foundation, Leicester, 1991.

[42] Ibid., pp. 26–34.

Muslim consumer behaviour or measuring the distribution of income in Muslim states. In a brief, but useful, review of the role of the state in Muslim economies, Naqvi supports the position of Iranian economists such as Bani Sadr who support government intervention to achieve a social balance, and Taleghani who advocate a state guarantee of minimum living standards. Nevertheless, the role of government is limited. The state may restructure property rights by abolishing uneconomic and unethical institutions such as feudalism, but the private sector can play a major role in producing goods and services.

Naqvi is unsympathetic to socialism, but distinguishes between capitalism as a mode of production and as a socioeconomic framework.[43] The former may be acceptable to Muslims, and indeed Naqvi views it as essential for the industrialisation of Muslim countries. The latter is less acceptable, not least because it represents a sub-system of Protestant ethics. Some aspects of these ethics may be quite legitimate when viewed from a Muslim perspective, but others are not, not least the exploitation by some capitalists. Viner's views in this respect are cited, although it is not clear if Naqvi is aware that Viner's interpretation was coloured by his desire to rehabilitate Roman Catholic views on commerce and industry.

AN ISLAMIC ALTERNATIVE TO MARXISM

One group of modern Muslim scholars can be best categorised as political economists, often originally adhering to socialist convictions, but seeking moral and ethical alternatives which are likely to find ready acceptance amongst Muslims. Their political economy solutions are presented as being fully compatible with an Islamic value system, and an alternative to the exploitative system associated with Western capitalism and imperialism which has been imposed at such costs in many parts of the Islamic world. This radical critique was associated with Iranian writers such as Muhammad Baqer as-Sadr and Abulhasan Bani Sadr. Muhammed Baqer as-Sadr's work, *Iqtisaduna, Our Economic System*, had a considerable influence on radical *Shi'i* economic thinking prior to the Iranian

43 Ibid., pp. 72–8.

revolution.[44] Much of *Iqtisaduna* was a critique of Marxism from an Islamic perspective, with a much shorter appraisal of capitalism.

Bani Sadr was much influenced by as-Sadr's thinking. His main economic work was *Eqtesad-e Towhidi, The Economy of Divine Unity*, based on his thesis for the Sorbonne, but here it is perhaps appropriate to review his most popular study, *Kar va Kargar Dar Islam*, translated as *Work and the Worker in Islam*.[45] This was written as an Islamic alternative to Marx's communist party manifesto, and is addressed to Iranian workers and the Islamic revolutionary masses in the same way that the *Tudeh* party, the Iranian Communist Party, had addressed an earlier generation back in the 1950s at the time of Mossadeq, the Iranian nationalist Prime Minister who challenged the Western oil companies' dominance of oil. The *Tudeh* party was ultimately to undermine Mossadeq and the *Mujahideen Khalq* resistance group which Bani Sadr was sympathetic to, and therefore they are denounced with some vehemence in *Kar va Kargar Dar Islam*.[46]

As with Marx, labour is seen as the key to value, and honest toil is to be commended as man has been endowed with talents which are to be used. Three types of labour are seen as necessary for society, manual labour, administrative work and innovative effort. Most people are capable of all three to varying extents, and it is desirable that they should engage in each, as a worker who confines himself to manual work in an unthinking way will loose his mental ability. On the other hand, those who only work with their brains will not develop manual dexterity. It is important to use even leisure time for thinking. Manual workers who spend their leisure hours watching television are not developing their mental powers, and are condemning themselves to a limited and unbalanced life.[47]

---

[44] Chibli Mallat, 'Muhammad Baqer as-Sadr', in Ali Rahnema, (ed.), *Pioneers of Islamic Revival*, Zed Books, London, 1994, pp. 251–72. See also Hanna Batatu, 'Iraq's underground Shi'i movements: characteristics, causes and prospects', *Middle Eastern Journal*, Vol. 35, No. 4, 1981, pp. 577–94.
[45] Abdulhasan Bani Sadr, *Work and the Worker in Islam*, Hamdami Foundation, Tehran, 1980, originally published in Farsi by the Payam Azadi Press, Tehran, 1978.
[46] Ibid., p. 4.
[47] Ibid., p. 19.

Although according to Bani Sadr work belongs to the worker, the worker is not entitled to the entire value of what he produces. At least three groups have a share in the value, nature which provides the raw materials, society which has provided the education and training for the worker, and capital, which has provided the tools the worker uses.[48] This capital accumulation is the result of past work which must be recognised. The worker's use of raw materials is recovered through resource rents, the social contribution is paid for by tax payments, and capital is rewarded through the profits the worker generates. All these are seen as legitimate rewards, which illustrates the distinction between Bani Sadr's views and a simple Marxist labour theory of value.

Bani Sadr realises that recognising the essential role of labour does not provide a guide to how the social product should be divided, nor will it ensure social justice. Workers themselves have different personal talents, creativity and earning ability which inevitably results in material inequalities. Material needs may differ from earning capacity. Should workers be paid simply according to their material needs and those of their families, with, for example, those with larger families getting paid more even though, because of their family responsibilities, they may have less time for their paid work? Alternatively, and closest to Western neo-classical theory, is the view that there should be material incentives, to encourage people to work harder, irrespective of material need.

Bani Sadr does not reject either of these two conflicting positions, but neither does he support one over the other. He states that the religious judicial authority may order additional religious taxes if they believe that excessive and inequitably distributed income is causing corruption in the society, as such taxes can help maintain the social equilibrium.[49] It is a matter of saving the rich from themselves, and ensuring the basic needs of the poor are met so that they can live in moral dignity, rather than bringing about a redistribution of income and wealth to ensure mere material equality. Ultimately, what Bani Sadr is concerned about is changing popular attitudes, so that there is more appreciation of the spiritual rather than an

[48] Ibid., pp. 29–30.
[49] Ibid., p. 31.

obsession with material goods. The ultimate reward for work is spiritual, it being a way of bringing the worker closer to God. Moderation should be the rule for consumption, but even in eating people cannot have unlimited personal choice, as if they harm their bodies through eating and drinking, they damage their own souls, and may impair unborn children. Bani Sadr stresses man's responsibility to God, as well as social responsibilities.

For Bani Sadr the question of the ownership of the means of production is less important than their use. The *Imam* or religious authority should ensure that there is fairness and justice in economic transactions. A small shopkeeper may own his premises, but if he has to deal with powerful wholesalers who decide how much he can buy and sell, and the prices and margins, the shopkeeper may have little control over his own business. The commercial laws should protect the weak from exploitation, and at the same time control monopoly power, and profiteering in particular. Profiteering is seen as a cause of inflation rather than a consequence of it, as Bani Sadr's attitude towards profiteering is that of the moralist rather than the analytical economist. Nevertheless, he recognises that profiteering frequently reappears even when moral campaigns are undertaken against it. Rather than exploring more fundamental economic causes of inflation, such as supply rigidities or excessive demand, Bani Sadr sees less emphasis on monetary values as the answer, almost a kind of spiritual demonetisation. Monetary policy is viewed as inappropriate and amoral, as excessive creation of money will result in inflation and those engaged in economic transactions being cheated. On the other hand monetary control will result in shortages, so that some deceive others in order to obtain a share of the limited supply.[50]

Bani Sadr's institutional framework is that of the nation state rather than some wider economic entity. His attention to international economic relations is confined to a few remarks on the oil industry, and a critique of the exploitation of Iran by international interests under the Shah, although what these interests are is not closely defined. There is a defence of *Sh'ism*

[50] Ibid., p. 32.

and Ali as symbols of the *Imamate*.[51] Although Bani Sadr spent much of his life in France, he makes no mention of French society, his interest clearly being confined to his own country of origin. Nor does he appear interested in the wider Islamic world, as there is no suggestion that his ideas are meant for anyone but an Iranian *Sh'ite* constituency. Those who have been educated in Iran and who leave for other countries for higher salaries are condemned, as they should feel an obligation to serve those whose sacrifices have helped pay for their education.[52]

The wider interest in Bani Sadr's work, and arguably its universality, is in his contrasts between the significance of Islamic revolution and communist revolution. He sees the latter as being false dogma: 'Oh you leftists who are against religion because, as you say, it's dogma, why now do you insist on sticking to your own dogmas?'[53] Islam according to Bani Sadr defines man in his relationship with God, but man is capable of movement and spiritual development towards infinity. In contrast he asks the leftists who reject this spiritual vision:

> Do we then have to conceive of man as some sort of creature who simply consumes . . . and justice as simply the equal consumption of those resources by all men? In that case our highest vision of man corresponds to a society of sheep.[54]

It is when contrasting the emptiness of communist dogma with the spiritual vision of Islamic revolutionaries that Bani Sadr is undoubtedly at his most persuasive.

ISLAM AND CAPITALISM

For Islamic economists the task is to design a system which can cope with the full range of economic problems of resource allocation and distribution. Neo-classical economics is seen as amoral, and equated with capitalism by the political economists

[51] Ibid., p. 35.
[52] Ibid., p. 12.
[53] Ibid., p. 78.
[54] Ibid.

and some of the mainstream economists, including Chapra and Siddiqi. As Umer Chapra has provided one of the most widely read and influential critiques of both capitalism and communism, it is appropriate to review his work first.[55] His book on *Islam and the Economic Challenge* raises many interesting philosophical questions about where the secular global economy is heading.

Chapra refers to the crisis in Marxism and the demise of the socialist economic system, as well as the resurgence of capitalism and free markets. Yet he points out the obvious failures of capitalism: deepening cyclical unemployment, rising prices, debt and growing inequality. Nevertheless, according to Chapra the Marxist alternative has proved to be a false dream. Market socialism appears to solve few problems, and is not even as economically efficient as capitalism. At the same time the western welfare state appears to be in crisis, as it places unrealistic demands on the state, and creates huge economic imbalances. Responses are clearly needed, and Chapra outlines a very different approach to economic difficulties based on the premises of Islamic economics, although the application of this to the industrialised economies is not spelt out.

Instead, Chapra concentrates on the Muslim economies and their development policies. He provides an especially convincing critique of development economics, pointing out its inconsistencies. He criticises the widespread acceptance of the 'vicious circle of poverty' and Nurkse's concept of a 'low level equilibrium that perpetuates itself.'[56] The assumptions of development economics regarding modernisation are basically ethno-centric.[57] In order to develop, countries are supposed to adopt the social institutions and values of the West, with the emphasis on personal materialism. Yet many in the developing countries, especially in the Islamic World, do not share these Western aspirations, and certainly do not see European or American life-styles as a role model to emulate. In fact, rapid development has occurred in many Islamic countries without

[55] M. Umer Chapra, *Islam and the Economic Challenge*, Islamic Foundation, Leicester, 1992.
[56] Ibid., pp. 149–51.
[57] Wolfgang Sacks, 'Progress and development', in Paul Ekins and Manfred Max-Neef (eds), *Real Life Economics: Understanding Wealth Creation*, Routledge, London, 1992, pp. 156–61.

the change in value systems that many Western economists regarded as necessary. Muslims have become more devout, not less, and the acquisition of new skills and advanced technology has proved to be quite compatible with the maintenance of traditional value systems.

In the literature on development economics there has been a move away from an emphasis on planning to a rediscovery of markets. The stress is on export promotion rather than import substitution, but through economic liberalisation rather than state direction and control. The Far Eastern economies are seen by many as the development model which other countries should follow. Yet as Chapra stresses there are many features of these economies that Western economists tend to neglect. He notes in particular the socio-economic justice and social harmony in countries such as Japan, Korea and Taiwan, with much less marked income disparities than those found in the West. There is also the high propensity to save and invest, associated with consumption sacrifice rather than lavish and unnecessary expenditure on material luxuries. The experience of these non-Western countries which have sought to preserve their traditional values and cultures has perhaps more relevance for the Islamic world than the development models of the West.

Chapra provides a clear and coherent account of the Islamic world view based on the three principles of *tawhid* (unity), *khilafah* (vice regency), and *adalah* (justice).[58] For Muslims these should be the guiding principles for development and economic relations. *Tawhid* concerns the one unique universe created by God which man must respect. *Khilafah* is the concept of man as God's agent on earth, empowered with considerable discretion to act for good or evil, but a duty to use the world's resources in the most effective and just way possible. The concept of socio-economic justice or *adalah* implies a duty to live by the *Shariah* Islamic law, and avoid all forms of *zulm*, which involves inequality, exploitation and oppression. Chapra outlines a strategy for putting these lofty ideals into practice involving a socially agreed moral filter mechanism. This involves collective value judgements, though these must be subject to divine sanction which limits the power of human

[58] M. Umer Chapra, *Islam and the Economic Challenge*, pp. 199–212.

discretion. Such limits are proper, as man has limited capabilities, and only Allah understands his true needs. Without the guidance of Allah, development would be meaningless, the material achievements hollow and worthless.

This raises fundamental issues regarding the economic challenge. What exactly are governments and peoples seeking to achieve? Is economic progress possible and how can it be defined? Should economic history be regarded as a linear process of improvement? Is there a perfect state to aspire to, or is it the striving that matters rather than the arrival at the end?

There are, of course, no simple answers to such questions, but Chapra's work at least provides some guidance to current thinking amongst Islamic economists. The stress on the 'right motivation' provides an important clue. Self-interest has its role, and is, according to Chapra, not necessarily bad. This is only one driving force, however; humans are also social beings. There is a contradiction here. Capitalism is about self-motivation, but it cannot accommodate social conscience. Socialism can, but it destroys self-motivation. Some other way is needed. For Chapra it is the accountability before an all-powerful being from which nothing can be hidden. Rational man is concerned not just with the physical world and the material, but the hereafter.[59] The economic challenge is ultimately a test. It is the human response which matters, not the material outcome.[60] Viewed from this perspective it is not at all clear that the developed countries are in fact developed in human terms, or that the so called less developed or developing countries are underdeveloped.

ISLAMIC ECONOMICS IN THE MODERN MIDDLE EAST

Some attribute the low level of development in the Middle East to the population's adherence to Islamic beliefs.[61] Secularisation, if not Westernisation, is seen as the key to development,

[59] Ibid., 28–36.
[60] M. Umer Chapra, *Islam and Economic Development*, International Institute of Islamic Thought and Islamic Research Institute, Islamabad, 1993, pp. 65–73.
[61] W. Montgomery Watt, *Islamic Fundamentalism and Modernity*, Routledge, London, 1989, pp. 3–8.

with religion viewed as an obstacle to be overcome if not actively discouraged. Needless to say, there are few in the Middle East who take this view, and any who do are an unrepresentative minority. Political demands are increasingly expressed in the language of Islam, and much of the political opposition now comes from the Islamists rather than the secularist left. These developments have been reflected in the economic sphere by the growth of interest in Islamic economics.[62] Funding from Saudi Arabian sources has, of course, encouraged research in this field, but the growth of interest in Islamic economics has more to do with politics than simply finance. The Iranian revolution in 1979 was the most dramatic manifestation of the desire to bring Islam into the political and economic sphere, but there are continuing indications of popular support for Islamic policies throughout the region. In Algeria the Islamic parties won the first round of the 1992 elections, which prompted the secularist government to cancel the second round. In Egypt many of the poor and low income earners look to local Muslim activists rather than the government, and the trend towards stricter religious adherence is apparent even amongst the highly educated youth in the universities. Islamic parties are well represented in the Jordanian parliament, although they suffered a setback in the 1992 elections.

In the Middle East there is not the same co-incidence of religious and nationalistic forces as in Pakistan, as national identity can be defined in ethnic and linguistic terms. This was as much the case for Nasser's Arab 'nation' as it was for Ataturk's Turkey. In such a context secularist economic policies were quite acceptable. There was, nevertheless, a desire for an alternative to the capitalist economic system, which was associated by many in the Middle East with colonialism and imperialism. For some in government and academic circles a socialist planned economy was viewed as the best alternative, although not necessarily a communist system, which outside Iraq and Yemen had few adherents in the Middle East. Even those who rejected Western economics in the 1950s and 1960s were secularised themselves in their economic thinking. There was little awareness, and no desire, to try to rediscover Islamic

---

[62] Akbar S. Ahmed, *Postmodernism and Islam*, Routledge, London, 1992, pp. 33–7.

economic ideas, at least amongst the intelligentsia and the ruling classes.

In most Middle East states the modern secularised education system existed side by side with traditional *Koranic* schools, but over time the latter were increasingly marginalised as resources were directed to state education. Even at university level religious education tended to be segregated from the new mainstream, with teachers at traditional religious universities such as Al Azhar in Cairo largely isolated and neglected. The Egyptian government tried to bring the latter under its control and influence, much to the dismay of many Islamists. Teaching and research on Islamic commercial practice was left to lawyers, with little interest in development, rather than economists. Most academic economists in Egypt were found in institutions such as the private American University, or the state financed Cairo and Ain Shams Universities. Few of these had much knowledge of or interest in Islamic economics. Those who were devout Muslims tended to separate their professional interests from their religious beliefs, partly because they were given no encouragement to do otherwise.

It is only during the last two decades that Islamic economics has started to be treated as a discipline in its own right with courses being offered in some state institutions. Part of the revival has been aided through private funding from Gulf sources as already mentioned, such as the assistance from the Al Baraka Islamic financial group for the Centre of Islamic Economics in the King Abdul Aziz University in Jeddah and the Islamic Foundation in Leicester, England. Both these centres promote research in Islamic economics and development. There has also been encouragement from the Islamic Development Bank in Jeddah which has helped to bring together Pakistani and Arab economists interested in this area. Needless to say, in Iran, since the Islamic revolution, there has been a proliferation of courses in Islamic economics in universities throughout the country, although the research effort is arguably weaker.

Economists who emphasis constraints on the supply side as an impediment to development often stress the importance of incentives for the individual businessman, entrepreneur or capitalist as the key to faster growth. How important are such material incentives in Islamic societies? Can a value system which condemns the individual pursuit of material self-interest be conducive to economic development? Does the downgrading of economic differentiation as defined by living standards impede material advance?

For many in Iran it is the Ayatollahs, Mullahs and other members of the *Ulamā*, the religious scholars, who are the most highly respected members of society. Business leaders, and even the government and lay members of the *majilis*, the Iranian parliament, do not command the same respect. The authority of the religious leadership comes from their knowledge of the *Koran* and the holy writings, and their ability to interpret the *Shariah* religious laws. An Ayatollah is able to recite the entire *Koran* without referring to the written text, a remarkable feat of memory which few can achieve. Many regard those who can manage this task as inspired by Allah.

The religious leaders are respected for their piety, not their possessions, as they have little personal material wealth, and no need or desire for worldly goods beyond what is necessary for sustenance so that they can perform their religious duties. Development for Khomeini was a tool, a means, but not an end. The objective of development was to strengthen the community of believers, the *ummah*, the true Muslim nation. Only then could they confront the *infidel*, the unbelievers, including the great Satan, the leadership of the United States who wallowed in their materialistic decadence, and repeatedly tried to corrupt the Muslim faithful.

Such views may sound extreme to many in the West, but in Iran where the CIA was credited with overthrowing the Mosaddeq government in the 1950s and reinforcing the power of the corrupt governments under the Shah, the rhetoric still strikes a popular chord. Elsewhere in the Middle East, especially in the Arab world, similar sentiments bring popular approval, and explain why the mourning for President Sadat of Egypt, when he was assassinated by extremists, was so muted. Mubarak is regarded by a significant element of the Muslim masses in Egypt as a tool of the United States and its agent, the much despised International Monetary Fund, which has dictated so much of recent economic policy in Egypt as a result of the government's indebtedness.

The mix of religious conviction and the politics of populist rebellion has proved a powerful force in the Middle East, which has somewhat sidelined economic debate in recent years. Against this background reforms that try to reduce the role of the state through privatisation or the reduction of regulation are seen as peripheral. It is not that Islamists are opposed to such policies, but rather the fact that they believe that most Arab governments are incapable of carrying out any worthwhile policy because of their moral corruption. The United States and the Western economies are not seen as role models which the Islamic economies should aspire to follow in any case, and therefore any Western economics policies which they pursue are at best inappropriate and perhaps *haram*, forbidden to the faithful.

IRAN'S ISLAMIC ECONOMY

As the only country to have experienced an Islamic revolution, it is interesting to examine Iran's economic structures and policies. How far did Khomeini's revolution affect the economy? Did it result in a real shift in priorities, with more stress on the spiritual, and an end to secular materialism? Did a new Muslim solidarity result, and were the revolutionary ideas sustainable when confronted with the practical economic realities of an underdeveloped country?

Observers of Iran's post-revolutionary economy seem to agree that the teaching of Khomeini had some impact on the Iranian economy, as did the ideas of Bani Sadr, outlined earlier, during the 1980–81 period when he was president of the Islamic Republic. The influence is difficult to evaluate however, as it was largely a question of affecting social attitudes, rather than institutional changes. Furthermore, as the economic objectives were not simply a matter of material advance, it is not appropriate to judge the success or otherwise of the Islamic revolution by examining conventional development indicators. In any case, comparing per capita gross national product growth rates with the earlier period under the Shah is meaningless, as the oil price rises of the 1970s inflated the gross domestic prices, whereas the 1980s were a period of falling oil prices. This period also brought the war with Iraq, which severely disrupted economic activity, and from which the Iranian economy has yet to recover.

Ayatollah Khomeini had little interest in economic matters, and was once reported as having said that the revolution
was about Islam and not the price of melons.[63] Economic growth
was not seen as important, the stress being on economic
justice and dignity for the poor, including those in the rural
areas and south Tehran. Khomeini himself led an austere
and puritanical lifestyle, and renounced the accumulation of
wealth. The Iranian élite who had amassed fortunes under
the Shah were seen as corrupt and un-Islamic. Khomeini
wanted a return to a type of simple idealised Islamic economy
which was thought to exist during the lifetime of the Prophet
himself 1400 years earlier. The key aim was to shift popular
attitudes, to convert, at least in Iran, *homo œconomicus* to *homo
Islamicus.*[64]

There was no economic blueprint for how an Islamic
economy could be created in Iran, partly because even those
involved in the revolution had not been preparing for government, and they themselves were surprised with the ease with
which the Shah was overthrown. Furthermore, those involved
in the revolution were a broad coalition of anti-Shah forces,
which included the clergy, moderate nationalists, the remnants
of the *Tudeh* communist party, and the *Mujahideen,* a diverse
grouping which included religious leftists. The clergy were
to win the immediate post-revolutionary struggle for power,
but this still left open the precise agenda of how to build an
Islamic state and society.[65] Perhaps inevitably the agenda
actually adopted was a compromise that fell well short of
the initial goals of the revolution as embodied in Articles 43
and 44 of the constitution of the Islamic Republic which
deals with the issues of economic sovereignty and economic
justice.[66]

[63] Jahangir Amuzegar, *Iran's Economy under the Islamic Republic,* IB Tauris,
London, p. 17.
[64] Hamid Hosseini, 'From *homo economicus* to *homo Islamicus*: the universality
of economic science reconsidered', in Cyrus Bina and Hamid Zangeneh,
(eds), *Modern Capitalism and Islamic Ideology in Iran,* St. Martin's Press, New
York, 1992, pp. 103–20.
[65] Mohsen M. Milani, *The Making of Iran's Islamic Revolution,* Westview Press,
Boulder, Colorado, 1988, pp. 273–317.
[66] Hooshgang Amirahmadi, *Revolution and Economic Transition: the Iranian
Experience,* State University of New York Press, 1990, pp. 5–6.

One of the priorities in the Islamic Republic was self-sufficiency in agriculture,[67] as the increasing dependency of the country on imported foodstuffs from the *infidel* was evident under the Shah, including meat which could not be guaranteed as *halal*, or fit for consumption by Muslims. Meanwhile, the agricultural sector had stagnated under the Shah, with much of the new investment directed towards joint ventures with Western agri-businesses on marginal lands that were to prove ill-conceived while the traditional farming sector was neglected. There were statements about the importance of planning for agriculture in the immediate post-revolutionary period reflecting the influence of Bani Sadr and the leftists, as well as Article 44 of the constitution which mentions planning.[68] With the war with Iraq and lower oil prices, the actual investments in agriculture were well below those envisaged in the 1983 Development Plan which gave priority to agriculture. Agricultural output increased, but this was largely due to higher prices, which made farming more profitable, but which increased urban food costs. These measures reduced the flow of people from the countryside into the cities, but with Iran's rapid increase in population after the Islamic Revolution from 37 million in 1979 to over 61 million by 1993,[69] self-sufficiency in foodstuffs remained a distant if not impossible goal for the Islamic Republic. Nevertheless, food production per capita increased by over 20 per cent over the 1979–92 period according to an independent World Bank index.[70]

Given the particular interest in Islamic teaching on the prohibition of *riba*, it was perhaps not surprising that the major Islamic reform measures in post-revolutionary Iran were in the field of banking. A law for interest-free banking was introduced in 1983 which was designed to eliminate *riba* from

---

[67] Asghar Schirazi, *Islamic Development Policy: the Agrarian Question in Iran*, Lynne Rienner Publishers, Boulder, Colorado, 1993, pp. 87–92.

[68] Ibid., p. 103.

[69] World Bank estimates. See *World Development Report*, Oxford University Press, 1981, p. 135 for the 1979 figure and *World Bank Atlas*, Washington, 1995, p. 8 for the 1993 figure.

[70] World Bank, *World Tables*, Johns Hopkins University Press, Baltimore, 1994, pp. 354–5.

the financial system and Islamise banking.[71] The banks had already been nationalised in 1979, following the demands of the Islamic leftists and support for the measures from Bani Sadr. Islamisation could be regarded as the more fundamental measure, however, as it involved changing banking methods and operations, rather than being a mere change of ownership.[72] The implication of the Islamic banking legislation was that profit sharing was introduced as an alternative to interest transactions, using the standardised Islamic financial contracts which will be discussed in the next section. As the existing bank staff were retained, almost 20 000 went on Islamic training courses.[73]

The extent to which the Islamisation of the banking system has been a success is difficult to judge. Bank deposits almost quadrupled when measured in rials between 1983 and 1991, but with the rapid depreciation of the rial, demand, savings and investment deposits all declined in terms of US dollars over this period.[74] In the absence of empirical evidence from bank clients it is impossible to ascertain whether this was due to the economic problems caused by the war with Iraq and the decline in oil prices, or a lack of customer confidence in the Islamised banks. Most surveys of Islamic banking in Iran discuss the financing methods, as outlined in the 1983 law and the commercial bank reports, but there has been no independent investigation of the volume of banking business.

ISLAMIC PROFIT SHARING INVESTMENT

In Western economies the rate of interest serves as a pricing mechanism to bring the demand for loanable funds into

---

[71] Zubair Iqbal and Abbas Mirakhor, *Islamic Banking*, IMF Occasional Paper No. 49, Washington, 1987. A complete translation of the law is provided; pp. 31–43.

[72] Hamid Zangeneh and Ahmad Salam, 'An analytical model of an Islamic banking firm', in Cyrus Bina and Hamid Zangeneh, *Modern Capitalism*, pp. 201–11.

[73] Hossein Aryan, 'Iran: the impact of Islamisation on the financial system', in Rodney Wilson, (ed.), *Islamic Financial Markets*, Routledge, London, 1990, p. 156.

[74] Estimated from data in the World Bank, *World Tables*, pp. 354–9.

equilibrium with the supply of savings. If the demand exceeds
the supply, interest rates rise, encouraging savings but deter-
ring borrowers. For business borrowers, the returns on the
projects for which they are seeking funding may be insuf-
ficient to justify the increased costs of borrowing. Some economists in the Islamic world believe that the prohibition of
riba only applies to personal loans and not business finance,
where interest can continue to act as a rationing mechanism
to determine how loanable funds are allocated. Most Muslim
economists reject this thinking, asserting that it would be
inconsistent to permit some transactions based on interest,
but not others.[75]

The Islamic alternative to *riba* finance is based on the concept of profit sharing between those who provide the funds
and those using the finance. This is referred to as the principle of *mudarabah*.[76] The return for the financier is related to
the income from the use of the funds after costs have been
covered. This implies a variable return which cannot be fixed
in advance.[77] The financier's return is justified by the risk taken,
as there will always be uncertainty over future returns. If there
are no profits then the financier will obtain no return. This
contrasts with fixed interest lending, where the borrower has
to service the debt regardless of the level of profit or losses.
When Western businesses get into difficulty, it is often the
banks who foreclose. Bankruptcy is less likely with Islamic
financing, where loan servicing obligations are eliminated when
there is no profit. It should be noted that the entrepreneur
being financed is not liable for any losses under a *mudarabah*
contract, as it is only the financier who can suffer from losses.

With Western *riba* based finance there are of course risks,
the major risk being that of default by the borrower. For this
reason collateral or some form of guarantee from a third party
is often required before funds are advanced. This reduces the
lender's risk. There can also be uncertainty over the return if

[75] Rodney Wilson, *Islamic Business: Theory and Practice*, Economist Intelligence
Unit Special Report, No. 221, London, 1985, p. 24.
[76] M. Umer Chapra, *Towards a Just Monetary System*, Islamic Foundation,
Leicester, 1985, pp. 71–7.
[77] Waqar Masood Khan, *Towards an Interest Free Islamic Economic System*,
Islamic Foundation, Leicester, 1985, pp. 28–33 and 73–9.

the loan is contracted at variable interest, but in such cases the variability will depend on government monetary policy and macroeconomic conditions, not on the return from the project at the microeconomic level. Islamic finance is by nature participatory in the sense that the provider of the finance shares in the project risk with the businessman undertaking the venture. Indeed, it can almost be regarded as a type of venture capital financing, especially when it is small businesses which are the recipients.

Within an Islamic financial system the role of banks is clearly different from that of conventional commercial banks as the banks tend to be more closely involved with both their depositors and those being funded. Nevertheless, Islamic banks aim to provide a similar range of services to Western banks. Depositors are offered current accounts for their everyday transactions, and are issued with cheque books and cash cards for use in automatic telling machines. No interest is offered on such accounts, but clients are usually expected to open current accounts if they are to qualify for bank funding. Overdrafts are not usually permitted by Islamic banks, although if a client accidentally goes into the red, the bank may at its discretion honour the cheque. A charge will not normally be levied in such circumstances, but the bank will write to the client seeking an explanation. The automatic telling machines are programmed to issue funds only to clients with credit balances.

Savings facilities are offered by Islamic banks on a *mudarabah* profit sharing basis with depositors sharing in the bank's profits. Such deposits are often designated as being in investment accounts, and are regarded as long-term precautionary balances rather than funds required for immediate transactions. There are often minimum periods required for notice of withdrawals from investment accounts, varying from one month to a year.[78] The longer the minimum period of notice for withdrawal, the larger the depositor's share in the bank's profit. Investment accounts are run in perpetuity, and are therefore different from time deposits which have to be renewed at regular intervals.

---

[78] John R. Presley, *Directory of Islamic Financial Institutions*, Macmillan, London, 1988, p. 22.

If a bank makes losses the depositors get no profit share, but the value of their deposits is guaranteed, and they have first call on the bank's assets in the case of liquidation. This puts them in a different category to shareholders, who can make capital losses as well as gains, and in the event of insolvency loose their investments. Shareholders are paid dividends based on the bank's profits, but these are discretionary rather than being formula based as with investment account holders.

For individuals with substantial funds to invest, Islamic banks can act as intermediaries between the investor and the fund user. In such cases the investor shares directly in the profit from the project being funded rather than the bank's profit. This of course may, and usually does, involve a higher risk for the investor. The bank charges the investor an arrangement fee for setting up such financing and a management fee for looking after the ongoing distribution of the profits. The recipient is also charged fees on the same basis. As stock markets are poorly developed in the Islamic World such funding can be a substitute for equity finance.

ISLAMIC FINANCING METHODS

Different types of financing are required according to the purpose for which funding is being sought and the period for which the finance is required. This applies regardless of whether the finance is provided by an Islamic or conventional bank. For example, short-term trade finance may be required by a Muslim merchant to cover stockholdings of imported consumer goods until they are sold. These financing terms will be quite different to those of a manufacturer investing on a long-term basis in new premises or equipment. Once-only lump-sum finance may be required or ongoing funding on a monthly, quarterly or irregular but frequent basis.

In practice in the Islamic World most longer term business finance is from ploughed back profits or borrowings from relatives rather than institutions. Governments fund large-scale investments by the large state sector businesses. This leaves the commercial banks, including the Islamic banks, mainly in the position of providing short-term trade related financing, often to cover import purchases. Islamic banks arrange this through an interest free *murabahah* arrangement rather than through commercial lending. *Murabahah* finance involves a bank purchasing a good on behalf of a client and reselling it to the client for an agreed mark-up. The bank assumes ownership of the good until it is resold, this risk justifying its reward. In practice the bank will not take physical possession of the good, which will be in transit to the client, or in a warehouse, or even on premises owned and used by the client. The bank will, however, have legal title to the good, with all the obligations which that implies.

The calculation of the *murabahah* mark up is quite different to interest as it is related to the administrative costs of providing the finance with an additional allowance for profits, a portion of which will be shared with depositors with the financial institution. It is unrelated to interest rates as dictated by the requirements of monetary policy or the fiscal needs of government. It is also unrelated to market interest rates as determined by the demand and supply of loanable funds. In an Islamic financial system savings may be determined by current income, expected future income in relation to needs and present and past wealth, but it is not determined by interest or the price of money. Financing requirements may be determined by business needs and opportunities, including marketing considerations, but not by the price of borrowing at any particular time.

Longer time finance for the equipment and other major items of capital expenditures can be made available through *ijara* or leasing, a recognised method of Islamic finance which is becoming increasingly popular with Islamic banks and their clients.[79] Under *ijara* finance, the bank maintains ownership of the equipment and the client pays an agreed rental on a monthly, quarterly or annual basis over a period of years, usually at least three and often over five. Rentals are fixed in advance and the bank will normally expect to more than recoup its investment in the equipment over the period of the rental. At the end of the contract, the bank may sell the equipment second hand, either to the client using it or to a third party. Under another variant, *ijara-wa-iktina*, the client has the automatic right to acquire the equipment at the end of the contract at a price agreed when the original arrangement

[79] Saad Al Harran, *Islamic Finance: Partnership Financing*, Pelanduk Publishing, Selangor, Malaysia, 1993, pp. 95–7.

was made. This represents a form of hire purchase rather than a leasing arrangement.

More directly participative Islamic finance can be provided through *mudarabah* trust financing which involves the bank taking a direct stake in the shareholding of the company. The Islamic bank is then regarded as the *rab al-maal*, the beneficial owner, while the business manager acts as *mudarab*, the entrepreneur. The *rab al-maal* should be regarded as more than a sleeping partner, as the bank acting in this capacity will expect to be consulted about all matters of financial policy, but the day to day running of the business will be left to the *mudarab*. The *rab al-maal* can be viewed as a non-voting shareholder, but unlike the holders of preference shares, the bank has a veto over financial dealings which it regards as imprudent or unwise. In the event of the business failing, the *rab-al-maal* may be required to dispose of the business assets and in such circumstances the *mudarab* will no longer be employed, but that is the extent of the latter's liability.

If a financier wishes to set up a partnership arrangement with an entrepreneur, it may prefer a *musharakah* arrangement whereby a new venture is formed between the Islamic bank providing the funding and the business seeking funding. Under this arrangement both parties share in the ownership of the new venture. If it fails, both parties lose, but the assets of the original company are not liable to be used to compensate the bank. From the bank's point of view *musharakah* investments are a greater risk, but the returns are also potentially higher, as any profits from the new venture will not be diluted by the obligations and costs of the existing business. Hence keeping the accounts of new ventures unconsolidated has powerful attractions, and it may be easier for the bank to sell its share in an unencumbered venture than disinvest from a *mudarabah* arrangement.

Islamic banks are, of course, commercial in nature rather than charitable agencies. Like other banks they aim to make profits for their shareholders, but in their case profits are arguably even more important as this determines the returns to those with savings and investment accounts. There is, however, provision for loans to be extended without any return to the bank through the Islamic principle of *Qard hasan*, lending which is not subject to either interest charges or profit sharing. Rather than foreclose on borrowers, and then make costly provision for bad debt to correct the financial position of the bank, Islamic banks try to directly help those in difficulty. *Qard hasan* loans are only available to bank customers, funds being made available to those who have already had finance but are in business difficulties due to unforeseen circumstances such as ill health. Such loans are not intended to reduce business risk, as this might encourage unnecessary risk taking. *Qard hasan* loans are designed to help those facing unanticipated personal or family hardship due to circumstances beyond the control of those involved.

ISLAMIC BANKING DEVELOPMENT

Financial dealings in compliance with the *Shariah* law date back to the early centuries of Islam, but these involved traditional money lending and money changing rather than commercial banking as understood today. Modern commercial banking was introduced into the majority of Muslim countries with the spread of European trade during the nineteenth century. The methods involved *riba* transactions, however, with no allowance made for Muslim susceptibilities.

It was only in the 1960s that serious consideration was given to how modern commercial banking could be adapted so that *riba* could be avoided. When Ahmed El Naggar, an Egyptian doctoral student was at university in Germany, he was impressed by the operation of mutual savings and loan associations. He thought that local savings banks could be organised in Egypt in a similar fashion, with savings being pooled, and distributed to members in need of funds. If a group of Muslim savers could follow this practice, there would be no need for interest. Ahmed El Naggar on his return to Egypt opened and managed a small savings bank in 1963 in the town of Mitr Ghams in the Nile delta. The venture was very successful in harnessing funds from landowners and small traders who had hitherto not used banks as they were devout Muslims who were concerned about any dealings involving *riba*. Within three years more than 60 000 Muslims has deposits with the bank.[80]

---

[80] Ann Elizabeth Mayer, 'Islamic banking and credit policies in the Sadat era: the social origins of Islamic banking in Egypt', *Arab Law Quarterly*, Vol. 1, Part 1, 1985, pp. 32–50.

The Egyptian government was unhappy about the new Islamic bank, especially some of Nasser's more leftist ministers who were suspicious of all Islamic institutions. The senior staff of the major state owned banks and the Central Bank of Egypt were also unhappy, especially the latter as they could not monitor the bank's activities. Rather than close the bank down however, which would risk causing widespread discontent, the decision was made to nationalise the bank. There was much delay and debate over this, but eventually in 1972 the Egyptian government injected £E1.4 million (more than $2 million at the then exchange rate) and effectively bought the bank. The institution was renamed the Nasser Social Bank, which survives till today, but it was not encouraged to become a major financial force in the countryside as Ahmed El Nagger had envisaged. He in fact left the bank as a result of these developments, becoming eventually the Chairman of the Association of Islamic Banks.

The major move forward for Islamic banking came in the Gulf in the 1970s. In these countries there had always been support from the merchants for the principles of Islamic financing, and many businessmen refused to use conventional commercial banks. Until the 1973–74 quadrupling in oil prices these merchants lacked the resources to found any type of bank, but with the oil boom new opportunities opened up. The Dubai Islamic Bank was founded in 1975 by a group of merchants, followed by the Kuwait Finance House in 1977, the Bahrain Islamic Bank in 1979 and the Qatar Islamic Bank in 1982.[81] All these banks have proved very successful in attracting depositors, and in harnessing funds from those who hitherto did not use banking services. The Kuwait Finance House accounted for almost 20 per cent of all bank deposits in the country by the late 1980s, and although the business was disrupted by the Iraqi invasion it has since recovered remarkably. It has purchased business and commercial property on behalf of its clients, who have then entered Islamic leasing and hire purchase contracts. It also offers transactions services to current account holders including the use of cash dispensers.

---

[81] Rodney Wilson, *Banking and Finance in the Arab Middle East*, Macmillan, London, 1983, pp. 80–6.

The oil price rises also enabled Saudi Arabian business-men to establish Islamic banking networks throughout the Muslim world. Amongst the most notable of these was Prince Mohammed bin Faisal who established the Faisal Islamic Banks in Egypt and the Sudan, both in 1977.[82] He also established the Geneva based Dar-al-Maal al-Islami to recycle Gulf funds Islamically into Western markets, with a particular emphasis on mark-up financing involving exports to Muslim countries. The Al Baraka Investment Company which is the Islamic Banking affiliate of Sheikh Hassan Kamel's Dallah Group, a leading Saudi Arabian trading company, has pursued a sim-ilar strategy, with branches in London, Bahrain, Tunis, Istanbul and even the Central Asian states and China. It helped the initial financing of the Jordan Islamic Bank, although this is now independent. The Al Rajhi group, which started as a money changing business to serve pilgrims to Mecca, has now become an international Islamic investment company with offices in London and Zurich. Islamic banking has also spread to Malaysia and Indonesia, and by the mid 1990s it was estim-ated that $65 billion was on deposit with Islamic banks world-wide, which has made these institutions a significant global financial force.[83]

PUBLIC FINANCE UNDER ISLAM

Islamic economics not only provides a framework for private financing through a banking system free from *riba*, it also sets out the rules for public finance through taxation. The most important Islamic tax is *zakat*, a tax based on wealth, which is paid annually at a rate of one fortieth of the value of personal or business liquid assets.[84] *Zakat* literally means growth, the notion being that giving leads to an increase in prosperity in

---

[82] Ahmad El Ashker, *The Islamic Business Enterprise*, Croom Helm, London, 1987, pp. 115–40.
[83] Figure quoted at International Business Communications conferences in Dubai and London in March 1985.
[84] Monzer Kahf, 'Zakat: unresolved issues in contemporary *Fiqh*', in Abdul Hasan Sadeq, Ataul Huq Pramanik and Nik Hassan, (eds), *Development and Finance in Islam*, International Islamic University Press, Selangor, Malaysia, 1991, pp. 173–90.

this world, and religious merit, *thawab*, in the next.[85] The payment of *zakat* was stated by the Prophet to be one of the five pillars of Islam, along with belief in one God, prayer, fasting during *Ramadan* and pilgrimage to Mecca.

Zakat applies to property, but this is generally interpreted as an ownership tax, tenants being exempted. In practice, personal residences are usually excluded, as is business plant and equipment, but cash holdings and financial assets, including shares in quoted companies, are subject to the tax at the standard rate of 2.5 per cent. The payment of the tax is viewed as a religious duty, and in such circumstances, there is little evasion, as this would be regarded as a moral sin. As with other economic injunctions in Islam, there has been much debate over what is included and what is exempt, and practice continues to vary widely. According to most schools of thought, including the influential Hanifites, inventories of traded goods should be included, as well as farm animals, but some argue harvest produce should be subject to tithes rather than *zakat*, the former being at four times the rate of the latter.[86]

Governments are usually responsible for *zakat* collection, although in the case of Iran before the Islamic revolution it was the *mullahs* and others working for the mosques. When the state is involved, however, it cannot treat *zakat* as general fiscal revenue, as *zakat* is regarded as a form of almsgiving for worthy causes. This limits the government's discretion and means the tax cannot be used as an instrument of fiscal policy. It is often administered by a special Ministry of Religious Affairs, with revenue earmarked for transfer payments to the poor and needy. It is, for example, permissible to use *zakat* expenditure for health care or education for the poor, but not for military expenditure or even infrastructure work. It tends to be used for recurrent spending to meet immediate needs rather than long-term investment.

In much of the Islamic World the tax base is limited, partly reflecting low incomes, apart from in the Gulf states and Libya, but also as a result of difficulty in the collection of direct taxes. Petroleum revenues and import duties are the major source of

---

[85] Nicolas P. Aghnides, *Mohammedan Theories of Finance*, The Premier Book House, Lahore, 1961, p. 207.
[86] Ibid., pp. 283–95.

government finance. There is no income tax in the Gulf states, where *zakat* represents the major form of personal taxation. In those non-oil states which do impose income tax, it is mostly collected from the government's own employees. The value of *zakat* is that it widens the tax base, with even the less well off, and those who are highly critical of governments willing to make voluntary contributions.

INSURANCE IN MUSLIM COUNTRIES

Entrepreneurial activity involves taking risk, and in developing countries such as those of the Islamic World, an aversion to risk is often cited as a reason for business stagnation. Commercial risks cannot be covered by insurance, but risks associated with the transport and distribution can, and this represents the major form of insurance business in Muslim countries. Life and endowment insurance is not regarded as legitimate, as life is in the hands of Allah, and if household income earners meet an untimely death, it is the duty of the *ummah*, the community of believers, to provide for the family. In closely knit societies there is less need for institutionalised support given the strong tribal and kinship support mechanisms.

Islamic law stipulates that gambling (*qimar*) is forbidden and all types of speculative activity are regarded as gambling.[87] Forward and futures dealings are prohibited in much of the Islamic world as, although such markets can be used for risk avoidance, there is always the temptation to speculate, indeed speculative funds to a large extent provide the liquidity for hedging activity. Risk sharing is advocated by Islamic economists rather than risk seeking, and *murabahah* and *musharakah* are regarded as appropriate instruments for this purpose. Mutual insurance is seen as preferable to insurance through publicly quoted companies who profit from the misfortunes of others.[88] Mutual insurance funds established by the *ummah* are referred to as *takafol companies*. Unlike conventional insurance

---

[87] Muhammad Nejatullah Siddiqi, *Insurance in an Islamic Economy*, Islamic Foundation, Leicester, 1985, pp. 27–46.
[88] Afzalur Rahman, *Economic Doctrines of Islam: Banking and Insurance*, Muslim Schools Trust, London, 1979, pp. 217–42.

companies *takafol* undertakings are not involved in *riba* transactions, as they avoid holding long-term bonds, but may hold
equities. Dar al Maal al Islami has a *takafol* insurance subsidiary
as do the Faisal Islamic Banks of Egypt and the Sudan.

CRITICAL WRITING ON ISLAMIC ECONOMICS

As the literature on Islamic economics and finance has prolif-
erated, so have its critics, most of whom dislike the prescriptive
character of much of the writing, and the fact that in countries
such as Iran, the blanket application of Islamic principles has
eliminated the conventional secularist alternatives. A more
profound criticism comes from Muslim economists who are
themselves conversant with the literature on Islamic economics, notably Timur Kuran of the University of Southern
California in Los Angeles.[89] Kuran is sceptical that the ethical behavioural norms which some Islamic economists see as
desirable for Muslims can be attained regardless of the stage
of development an economy has reached and its political and
social structures. Altruistic behaviour usually depends on being able to identify closely with the beneficiaries, as within
households or even extended families. At the national level
such behaviour is less likely, even in Muslim countries because
of the diversity of interests, and at the level of the Islamic
world, religious affiliation does not necessarily imply economic
solidarity. Putting the interests of society above personal interests may mean behaving altruistically towards the entire Muslim *ummah*, which comprises one sixth of humanity.[90]

Kuran distinguishes between the production and consumption norms specified by Islamic economists. Muslims are free
to produce and trade for personal profit, but in exercising this
freedom they have a responsibility not to harm others. This
means paying 'fair' wages, charging 'reasonable' prices and
being content with 'normal' profit, however these concepts are
defined. Moderation is stressed in consumption, and abstinence

[89] Timur Kuran, 'The economic system in contemporary Islamic thought',
in K.S. Jomo (ed.), *Islamic Economic Alternatives*, Macmillan, London, 1992,
pp. 9–47.
[90] Ibid., p. 12.

in the case of alcohol or pork products. It is this moderation which reduces the scarcity problem, and makes demand generated inflation less likely. Kuran argues that not harming the position of others through seeking personal gain, and restraint in consumption are perhaps too much to expect given the state of most Muslim economies. He believes that implicit in the view of Muslim economists is the assumption that the Islamic norms perform equally well in any society regardless of its history, level of development and degree of heterogeneity.[91] This, Kuran asserts, is idealistic rather than realistic.

Many Islamic economists reject neo-classical premises, as they assert these evolved in Western, largely Christian or secularist, societies and, therefore, have little applicability in the Muslim world. Kuran rejects this criticism, as he believes that Islamic societies share many of the characteristics of their Western counterparts, and that there are universal traits, and indeed weaknesses, in human behaviour. He identifies in particular the free rider problem, of individuals or groups who may seek to take material advantage of the efforts of others. This can be overcome to some extent by coercion or material incentives and penalties, and no doubt Islamic economists would appeal to moral persuasion, to encourage potential free riders to act in the public interest rather than their own personal interest. Many may feel that such unselfish behaviour will make little impact in large economies, especially when others continue to abuse the system. Kuran points to the corruption in many Muslim societies, and the abuse of authority by the rulers for personal ends that is hardly likely to encourage unselfish behaviour from their subjects.

Islamic economists hold widely divergent views on the role of the state, but most seem to agree that its role should be limited. Kuran cites Inamul Haq and Syed Naqvi as asserting that the problem with communism is that it seeks to establish the state as an agent of man, with no divine role.[92] An Islamic state's economic objectives are to prevent violations of

---

[91] Ibid., p. 11.
[92] Ibid., p. 15. Kuran cites an unpublished paper by Inamul Haq, *Principles and Philosophy of Democratic Socialism in Islam*, Karachi, 1996, p. 2. He also cites Syed N.H. Naqvi, *Individual Freedom, Social Welfare and Islamic Economic Order*, Pakistan Institute of Development Economics, Islamabad, 1981, pp. 9 and 25.

the norms as defined in *Koranic* teaching and the *Shariah* law. This includes imposing price ceilings where sellers charge unreasonable prices, although how this is defined is by no means clear. Kuran is sceptical about Islamic economists who advocate a minimal role for the state in economic affairs, but then go on to urge employment creation programmes, active policies towards agriculture and natural resource measures and many other types of intervention. His greatest reservation is about the behaviour of the rulers and state bureaucrats, which even in an Islamic state may not necessarily be in the wider public interest, even if it claims to be divinely inspired.

Although some Islamic economists resent Kuran's questioning and his scepticism, most serious scholars working in this area welcome the debates he has provoked. His critique of how economic justice is defined in Islam has been particularly useful, as it has sharpened up the arguments, and resulted in more precise definition, where there was arguably a rather blurred and fuzzy discussion hitherto. As the *Koran* itself is precise and explicit on economic matters, Muslim economists should also seek to clarify their thinking.

According to Kuran the two overriding principles of Islamic economic justice are equality and fairness.[93] Moderate inequality is acceptable, but not extreme disparities in income and wealth. Fairness means that economic gains are to be earned and losses deserved. Injunctions such as those already reviewed including the inheritance laws and the prohibition of *riba* ensure equity and fairness. Kuran is not concerned to question the individual injunctions, but rather raises more general issues regarding what he describes as the 'illusions' of Islamic economists concerning the injunctions.[94] One issue is their static nature, as Islamic economists view them as eternally applicable, without revision, to all societies. Kuran asserts that this means that the attainment of substantive justice is merely a procedural matter, as the injunctions are to be applied irrespective of economic and social conditions. It follows that there must be conformity to the injunctions, and that all Muslims at least are capable of such conformity. Yet as Kuran points out, human

[93] Timur Kuran, 'Economic justice in contemporary economic thought', in K.S. Jomo, *Islamic Economic Alternatives*, p. 51.
[94] Ibid., p. 56.

abilities to acquire, store, retrieve and process information are severely limited, and not everyone may be capable of always distinguishing between what is Islamically just and unjust. He believes that Islamic economists are over optimistic about human nature and capabilities.

Kuran is perhaps most controversial when he questions whether some of the Islamic injunctions will result in economic justice. The prohibition of *riba* may result in a borrower gaining at the expense of the lender under inflationary conditions. Islamic economists disagree over the merits of indexation in such circumstances, but if this is introduced, further distortions may result, which result in other injustices. The proportionate rather than the progressive nature of *zakat* has also been a source of disagreement amongst Islamic economists as already indicated. Kuran identifies injustices in both progressive and proportionate taxes, as no system of taxation is perfect as the extensive literature on public finance makes clear. Furthermore, Islamic economists are also concerned with other priorities as well as justice, including economic growth, efficiency, employment and industrialisation, all of which are subject to disagreement, and on which Islamic injunctions have little or nothing to say. All this results in a confused picture according to Kuran, rather than Islamic economics representing an agreed set of principles and practices.

In spite of Kuran's criticisms, it is evident that Islamic economic teaching does provide a comprehensive set of principles governing commerce, banking, public finance and even insurance. Many Muslims see an Islamic economic system as an alternative to capitalism, socialism and communism. The definition of what constitutes Islamic economics may not be as clear cut as some Islamic economists suggest, but similar criticisms can be made of neo-classical and Marxian economics. How far Islamic economic principles can be put into practice in the modern world is likely to be subject to continuing debate. It is undoubtedly too early to judge on the economic success or failure of the Islamic Republic of Iran. A significant proportion of the younger generation in the Muslim World are looking to it as a model for development. Just how it evolves in the coming years deserves to be studied closely, but care is needed in the choice of criteria for evaluation. Not all Muslim economists even agree that Iran's economic system is actually Islamic.

5 Business Ethics

Is it possible to be successful in business and at the same time behave in a manner which is thought to be morally acceptable? This is an issue which has been addressed by moralists who see a conflict between the profit seeking motive determining business decisions and the wider social responsibilities of those in business to their fellow citizens. Business ethics encompasses all aspects of business, from issues of pricing to marketing, production methods and employment practice. One aim is to establish codes of 'good practice' which take account of the moral consequences of business decisions and not simply their financial impact.

The job for those involved in teaching courses in business ethics is to question, and point out the moral dilemmas which face everyone in business. Are market determined prices exploitative? Is it morally legitimate for firms trading in monopolistic or oligopolistic conditions to levy high charges to boost their profits? Is a hire and fire employment policy morally acceptable even if it does ensure more flexibility for business? Can production methods that result in pollution and environmental damage be acceptable in any circumstances? Are marketing campaigns really honest if they seek only to promote brand image and give little real information about the products being sold?

Before even attempting to provide answers to some of these questions, it is important to have some understanding of what business ethics involves. Can it be considered a discipline in its own right like economics or theology? Has business ethics an agreed approach and methodology? Are the objectives of those who teach business ethics prescriptive, or is it simply about evaluating choices? It could be considered morally dubious, and possibly presumptuous, for teachers to prescribe their own ethical values on others. What is the source of their authority? Even if business ethics is simply about evaluating choices, the question arises of what criteria should be used, and the grounds on which these can be justified. These issues are explored in the first part of the chapter.

Business ethics also naturally concerns those with religious convictions. Is it possible to follow Jewish law and be successful in modern business? Should good Christians avoid the world of commerce with its emphasis on material gain? Can devout Muslims serve God if they work for Western multinational companies? Theologians are aware of and interested in the questions posed by those involved business ethics, and indeed there is much common ground between those who take an essentially secular and humanist approach and those who are primarily concerned with the possible conflicts between modern business practice and religious adherence. Judeo-Christian and Muslim writings on modern business practice are surveyed in the second part of the chapter.

BUSINESS ETHICS AS A DISCIPLINE

Those who write and teach business ethics come from a variety of backgrounds, from accounting and finance to commercial law, economics, marketing and information technology. Often they have been asked to teach a course on ethical issues in business even though this is not their main field of research or teaching; indeed, sometimes they may have little experience and have to start from scratch. The business school or management faculty may feel obliged to offer a course in ethics, and perhaps add it to their research portfolio. This may be a consequence of others doing the same, following academic fashion or simply political correctness. The number who write or teach exclusively in the field of business ethics is very limited, arguably constraining the development of the subject as a distinct discipline in its own right.[1] Even many of the books on business ethics are edited volumes, with contributors approaching the issues from a wide range of perspectives.[2]

[1] The issue of whether business education itself can be classified as a humanity or as subject in a class by itself has been addressed by leading scholars in business ethics. See Thomas J. Donaldson and R. Edward Freeman, (eds) *Business as a Humanity*, Oxford University Press, New York, 1995.

[2] Popular texts include William D. Hall, *Making the Right Decision: Ethics for Managers*, Wiley, New York, 1993. This is based on the Arthur Anderson business ethics programme. In Britain texts used include Brian Harvey (ed.), *Business Ethics: A European Approach*, Prentice Hall, New York, 1994 and John Donaldson, *Business Ethics: A European Casebook*, Academic Press, Harcourt Brace Jovanovich, London, 1992.

An interdisciplinary approach can, of course, be seen as a strength rather than a weakness, but, as Norman Bowie asserts, seeking to make business ethics a discipline is part of the search for legitimacy.[3] Before there can be peer recognition and academic respect, however, it is necessary to define what the methodology of business ethics involves, and what objectives are served through its study. Bowie's starting point is to question the objectives of business school teaching. Are they vocational institutions, with the aim of imparting skills, or is the aim education – in the traditional liberal arts sense of imparting not only knowledge but civic values, including a sense of moral responsibility? Bowie includes this as one of the qualities of professional training,[4] as in the case of medical education or law school, where there is usually a component included on ethics. Training for managers at business school arguably requires a similar ethical component.

Disciplines are often regarded as scientific, in the sense that they involve the formulation of theories that can be tested either experimentally, as in the case of natural sciences, or empirically, as in the case of social sciences, including economics. Business ethics is not usually regarded as a discipline in this sense, as it is not clear how the superiority of one value over another can be scientifically proven through either experimentation or empirical work. Nevertheless, it has evolved a distinctive methodology, that draws more on other fields of business study. This involves investigation, usually in the form of discovery of the facts of a particular business situation, and an evaluation of the options which are open to management. Often case studies will be examined, not so much to establish general rules for decision taking, as to reveal the ethical implications of particular situations confronting managers. These case studies may bring the ethical consequences of decision making sharply into focus, with those who read the material, and perhaps participate in class discussion, gaining greater insights than would otherwise be the case.[5]

[3] Norman E. Bowie, 'Business ethics as a discipline: the search for legitimacy', in R. Edward Freeman, (ed.), *Business Ethics: the State of the Art*, Oxford University Press, New York, 1991, pp. 17–41.
[4] Ibid., pp. 18–19.
[5] A useful volume of case studies has been compiled by Robert F. Hartley, *Business Ethics: Violations of the Public Trust*, John Wiley, New York, 1993. Cases include Union Carbide, Lockheed, ITT, Nestlé and Johnson and Johnson.

Economics may be the core discipline for the study of business, but Bowie criticises the narrow view of many economists that human behaviour is based on self-interest and that altruism has no role in business dealings.[6] He accuses some economists of being discipline imperialists in trying to apply cost-benefit concepts to all decision making, even in the political and legal spheres. This can undermine democracy and the individual rights which legal systems seek to protect. For Bowie, one task for business ethics is to bring a halt to this discipline imperialism, by drawing attention to the fact that human behaviour has a moral dimension, and that individuals have duties which may override their economic self-interest.[7]

Business ethics involve judgements, and weighing up rights and wrongs, openly using subjective criteria, rather than attempting to appear objective by being impersonal. Competition, for example, may bring the benefits that many economists suggest, especially for consumers, but there are also costs which are borne by the producers who do not survive. Co-operation can bring gains for producers, yet collusive arrangements can mean costs for consumers. Economists are aware of these trade-offs, but the whole purpose of welfare economics is to avoid making interpersonal comparisons. In contrast, students of business ethics can make these comparisons, the issue being whether competition or co-operation in a particular case best ensures adherence to the code of moral values held by those affected. Those who lose may not feel resentful if the system itself is morally just, and if those who gain show compassion and respect for the less successful rather than merely trumpeting about their gains.

Richard DeGeorge in his contribution to the same edited volume as Norman Bowie asks whether the popular success of business ethics could pose a threat to its continued survival as a coherent field of enquiry.[8] He sees business ethics as essentially a philosophical area of inquiry, which has evaluation as

---

[6] Norman Bowie, 'Business ethics', pp. 39–40.

[7] Some economists have addressed these issues and are well acquainted with the literature on business ethics. Mark Casson, for example, draws on the literature on transactions costs to build an economics of trust which moves from economic to ethical man. See Mark Casson, *The Economics of Business Culture*, Clarendon Press, Oxford, 1991, pp. 23–6.

[8] Richard DeGeorge, 'Will success spoil business ethics?', in R. Edward Freeman, *Business Ethics*, pp. 42–56.

only one part of its task. The problem, DeGeorge believes, is that too much is expected from business ethics, with those involved in the subject being overwhelmed with demands that cannot be met. This is resulting in diluted competence, as people are drawn into the area with little knowledge of either ethics or philosophy. Critical ethics is being replaced with descriptive ethics, with excessive attention to the detail of the case material being used, but less appreciation of the broader issues in the field of moral philosophy.

SELF-REGULATION, CONSCIENCE AND MORAL CODES OF CONDUCT

Within companies the interest in business ethics has often arisen reactively rather than being a result of a pro-active policy. It was the business scandals of the late 1980s and early 1990s in the United States, the United Kingdom and Germany that prompted an increasing interest in the subject.[9] Scandals had long been commonplace in Italian and to a lesser extent French and Japanese business, but there was increasing moral indignation in the United States and northern Europe, and growing discomfort elsewhere. Companies became defensive in the face of public disquiet, and there was a feeling that there had to be a better way of being seen to conduct business dealings. Public image was more important than ever, especially as pressure groups lobbying for the protection of consumer interests and environmental concerns became ever more outspoken. At the same time, with the privatisation of nationalised industries and utilities, the public complaints which used to be voiced about the state sector undertakings were increasingly directed at the private sector. Regulators were expected to ensure the privatised companies charged 'fair prices' and did not abuse their monopoly position.

[9] Although such scandals were not new. For an account of earlier wrongdoing in Britain see Michael Clarke, *Fallen Idols: Elites and the Search for the Acceptable Face of Capitalism*, Junction Books, London, 1981. For a more historical account of business values in the United Stages through case studies of leading entrepreneurs and companies see Peter Baida, *Poor Richard's Legacy: American Business Values from Benjamin Franklin to Donald Trump*, William Morrow, New York, 1990.

For some critics of business behaviour, especially politicians on the left of the political spectrum, the notion of 'business ethics' was regarded as a contradiction in terms. Capitalism was regarded as an unethical system, and those who worked as managers in private companies were viewed as morally inferior to the public-spirited employees who were employed in the civil service, or as professionals in state schools, public health or social services.[10] With considerable publicity over scandals involving abuses and wrongdoing in public services in the 1980s attitudes started to change, and fewer and fewer held the view, which had arguably always been mistaken, that those who worked in public services were in some sense more morally pure and clean than those in business. Human moral frailties and the potential for corruption were seen as universal traits, which applied irrespective of occupation.

Because private sector companies were increasingly seen as the prime agents for economic advance by those of all shades of political opinion, intellectual attention was no longer focused on how capitalism could be replaced, but rather how it could be made to work consistently with the public interest. Companies were no longer under the threat of nationalisation, but managers felt obliged to respond to the moral concerns expressed by parliamentarians, the media and public pressure groups. One response has been to have a company policy on business ethics, a mission statement clearly setting out the goals of the company, and codes setting out what is viewed as acceptable behaviour by employees. There are lectures, seminars and workshops to make employees aware of company policy on what practices are morally acceptable, and training sessions which include discussion of business ethics.

Nevertheless, managers cannot simply use as an excuse for unethical behaviour the fact they have not been on an ethics course, or were unaware of the ethical implications of their actions. They have a duty to find out, to seek full information. Sir Adrian Cadbury suggests that 'ethical managers make their own rules.'[11] Managers must determine, as precisely as possible,

[10] For a discussion of the morality of 'enterprise values' and the ethics of the 'enterprising self' see Paul Heelas and Paul Morris, (eds), *The Values of the Enterprise Culture*, Routledge, 1992, pp. 83–138 and pp. 139–214.
[11] Sir Adrian Cadbury, 'Ethical managers make their own rules', in *Harvard Business Review, Ethics at Work*, Harvard University, Boston, 1991, pp. 3–9.

what their own rules of conduct are. They should examine their own decisions in the past, and consider what principles they adopted in taking those decisions. If those decisions were mistaken, then the manager can learn from his or her mistakes. The key issue however is to stand back and take personal stock. Managers should be judged by their actions, and not merely by their statements of intent, but they can also judge themselves through a personal evaluation of their own past actions.

Standards expected from sales personnel have risen. They are expected to inform and enlighten customers, and not to mislead or pressurise clients into signing contracts or buying products. Codes of best sales practice suggest that it is not merely enough to sell satisfactory products at fair prices in an open and transparent fashion, but also to ensure that the products are well suited to the customers' actual and potential needs. The sales representative's responsibilities extend to intelligence gathering as well as to information dissemination. Honesty is essential when explaining the details of a particular product, but the sales representative also has a duty to ensure, as far as possible, that the client understands the nature of what is being offered. Information overload can be as perplexing for the customer as withholding important facts, and even providing information in standardised form may not be optimum, as different customers will have varying abilities to absorb and understand what is being explained.

Hence it is not simply a question of the sales literature being given an ethical seal of approval, and the sales representative always behaving in the same way. Rather it is a matter of continual trial and error to arrive at as morally just a position as possible. Experience will clearly matter, but everyone has to start somewhere. As far as selling is concerned, the morality of the transactions cannot simply be measured by outcomes, it is rather a matter of the intentions in the mind of those involved.

For many in business national laws are regarded as a major ethical source, as deceptive human behaviour may be a cause for some concern, but breaking the law is to be avoided at all costs.[12] It is not merely a matter of the potential bad publicity

---

[12] Jack Mahoney, 'How to be ethical: ethics resource management', in Brian Harvey, (ed.), *Business Ethics: A European Approach*, Prentice Hall, New York, 1994, pp. 32–55.

if found out, but, as Mahoney stresses, a sense that anything less than legal compliance is immoral,[13] and that the company should behave and be seen as a 'good upright citizen'. Telling a lie is not a crime, but breaking a contract is often a matter for the criminal law which exists to enforce compliance. Civil and criminal laws are a recognition that people cannot be trusted to respect agreed codes of conduct, and that some penalty is appropriate for those who fail to comply. Laws, of course, are not necessarily ethical, and there may be conflicts between different laws, and the moral values which are held by significant groups in society. In such cases the law may be brought into disrepute, necessitating its repeal or amendment. Companies, however, are seldom involved in campaigns of civil disobedience to have laws changed. They may lobby to have laws changed, but few will deliberately flout the law.

The law can be regarded as an external ethical resource, like religious values which are discussed later in the chapter. Mahoney also considers internal ethical resources including self-regulation through conscience and moral skills. Individuals working as managers or employees have a 'feeling' about what is right or wrong, which comes from conscience, a kind of voice within themselves that people 'consult', 'follow' or 'obey'.[14] For the religious, conscience may represent 'the voice of God', but those without religious beliefs may still have a developed sense of conscience, which could be regarded as an instinct within humans conditioning their behaviour. Law breakers, the unethical or the morally corrupt are said to have little or no conscience, at least with respect to the wrongdoing they are accused of. Conscience can be regarded as part of the decision making process, perhaps the most vital part, acting alongside the external resources determining behaviour such as law or religion. Indeed, the external resources may exert their influence through conscience, which provides a positive force to obey, rather than through the negative force of coercion. As Mahoney asserts, humans are not 'moral calculating machines'.[15] Their consciences work through feelings and emotions, these providing the weights

[13] Ibid., p. 33.
[14] Ibid., p. 36.
[15] Ibid., p. 37.

which determine what is important for the person, and what is less significant.

Mahoney stresses that moral skills are not static, but can be developed like other skills.[16] The traditional approach to virtue views it as a permanent tendency which an individual has and makes that individual react in a certain way when confronted with various situations as if it was second nature. Virtues are regarded almost as habits, instinctive reactions, such as an unwillingness to betray colleagues or business associates, as the individual himself or herself may regard this as a breach of trust or confidence. The question is whether these reactions are inborn traits, or if they can be developed. Mahoney subscribes to the latter view, believing that 'accumulating ethical capital through regular investment in acting virtuously can, then, provide one with a capacity for moral insight into various ethical issues as they arise in business, and for identifying the just, honest or loyal course of action in such situations.'[17]

The discussion of moral virtue by Mahoney owes much, as he openly acknowledges, to the philosophy of Aristotle, who saw virtue as moral courage, of coping with personal fears. It is a matter of being neither too timid or too impulsive, but of working out a balance which can only come through experience. This notion that ethics can be viewed as character development is taken up by Lynn Sharp Paine, who reflects on the objectives of ethics education.[18] She sees the development of character as a process, and virtue and faults as characteristics that can be extended or contracted over time. Character traits can be strengthened or weakened, and personal integrity can, she believes, be developed.[19] Integrity may involve a commitment to particular causes, ideals or people, including loyalties to a company and its mission. This, however, implies first acquiring knowledge of the cause or ideal. Ethical inspiration often comes through effort, and conscience can develop with the accumulation of knowledge.

Paine sets out a practical programme for ethics education

[16] Ibid., pp. 38–9.
[17] Ibid., p. 41.
[18] Lynn Sharp Paine, 'Ethics as character development: reflections on the objectives of ethics education', in Freeman, *Business Ethics*, pp. 67–86.
[19] Ibid., pp. 74–6.

involving the development of sensibility, reasoning, conduct and leadership.[20] Sensibility involves enriching the students' vocabulary of ethics, and in providing a sense of what honesty, fairness and trust can mean in practice in a business context. Ethical reasoning may involve setting out the arguments about particular business dilemmas and showing the virtues and vices of the possible alternatives. Ethical conduct is about how to exhibit integrity, and demonstrating how managers can be led astray in their business dealings. Ethical leadership is about setting an example through moral behaviour regardless of the position that a person occupies on the corporate hierarchy. The office cleaner can just as easily exercise ethical leadership as the chief executive, indeed he or she may teach their superiors a lesson through their daily behaviour.

CORPORATE VALUES AND BUSINESS MOTIVATION

It is misleading to speak of a company as having values, as corporate behaviour depends on the values of those who have a stake in it, whether as directors, managers, employees, shareholders, customers or suppliers. Companies are also bound to be influenced by the value systems prevailing more generally in the countries in which they are operating, it being arguably difficult, for example, to survive as a business by never giving bribes in an environment where illicit payments to government are a prerequisite for successful tendering.[21] In such circumstances competitors who are willing to resort to bribery are likely to gain financially at the expense of companies which are not. The morally upright company can, of course, stay out of such markets, but that deprives citizens of those countries of the goods and services which the company has to offer. Not giving bribes may also disadvantage the company's own employees, who may be laid off if business is slack, or even end up being recruited by the corrupt rival.

Similar arguments can be advanced over corporate tax

---

[20] Ibid., pp. 77–83.
[21] Jeffrey A. Fadiman, 'A traveller's guide to gifts and bribes', in *Harvard Business Review, Ethics at Work*, op.cit., pp. 29–35.

evasion, or attempts to circumvent environmental laws or regulations. There may be a conflict between being socially responsible to the wider community and serving the interests of the company's stakeholders. The business ethics literature, and most Western media commentators assume that the wider public interest should always come first, but it can be argued that it is more human to give priority to those within the corporate family rather than the impersonal public interest. Effects on company stakeholders are usually known and measurable, whereas the impact on the national community may be marginal at best, and perhaps highly uncertain.

Political economists, especially those who are employed within political science departments, often assume that elected politicians have a greater legitimacy than business leaders. The former are chosen by a wide constituency on the basis of one vote for each citizen, whereas those in business may be recruited as a result of consultations involving a small circle of people, or perhaps even by a sole individual taking an initiative. The greater legitimacy of an elected government compared with a private company means that the objectives of the two institutions do not carry equal moral weight, the interests of the democratic state being always paramount. Companies have a narrow commercial focus, and the owners, in most circumstances, have greater power than the other stakeholders. In contrast, the state has a wider national interest, involving obligations to all its citizens, including the protection of human rights, and not simply in striving for material advance. It is this legitimacy of the state that makes it morally correct for companies to uphold national laws, whereas when governments give way to business lobbying they are portrayed at best as bowing to commercial pressures, or at worst as behaving corruptly.

Within businesses, careerist behaviour is the accepted norm, as executives strive for greater personal reward and positions of power and prestige. The corporate culture may encourage materialism and a striving by employees for the rewards of their superiors. Symbols of power and position are revered and coveted, such as the largest or better positioned offices, quality desks and office furnishing, the best computer equipment or the most superior company vehicles. Not all achieve the highest positions, and the senior executives may derive part of their satisfaction from their achievement in climbing the corporate ladder, and perhaps even from leaving some of their fellow employees behind.

Is such behaviour ethical, and are the corporate conditions which encourage it to be condoned? According to Kenneth Goodpaster, business behaviour is usually moulded by competition, which is externally driven by a market ethic, and internally driven by the executive's self-interest and rationality.[22] Co-operative behaviour in contrast is externally determined by the legal ethic, and internally driven by the ethics of respect. Businesses can adopt co-operative behaviour, but this requires the external force of legal regulation, and internal adherence to humanist or religious values by executives regardless of corporate competitive pressures.

Goodpaster believes that corporate leaders should mould business behaviour, and not vice versa, as the ability to instil ethical values is one aspect of leadership. For leaders to modify their organisations' shared values, these must first be identified, an essential step in the orienting process. Next, the corporate leader, having identified characteristic values of the organisation and clarified the values which it is aimed to impart, should try to institutionalise the attainment of the new values by decisive actions, statements of standards, and appropriate incentives to ensure compliance. The latter may be least important, the crucial action being to inspire middle management and other employees by example. This should help ensure the new ethical standards are sustained, even after the corporate leader retires or resigns.[23]

Mark Pastin examines the question of whether ethics can be an integrating force in management.[24] Often, he asserts, critics of business use ethics as a fortress from which to attack corporate actions. This, Pastin believes, is a negative use of ethics. Instead he proposes a more constructive approach, plugging in ethics at the outset to business decision making, which will result in it shaping the character of the company. Ethics is not about goal or target setting, as once a goal is achieved a

[22] Kenneth E. Goodpaster, 'Ethical imperatives and corporate leadership', in Freeman, *Business Ethics*, p. 98.
[23] Ibid., pp. 100–6.
[24] Mark Pastin, 'Ethics as an integrating force in management', in John Drummond and Bill Bain, (eds), *Managing Business Ethics*, Butterman Heinemann, 1994, pp. 76–88.

process is finished, and a new goal has to be agreed. Rather, ethics is about purposes, such as how the corporate managers can realise themselves and achieve satisfaction through attaining their goals. This comes back to the notion of Lynn Paine, which has already been discussed, of the appreciation of ethical norms as part of character development. Within the corporation establishing purposes is about setting ethical standards to which managers and other employees will be expected to adhere. Not only is this desirable from the point of view of management behaviour, but it may also serve the business well by ensuring consistency and continuity of purpose.

Pastin cites the case of a large electronics manufacturer that attempted to institute a programme of shared values or purposes. It found its lower level employees put great stress on product values, the need for quality output. Senior executives stressed economic values, the importance of ensuring a favourable return on assets. Middle managers had conflicting values, but none of the groups put much stress on human values, the notion that committed, quality people are the source of success.[25] The company was unable to establish consistent values across these different groups, the consequence being a lack of purpose and drift, with the inability to resolve internal political conflicts or to respond adequately to external forces such as foreign competition.

In order to establish a value framework selectivity is necessary, according to Pastin. The first issue is who should be consulted: senior management, all management, all employees, shareholders or customers. The wider the consultation, the more difficult the process. A time frame has to be established for the process, otherwise it will never be completed. The value framework itself should provide a coherent picture of the choices available to management, and be sufficiently comprehensive to encompass the variables relevant for the choice. It should encourage questions which challenge beliefs, keeping executives on their toes, and facilitating healthy open debate. The value framework should, in other words, promote management awareness, and serve the interests of the business.

Pastin's view of business ethics as a management tool, and a facilitator of decision making illustrates the direction which

[25] Ibid., p. 80.

some of the business ethics literature is taking. There is much talk of values, but little discussion of these values in a moral context. It is unclear what the underlying morality is, or indeed if there is any. The human values seem one dimensional, concerned with self-fulfilment, but not personal responsibility beyond that to the company and its stakeholders. There are no laws to constrain management behaviour, just codes of practice worked out by the company itself, which by definition lack any wider legitimacy. Such legitimacy could come from national law, natural law or divine law, but many of those involved in business ethics avoid referring to such sources, recognising the complexities which this introduces, which may in any case be beyond the remit of the company, and perhaps the competence of its management.

Douglas Sherwin addresses these issues, at least indirectly, when he considers the ethical roots of the business system.[26] He sees the purpose of business as being more than serving its individual stakeholders, which for owners is profits and capital gains, for employees is remuneration and for consumers furnishing goods and services. Businesses also serve society more widely by being the most efficient means of securing given ends with least means. Through competition they come up with the economically efficient solutions which society expects, and which cannot be brought about by governments through command economies. Businesses are economically motivated institutions, but serve a larger social purpose in a pragmatic way which is more effective than alternative institutional arrangements involving state direction of production and distribution.

Ethical problems arise when the business confines itself to serving the interests of some of its stakeholders and ignores its wider social role. Sherwin cites the way Peter Drucker's concept of management by objectives has become distorted by evaluations being made through the use of employee performance appraisal.[27] Under most appraisal systems performance targets are set by managers and employees without reference to other stakeholders. Such cosy arrangements are arguably unethical if not immoral, as the employee is assessed through

---

[26] Douglas S. Sherwin, 'The ethical roots of the business system', in Kenneth Andrews and Donald Kay, (eds) *Ethics in Practice: Managing the Moral Corporation*, Harvard Business School Press, Boston, 1989, pp. 144–55.
[27] Ibid., pp. 149–50.

largely subjective criteria without regard for wider responsibilities beyond, as the system has been distorted largely to
serve self-interest and individual career advancement. If remuneration is then linked to appraisal this can become especially
damaging, as managers become ever more self-centred, and
the business focuses inward rather than outward.

Kenneth Goodpaster in an article written with one of his
Harvard Business School colleagues, John Matthews, asks
whether a corporation can have a conscience.[28] An obvious
retort is that only human beings can have consciences, not business entities which are mere legal constructions and vehicles
for mobilising investment. Corporations as legal entities can
be sued, however, as many businesses involved in expensive
litigation know to their cost, and it is possible to identify corporate values which represent more (or less) than the values
of the stakeholders working for or involved with the company.

Furthermore, although corporations are concerned with
survival, stability and growth, and financial health is a prerequisite for all of these objectives, this does not necessarily conflict with moral health. Rather, corporate moral responsibility
is a containment, not a replacement, for the self-interest of the
corporation. This containment comes not only from the invisible moral force of the market (Adam Smith's invisible hand)
and the visible moral force of government through regulation,
but also from the hand of management itself. For Andrews the
invisible hand of the market is not sufficient to moderate the
injury done by the pursuit of self-interest, in addition corporate moral leadership is needed.[29] Ethical dereliction, sleaziness
or inertia is not merely an individual failure but a management
problem. Goodpaster and Matthews identify a principle of
moral projection as underwriting corporate conscience, which
is patterned on the thought and feeling process of the person.[30] There is a corporate personality which, like individuals,
is capable of being either moral or immoral. Neither state is

[28] Kenneth E. Goodpaster and John B. Matthews Jr., 'Can a corporation
have a conscience?' in Kenneth Andrews and Donald Kay, *Ethics in Practice*,
pp. 155–67.
[29] Kenneth R. Andrews, 'Ethics in practice', in *Harvard Business Review, Ethics
at Work*, op.cit., pp. 39–44.
[30] Kenneth E. Goodpaster and John B. Matthews Jr., 'Can a corporation
have a conscience?' pp. 159–62.

inevitable, rather the ethical standards of the business will depend on those projected through the markets in which it operates, from government and from its stakeholders.

MULTINATIONAL COMPANIES, NATIONAL INTEREST AND CORPORATE RESPONSIBILITY

If the personality of a business and its moral behaviour is determined by the environment in which it operates and the ethics of its stakeholders, then multinational corporations which adapt to the standards of the countries in which they operate might be regarded as having split personalities. Yet companies with a relatively homogenous management style determined largely by the value systems of their home countries are often accused by other governments of being cultural imperialists. At least some politicians in developing countries see multinationals as being neo-colonialist and exploitive, while politicians in the industrialised countries see multinationals as exporting jobs and taking advantage of cheap labour at the expense of home nationals. Critics from the home countries in which the multinationals are based often accuse the companies of 'going native' in their overseas operations, through giving into demands for bribes to win government contracts, or of taking advantage of the lack of pollution control or safety at work legislation in developing countries.

It seems that multinational companies are in an impossible situation, where the criticisms of home country critics cannot be reconciled with those from the host countries in which the subsidiaries are located. The problem is the lack of universal standards of business ethics, and the culture specific morals of many of the critics. Thomas Donaldson addresses these issues, and attempts to suggest a way forward through defining minimal corporate responsibilities where it is perhaps easier to get international and cross-cultural agreement.[31] Minimal duties are defined as mandatory by Donaldson, in contrast to maximal duties which may be praiseworthy, and an example of best practice by a multinational company, but not obligatory.

---

[31] Thomas J. Donaldson, 'Rights in the Global Market', in Freeman, *Business Ethics* pp. 139–62.

Minimal duties might include the prohibition of child labour and an obligation not to deprive workers of freedom of speech or association, the latter presumably being denied by companies that refuse to recognise trade unions.

Donaldson sees duties and rights as two sides of the same coin, which enables him to identify fundamental international rights and then translate these into duties for multinational companies. The right to a minimal education, for example, precludes multinational companies from employing children on a full time basis. Donaldson compiles a list of minimal correlative duties for multinationals which will avoid depriving people of their rights as defined in the United Nations Declaration of Human Rights, which most governments have signed, even if they do not always implement its provisions in practice. These rights include freedom of physical movement, freedom to own property, freedom from torture, fair trial, non-discriminatory treatment and political participation.[32]

At first sight these rights might seem more matters for governments than multinational companies, but imposing conditions of residence or threatening employees with redundancy if they reject a transfer to another plant could be regarded as infringing the right to physical movement. Similarly, denying a hearing to an employee accused of misconduct could be said to be in conflict with the right of fair trial, which is not only restricted to courts of law. Discrimination by multinationals against workers on grounds of race, religion or even political affiliation would also be a breach of basic rights.

The rights enshrined in the United Nation's International Covenant on Social, Economic and Cultural Rights are regarded by Donaldson as being in a different category to basic rights.[33] They are positive rather than negative rights in the sense that they imply that governments must undertake some specific action, such as making welfare provision for the poor, rather than merely refraining from undermining human rights, as in the extreme cases of torture or racial or religious discrimination. Interpreted in terms of multinational companies, such positive rights could refer to payment of a just wage or charging a fair price and providing reliable service. These are more

[32] Ibid., p. 151.
[33] Ibid., p. 142.

controversial areas, as few suggest that multinationals should pay the same salaries or wages to local nationals in a poor developed country as they do in a rich industrialised state. Rather, it is widely accepted that they should pay the 'going rate' for a given job in the country where their subsidiary is located. In practice, multinational companies usually pay above average rates in developing countries, but this is more a reflection of market conditions than ethics, the objective being to attract high quality employees. Donaldson does not see multinational companies as having an obligation to aid the deprived, as they may be a victim of their own government's policies, and not a system of international exploitation.

In the literature on business ethics compliance with the law is usually regarded as a moral duty as well as a legal obligation. However, if the laws are immoral, as was arguably the case with the pass laws preventing free movement and residence in South Africa under the apartheid system, then multinational companies with subsidiaries there during the period of white domination were clearly in an ethical quandary. This was one of the arguments used by opponents of apartheid against companies investing there, as being just under an unjust system is clearly difficult. Others said that multinational companies should keep their subsidiaries in South Africa open, and attempt to change the system from within, by adopting non-discriminatory employment practices and paying equal wages to black and white workers. This could be regarded as showing positive respect for rights, doing more than the law demanded, and changing social attitudes and behaviour through the demonstration of good practice.[34]

Multinational companies are normally expected to be honest in their tax declarations, but Donaldson cites the case of an American bank in Italy which was urged by its lawyers to underestimate its income to reduce its tax liability, as this was the normal practice for Italian banks.[35] When it insisted in

---

[34] Edwin, M. Hartman, 'Donaldson on rights and corporate obligations', in Freeman, *Business Ethics*, p. 164. This was what the Sullivan principles implied, which set out a code of conduct for United States multinational companies operating in South Africa under the apartheid system.

[35] Thomas Donaldson, 'Multinational decision making: reconciling international norms', in John Drummond and Bill Bain, *Managing Business Ethics*, pp. 137–8.

submitting an American-style tax return, it was overcharged by the tax authorities which expected all banks to underestimate their incomes. As a consequence, in subsequent years it followed the practice of Italian banks, so that it would avoid being treated unfairly because of exact disclosure. The importance attached to honesty, and perhaps even the concept itself, would appear to vary cross-culturally, with honesty regardless of cost, including employee well being and job security, not necessarily the best policy in all circumstances.

Multinationals may be honest in their declarations, but financial information is not always what it seems to be as the literature on transfer pricing makes clear. Transfer pricing refers to the prices charged by one subsidiary of a multinational company to another or to the parent company.[36] Vehicle engines, for example, do not have to be supplied by Ford in Germany to Ford in Britain at the market price, as the transaction is entirely within the company. If corporate taxes are lower in Britain than in Germany, then Ford might decide to charge a lower price for its engines, perhaps only covering costs so that no profits are declared. The British subsidiary will acquire the engines at an artificially low price, and record a larger profit than would otherwise be the case. It will be subject to corporate taxes, but Ford as a whole will have a lower tax liability internationally, which should improve the company's net profits. The ethics of such practices are questionable, as although the British government gains, the German government loses. It is not clear, however, what exactly is implied in saying that the transfer price should be a just price, especially as Britain has a lower living standard than Germany, and, therefore, there is an international income redistribution with a low transfer price.

ETHICS IN FINANCE

It is undoubtedly in the field of finance that unethical practices have received most attention in recent years, perhaps

---

[36] David K. Eiteman, Arthur I. Stonehill and Michael H. Moffett, *Multinational Business Finance*, Addison Wesley, Reading, Massachusetts, 1995, 7th edition, pp. 604–14.

reflecting the fact that financial engineering and the development of derivatives such as futures and options have opened up new possibilities of fraud, and new temptations to cheat. At the same time the greater transparency demanded by the public over matters such as commissions on insurance sales or how investment funds are deployed is highlighting abuses which in the past may not have been so apparent. There has been an encouraging response to this public concern by both academics in business schools and financial practitioners, which has resulted in financial ethics being one of the major growth areas in the business ethics literature. Banking ethics has emerged as a separate field in its own right, there being some parallels with the emergence of Islamic banks, a phenomenon reviewed in the last chapter, and explored in further detail below in the context of Muslim financial reporting.

Bimal Prodhan points out that as finance is a relatively new discipline with much of the literature dating from the 1970s onward, it has a late twentieth-century ethos which is obsessed with identity, individualism, existentialism and deconstructionism.[37] Financial economists have demonstrated the efficiency of utilitarianism, and disregarded the societal effects. The emphasis is on professionalism which is equated with rationality, and the profession rather than other groupings such as communities, nations or families. Hence the search for codes of conduct for finance professionals, regardless of where they work and live. An individual's ethical position and their responsibilities to others in society are defined by his or her occupation, rather than nationality, culture or religion. Whether a stockbroker or futures and options trader is a Jew, Christian, Muslim or atheist makes no difference to his or her business dealings. They are obliged to play the rules of the game, often within a depersonalised screen based market. The traders are usually acting as agents without knowledge of the identity of those on whose behalf they are trading, their experience being of prices and market behaviour, their skill being to have a 'feel' for the market rather than for their fellow human beings.

[37] Bimal Prodhan, 'Ethics, finance and society', in Andreas R. Prindl and Bimal Prodhan, (eds), *Ethical Conflicts in Finance*, Blackwell, Oxford, 1994, pp. 11–12.

Many of the ethical issues in finance involve resolving conflicts of interest between different parties to a transaction or deal. Often some parties have an advantage over others, perhaps because of the asymmetrical way information is diffused and interpreted. Bankers providing finance may be in a powerful position in relation to other stakeholders in a company.[38] It is they who can authorise a take-over of another company by one of their clients which may affect the livelihoods of thousands of employees. Indeed, merchant banks often have special mergers and acquisitions divisions that engineer the actual take-over plans in consultation with their clients, but in secret so that the target for the dawn raid or hostile bid has no time to prepare a defence. As financiers have less contact with the stakeholders who will be adversely affected by their actions than the managers in the affected businesses, they can pursue their strategies shielded from the ethical consequences. Their focus is purely on the financial side, in obtaining fee income for their banks, and ensuring their clients get the maximum return on their assets.

In such circumstances there is a strong case for arguing, as Prodhan does, that questions of ethics need to be in the mainstream of finance, just as they are in the professions of law and medicine.[39] Only then will cognitive development of financiers and bankers as individuals be possible. Prodhan believes voluntary codes of conduct have a role to play, but they cannot be a substitute for individual integrity. This, however, cannot simply be assumed to be a question of character. Financial issues are often highly complex, with consequences that can only be foreseen by those with knowledge and experience. An education in finance needs not only to include training in techniques, but also a wider understanding of the moral dimension of the situation likely to confront those involved.

Bankruptcy proceedings are a good example of some of these ethical issues.[40] When borrowers get into difficulties, banks aim to protect their own interests including those of their

[38] F.W. Pointon, 'Conflicts of interest for lending bankers', in Andreas R. Prindl and Bimal Prodhan, *Ethical Conflicts*, pp. 70–3.
[39] Bimal Prodhan, 'Ethics, finance and society', in Prindl and Prodhan, *Ethical Conflicts*, p. 22.
[40] Adrian L. Cohen, 'Bankruptcy: who sacrifices', in Prindl and Prodhan, *Ethical Conflicts*, pp. 83–94.

shareholders and employees. It can also be argued that banks have a moral duty towards their depositors who have placed funds in good faith. Banks will usually reschedule loans if borrowers cannot make repayments, as long as at least some interest obligations are honoured, so that the assets can be counted as performing. If, however, a borrower unilaterally suspends both interest servicing and repayments, the bank may have little option but to instigate bankruptcy proceedings, so that it can have first call on the borrower's assets. This will obviously be to the detriment of the indebted company and its shareholders, who may lose everything. Bankruptcy implies the company assets will be placed in the hands of a receiver who will act in the creditors' and not the other stakeholders' interest. The company can no longer raise capital from banks or other sources, and can only continue trading if that is in the interests of the creditors until a buyer is found for the company or its constituent parts, or until the physical assets and equipment are auctioned.

The moral dilemma in bankruptcy is that although the shareholders should have been aware of the risks they were taking, with the risk reflected in the share price, and the danger signs in company statements, often the employees are in a weaker position. The shareholders have the option of selling their shares up until bankruptcy, and writing off their losses, but the employees may find it more difficult to find alternative work. Labour markets are seldom as flexible as capital markets, as they involve humans moving and not merely finance. The bank may be effectively driving people into unemployment, in order to safeguard its own employees and depositors. In recognising where its prime responsibilities lie, it is making interpersonal comparisons, with its decision making harming some but not others. On the other hand, banks are not charities, and bankruptcies are an inevitable part of capitalist market systems.

Contributors to the business ethics literature cannot provide solutions to these dilemmas, short of calling for a completely different economic and financial system, which is arguably more unrealistic than ever since the collapse of communism and the demise of traditional socialism. Most writers instead concentrate on the issue of disclosure, so that at least all parties are kept informed about the likely or impending bankruptcy.

Disclosure of the full facts about the difficulties surrounding a company may, however, adversely affect the share price, make the company appear heavily geared, and undermine the confidence of creditors. Full and honest disclosure may, in other words, help precipitate bankruptcy. Usually companies get round this by stating that their difficulties are temporary, due to 'adverse trading conditions', but that they have a strategy to survive and recover in the longer term. The aim is to encourage shareholders not to sell, creditors to be patient, and employees not to look to competitors for jobs.

There has been considerable interest by those concerned with business ethics in the issue of insider dealing, which is usually regarded as immoral, and can constitute a criminal offence as it amounts to an attempt to defraud.[41] This interest has come from those involved in law and ethics as well as from financial economists. Insider dealing involves taking advantage of information which has not been revealed to the public, the classic example being when the executives in a company use information which they have acquired in the course of their job to buy shares in another company which they know will be the target of a take-over bid from their own company. The investing public may be surprised by the dawn raid which dramatically increases the share price of the company subject to the bid, but those involved in the take-over may have purchased shares in their own name or those of relatives a few days, or even a few hours previously, in anticipation of such developments.

As Jennifer Moore points out, taking advantage of inside information for financial gain which others do not have access to is usually regarded as unfair.[42] Insider dealing is also regarded as harmful, as ordinary investors may loose out as the insiders make their gain, or in the case of falling prices, make larger losses, as the insiders may have sold their shares first, and helped undermine the market. Stock market regulators of the world's leading exchanges take a serious view of insider dealing, as they believe it harms investor confidence, and leads to a weaker market with fewer participants.

---

[41] Jennifer Moore, 'What is really unethical about insider trading?' in Prindl and Prodhan, *Ethical Conflicts*, pp. 113–42.
[42] Ibid., pp. 115–22.

A contrary view is that insider knowledge is only acquired as a result of effort, and that those who possess or own the knowledge have a right to exploit it. Insider knowledge according to this view is a form of intellectual property right, which insiders have the skills to interpret as a result of education and training which they may have acquired at their own or their family's expense. It may also result from investment in processing systems. Major banks which have invested large amounts in computer systems for their foreign exchange dealing rooms may feel they have a right to exploit arbitrage opportunities which their software has been especially programmed to detect. The information is potentially available to rivals if they had made similar investments in their computer systems. Arbitrage in the foreign exchange market is quite legal, as the exchange rate quotes are regarded as in the public domain, even though banks may have to invest in expensive information systems to get spot, forward and futures quotations in real time, second by second.

ETHICAL BANKING AND INVESTMENT

The development of specifically ethical banking and investment products is a phenomenon that emerged during the 1970s in response to the demands of particular types of customers. Some see the concept as a mere fad, a pandering to political correctness, while others see it as a cynical attempt by some financial institutions to exploit their clients' potential benevolence, perhaps paradoxically in an unethical way. An investment company or bank may claim it is not investing in armaments companies or in ventures which cause environmental damage, and explain that as a result it is having to pay a lower return. There may be an economic argument for this, as excluding some potentially profitable activities may reduce the return on any portfolio in relation to the risks involved. If, however, the return is much lower than that offered by non-ethical institutions, and the criteria for exclusion is narrowly defined, then the poor rewards to the investor may simply disguise incompetent management or the fact that the institution is siphoning off profits to its executives or other insiders.

Ethical banking and investment may simply be viewed as a marketing ploy to appeal to the environmentally concerned, pacifists or leftists who view all private financial institutions with suspicion. It is related to the politics of direct action which was invigorated by the anti-Vietnam war protests of the late 1960s and the green and ecology movements of the 1970s and 1980s. It is an attempt to appeal to the beliefs and values of individuals who have taken part in or been influenced by these movements. The aim is to get potential clients to translate their political preferences into their financial practices, by convincing the investor that the institution concerned shares his or her point of view. From a marketing perspective this is a way of winning client trust and encouraging loyalty, while persuading the investor that more is being offered than a mere financial return, and that the institution is adding value in a qualitative sense. The aim is to produce a 'feel good' factor for the investor, so that he or she can have a good conscience about the returns on their assets.

The concept of ethical banking is controversial, as it implies that traditional or conventional banking is somehow unethical. This may be because of how its methods or practices are viewed. An example of this is where interest dealings are equated with usury, as in the case of modern Muslim thinking or Christian thinking historically. It may also be the result of secular leftist thinking, that regards banks as capitalistic institutions. In this case it is regarded as morally wrong that wealthy shareholders should be profiting from less wealthy bank clients, especially in a situation where interest rates are fixed by monetary policy, and there is little real competition amongst the banks over pricing for their services. The banks may exploit a monopoly position thanks to banking licences which restrict the entry of competitors, and benefit from windfall gains if monetary tightening raises interest rates. One answer for these leftist critics is a co-operative bank or credit union, where the bank customers and employees are the shareholders, and obtain the benefit of any windfall gains or monopoly profits. This avoids the conflict of interest between shareholders, clients and employees, but means the institutions will not have access to markets for risk capital.

James Lynch reviews some of the trends in alternative banking, including social collateral banking and viewpoint banking.[43]

[43] James J. Lynch, 'The future shape of ethical banking', in Drummond and Bain, Managing *Business Ethics*, pp. 175–6.

The former is especially relevant to developing countries where the poor lack collateral for loans. Under one scheme in Bangladesh, run by the Grameen Bank, potential clients organised themselves into groups of fifty and sub-groups of five. Members of each sub-group act as guarantor for each others' loans. Each group and sub-group act as the evaluator and approver for each loan, thus moving credit scoring from the bank to the community. The Grameen Bank has a 97.3 per cent record for repayments being on time, and by 1992 had advanced over £54 million ($83 million) to 290 000 customers.[44]

Viewpoint banking is Lynch's term for alternative banks which share a common philosophy with their clients, Islamic banks being an example. Lynch also cites the case of Mercury Provident, a licensed deposit taker in Britain, whose founder, the ecologist Rudolph Steiner, believes money represents social and spiritual energy which should be used in a conscious way.[45] Rather than merely putting funds on deposit, clients can specify the purposes for which they are to be used, and even their own terms for withdrawal and rate of interest up to a specified ceiling. Funding has gone to projects such as retirement homes, alternative schooling, organic farming and a women's co-operative making shoes in Wales. Because depositors have faith in what they are backing, they are usually charitable, and do not demand maximum interest returns.

Lynch discusses ethical investment briefly,[46] but a much more comprehensive discussion is provided by Christopher Cowton.[47] He defines ethical investment as the use of ethical and social criteria in the selection and management of investment portfolios, generally consisting of company shares. Ethical investors are not only concerned about the financial returns on their portfolios and the risks involved, but also with the characteristics of the companies in which the funds are placed. This involves the nature of the company's goods or services, the location of its business and the manner in which it conducts its affairs. The strategy for ethical investment can either be positive or negative, the former being supportive of

[44] Ibid.
[45] Ibid., p. 176.
[46] Ibid., pp. 177–8.
[47] Christopher J. Cowton, 'The development of ethical investment products', in Prindl and Prodhan, *Ethical Conflicts*, pp. 213–32.

companies which are particularly approved of in terms of their products, activities or business methods. The latter aims to avoid investing in companies which are involved in unacceptable products or countries, or whose business methods are regarded as unethical. Negative criteria are more usual than positive criteria, with investors starting with a complete listing of quoted companies, and then excluding the unethical minority.

Cowton discusses product design issues, as although it is possible to have a customised professionally managed ethical portfolio, in practice most ethical investment is placed in standardised offerings.[48] For individuals and institutions with more than £100 000 ($153 000) to invest, a personalised ethical stockbroking service can be provided. It is only worth constructing tailor made portfolios to meet the client's income or capital growth and ethical objectives if substantial amounts are involved, as fund monitoring costs are relatively high for a stockbroker offering a conscientious service, and a large portfolio is necessary to ensure adequate diversification to reduce risk. The standardised products can be purchased through a stockbroker or directly from the investment institution managing the ethical fund, with investments of as little as £1000 ($1530) accepted, or savings of £50 ($76.50) a month for regular investment plans.

The earliest established and largest ethical fund in the United Kingdom is the Friends Provident Stewardship Fund. It started operating in June 1984 and by 1994 had funds worth over £414 million ($633 million) under management.[49] Friends Provident is one of Britain's oldest mutual insurance companies, established by the Society of Friends, better know as the Quakers, because of their fear of God, in the mid-nineteenth century. Although Friends Provident has long catered for the wider public regardless of religious affiliation or belief, and its employees can be of any or no religion, it still tries to conduct business in accordance with the ethical beliefs of its founders. It offers a full range of investment services, and most of its funds are not employed on a specifically ethical basis, but the provision of ethical investment seemed a natural extension of

---

[48] Ibid., pp. 222–7.
[49] Information supplied by Holden Meehan.

its activities following the start of similar funds in the United States.

Positive ethical criteria used by the managers of the Stewardship Fund when examining companies for possible investment include a good record for quality products, safety, staff management and customer relations. Companies involved in environment improvement and pollution control are favoured as well as those with interests in sustainable woodland management and energy conservation. Negative criteria means the exclusion of companies which promote gambling or pornography, or are engaged in tobacco or alcohol production or distribution. Military suppliers are also excluded, as well as companies involved in the exploitation of animals for cosmetics or the fur trade, or in factory farming for the meat trade. The rulings of the Health and Safety Executive, the National Rivers Authority and the Advertising Standards Authority are studied in the UK, as companies which are subject to prosecutions or complaints from these authorities are excluded.

Friends Provident do not take a proactive approach to ethical investment, their policy being simply not to invest in, or to withdraw from involvement with, companies which do not meet their guidelines. In contrast, Britain's second largest ethical fund, the Merlin Jupiter Ecology Fund, 'pushes' companies to respond beyond the letter of the law to issues raised by their sustainable development agenda. The Merlin Resources Unit is engaged in a continuous dialogue with the companies they fund, and their research unit produces a bi-annual newsletter. Investors are invited to fill in regular questionnaires so that their views on the Fund's policies can be ascertained, the emphasis being on constructive and open exchange of views. Although only founded in March 1988, by 1994 the Merlin Jupiter Ecology Fund had £62 million ($95 million) under management which was invested internationally,[50] including worthwhile projects in developing countries.

The table shows the major ethical funds in the United Kingdom, which had assets worth over £766.5 million ($1173 million) under management in 1994. The Friends Provident Stewardship Fund was by far the largest player accounting for over 54 per cent of the market, with some of the other funds

---

[50] Figures from Holden Meehan.

Table 5.1 British Ethical Funds (£1 = $1.53)

Fund	Assets (£million)	Market spread[1]	Launch date	Screen[2]
Friends Provident Stewardship Fund	414.0	UK+	6/84	5
Credit Suisse Fellowship Trust	5.2	UK	7/86	4
Framlington Health Fund	11.8	Int	4/87	4
Abbey Life Ethical Trust	22.1	UK+	9/87	5
NIM Conscience Fund	12.3	UK+	9/87	4
Allchurches Life Amity Fund	19.0	UK	2/88	4
Jupiter Merlin Ecology Fund	62.0	Int	3/88	5
City Financial Acorn Ethical Unit Trust	3.6	Int	3/88	2
Scottish Equitable Ethical Unit Trust	25.5	UK	4/89	5
Sovereign Ethical Fund	9.1	UK	5/89	2
Eagle Star Environmental Opportunities Fund	13.5	UK+	6/89	1
TSB Environmental Investor Fund	23.3	UK+	6/89	2
Homeowners Friendly Society Green Chip Fund	13.5	UK+	11/89	3
Commercial Union Environment Exempt Pension Fund	33.0	Int	12/89	2
Clerical Medical Evergreen Fund	15.9	Int	2/90	5
CIS Environmental Trust	26.9	Int	5/90	3
NPI Global Care Fund	6.7	Int	8/91	5
Abtrust Ethical Fund	1.3	Int	9/92	2
Sun Life Global Management Ecological Fund	4.0	Int	12/92	2
Mercury Provident Personal Pension Plan	15.5	Int	1/94	5
Co-operative Bank Ethical Unit Trust	12.8	UK	9/93	3
Equitable Ethical Trust	15.5	Int	1/94	3

Notes: 1. 'UK+' is mostly domestic with limited international exposure, 'Int' is world wide.
2. Resources applied to screening – an assessment by Holden Meehan of the time, care and expertise applied to selecting shares. A higher number indicates a more comprehensive screening process.

Source: Holden Meehan, Bath, September, 1995.

being very small. Holden Meehan ranks the funds according to the resources applied to screening which is obviously important for ethical management. Friends Provident scores well, as does the Jupiter Merlin Ecology Fund, but it is evident that some of the major insurance companies which are very new to ethical investment and have relatively small amounts of funds deployed in this way are not devoting sufficient attention to the screening. The question is whether Eagle Star, the Commercial Union and Sun Life would attract more funds if they treated ethical investment more seriously, or if the lack of company support reflects a perception that their ethical funds have not been a success, and therefore that it is not commercially viable to channel resources in this direction? Cynics might suggest that they were merely jumping on an ethical bandwagon, and using ecology and the environment as marketing ploys.

THE PERFORMANCE OF ETHICAL FUNDS

Although some investors may be more than willing to sacrifice returns for the sake of funding an especially good cause, the performance of ethical funds is of as much concern as any other fund, as the ethical investment industry does not want to see its backers lose out in relation to those with holdings in purely commercial funds, otherwise they will have relatively less to invest in the future. Ethical investors themselves still hope for above average performance, usually defined in terms of capital gains in relation to benchmark indices such as the FTSE 100 or FTSE All Share in the case of the United Kingdom or the Dow Jones index in the case of Wall Street. It can be argued that placing restrictions on share selection on ethical grounds results in a smaller universe from which to select potential purchases, which must adversely affect returns. Ethical fund managers argue, however, that the overall stock market is large, with a capitalisation of £800 billion ($1224 billion) in the United Kingdom alone. They suggest that stock worth over £320 billion ($490 billion), representing 40 per cent of the total, is eligible for ethical investment. Given this large pool available for ethical investment, performance is unlikely to be any different from that of unrestricted investments.

There is a bias in ethical investment towards medium sized and smaller companies in both the United Kingdom and the United States, with 80 per cent of the companies listed in the FTSE 100 not eligible for ethical funding for one reason or another.[51] As the medium sized companies in the FTSE mid 250 index and the FTSE smaller companies index typically outperform those in the FTSE 100, reflecting the greater risks involved, ethical investment in medium and smaller companies might be expected to perform better than that in larger companies. Over the 1988 to 1993 period in the United Kingdom the average ethical pension fund grew by an average of 14.2 per cent per year, compared with 13.4 per cent for the average conventional pension fund.[52]

Performance within the ethical investment sector varies widely however, although these differences are similar to what is found within other sectors. The Allchurches Life Amity Fund rose by 12.6 per cent over the year to September 1995, 2.7 per cent less than the Financial Times All Share Index, while the Abbey Life Ethical Trust rose by 6.1 per cent over the same period, 8.3 per cent below the FT All Share Index.[53] The Scottish Equity Ethical Unit Trust recorded a 13.6 per cent rise over the twelve month period to September 1995, while the Friends Provident Stewardship Fund recorded the largest rise of the major ethical funds of 14.2 per cent, only 1.3 per cent below the rise of the FT All Share Index.[54] The so called 'high low' chart illustrates the price trends and annual price variations of the Friends Provident Stewardship Fund since its instigation in 1985. Quarterly data were used, the top of the bar for each year showing the highest price attained at the end of a quarter and the bottom the lowest quarterly price. So-called opening and closing prices are also shown. As the bars refer to years rather than days, the line to the left of each bar shows the price for the end of the first quarter of each year, usually 31 March unless this falls on a weekend or the Easter holiday. The line to the right shows the price for the end of the

---

[51] According to Holden Meehan.
[52] Ibid.
[53] Figures from Datastream, London, September 1995.
[54] Ibid.

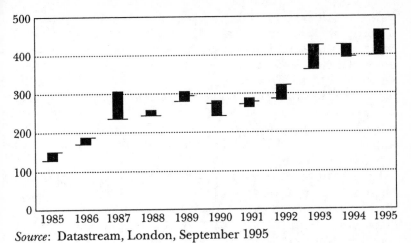

Source: Datastream, London, September 1995

Figure 5.1 Friends Provident Stewardship Fund: Price Trends and Annual Variations (in pence: note that 100 pence = £1; £1 = \$1.53)

final quarter, typically 30 December, as the 31st is not a trading day.

As with any equity based investment, with ethical funds the size of capital gains or losses depends crucially on the timing of purchases and sales. The problem is to anticipate the price peaks and troughs in any particular time period when the investor has funds to deploy. One way round the difficulties in timing purchasing decisions for small investors is to subscribe to a monthly savings plan, which irons out the peaks and troughs.[55] This facility is offered by most ethical funds, the minimum subscription being £50 (\$76) per month. The larger ethical funds also offer personal equity plans which can improve returns, as under these United Kingdom government provisions investors can realise capital gains of up to £6000 (\$9180) per year without paying tax. Tax advantages can also be realised by linking investment in ethical funds to pension plans, which increases benefits in relation to monthly contributions.

Most of the ethical funds are set up on a unit trust basis,

---

[55] Holden Meehan provides a list and details of the ethical funds offering this facility.

with the prices of the units related to a weighted average of the prices of the underlying shares held. Ethical investment company shares represent a slightly more risky investment, as these companies can borrow from banks for share purchases unlike unit trusts. This added gearing gives the fund managers more flexibility over the timing of investment acquisitions and sales, which do not have to be adjusted immediately to withdrawals as in the case of unit trusts. Substantial capital losses with borrowed funds can be disastrous for any investment company, including those run on ethical lines.

In the United States ethical investment has been part of the financial scene for over two decades. There are two measures of the performance of American ethical funds compared to conventional funds. The first by the Lipper Corporation shows ethical mutual funds, the United States equivalent of unit trusts, rising by over 95 per cent over the five year period up to December 1992, compared to an 80 per cent price rise for conventional funds. The second, the Domini Social Index, comprises 250 ethically screened companies from the Standard and Poor's 400 largest American companies, plus 150 socially acceptable smaller companies. When this index is tracked against the S and P 500 largest companies, it reveals a 10 per cent advantage over the July 1990 to December 1993 period.[56]

In the United Kingdom the Church Commissioners who look after the financial assets of the Anglican church do not use ethical screening, although in the 1970s and 1980s they avoided investments in South Africa. The Church Commissioner's policy on investment in the late 1980s caused much controversy, not so much on ethical as on financial grounds, as they lost a considerable amount of money in ill-judged property investments, by buying at the peak of the price cycle, and then experiencing a drop in the value of their assets, and a fall in rental income as tenancy contracts came up for renewal. Rather than attempting to manage their finances 'in-house', other churches, including the Methodists and the Presbyterians, have used professionally managed ethical funds, the Allchurches Life Amity Fund, as its name implies, being particularly tailored to this market, as is Clerical and Medical, which has handled pensions for the clergy.

---

[56] Information quoted by Holden Meehan.

CHRISTIAN BUSINESS ETHICS

Although much of the business ethics movement draws on a humanist tradition concerned with respect for the dignity of man, and writing in the field of moral philosophy more generally rather than religion, it is to the latter that we now turn to complete the survey of the development of business ethics. Those involved with ethical issues cannot ignore the contributions of the Judeo-Christian and Muslim traditions as set out in these final pages. Laura Nash has described good business behaviour as 'ethics without the sermon', but perhaps there is a case for including the sermon.[57]

For many Christians in the modern world, religious belief is primarily a private matter, although not necessarily an individual matter. They may belong to a church, and worship with their fellow believers on Sundays and during religious festivals. As church members they may participate in social events and give regular charitable donations. Their beliefs may shape their family lives, and determine their basic social attitudes and personal values. Christians may be reluctant to declare these values in their business dealings, and any attempt to proselytise in the workplace may be met with open hostility. Those in authority who engaged in such activity would be open to the charge of abusing their position. Where groups of Christian employees have organised lunch-time meetings for Bible study and prayer, they are at best regarded as slightly odd by other employees, including those who are regular church attendees themselves. At worst they are thought of as fanatics, wasting company time and not giving sufficient priority to their work, especially under the pressurised business conditions that are increasingly the norm with many employees working through their lunch breaks.

Within the modern business corporation many Christians almost feel a sense of embarrassment about their beliefs, even when many of the other employees are Christian. In the nineteenth century in the United States and Britain many business leaders openly professed their Christian beliefs, and often their paternalism towards their employees was driven by

---

[57] Laura Nash, 'Ethics without the sermon', in Andrews and Kay, *Ethics in Practice*, pp. 243–57.

Christian values such as compassion and charity. In the closing years of the twentieth century anti-discriminatory legislation means that while the beliefs of individual employees are supposedly protected, a corporate business culture overtly based on Christian beliefs is regarded as inappropriate. An employment policy that favoured Christians, or particular Christian denominations, would be illegal. One problem is that while the law protects individual rights, 'political correctness', which implies adherence to a particular set of social values, undermines those rights. Christians may be subject to harassment, or even discrimination, in the workplace for the sake of 'political correctness', the position of Roman Catholic medical workers who are concerned with the rights of the unborn being an example.

Management decisions appear to be taken without reference to the teachings of the Gospels, even by those who are practising Christians. There is a view that business is business, and that corporate and Christian values do not mix. Williams and Houck quote the common belief that 'there is no need to mix the oil of religion with the water of business.'[58] The goals of business may include profit maximisation and enhancing shareholder asset values. Company mission statements may speak of providing value for money, customer satisfaction, responsibilities to employees and the community and other morally desirable objectives, but these are often the means to monetary gain, the latter being the end. In contrast, for Christians the objectives are spiritual, money and the stewardship over resources merely being the means for serving God.

Does this mean that Christian values and managerial objectives are irreconcilable, and that believers in Christ cannot work in modern business? Should church leaders be calling for a transformation in business culture? Some are, but their voices do not appear to be heard. Does this mean that secularism has triumphed, and that the Christian message is increasingly irrelevant for modern commercial life?

Such an interpretation of economic and social development is possible, and indeed there are many who take this view. Much depends on the Christian's view of work and its place in

---

[58] Oliver F. Williams and John W. Houck, *Full Value: Cases in Christian Business Ethics*, Harper and Row, San Francisco, 1966, p. 3.

life. Those that live to work have a problem if the ultimate objective of the organisations they work for is monetary gain. If instead work is seen as a means to winning control of resources, so that they can be utilised according to the principles of Christian stewardship, then this casts a different light on the role of salaries, dividends, capital gains and other forms of remuneration in cash and in kind. What becomes crucial are the beliefs and attitudes of the individual Christian managers and employees. If work itself is seen as simply the means and not the end, then business is kept in its place, with the company as the servant, not the master. It may not be so much a question of transforming modern business corporations, but of changing how they are perceived, and of seeing their role in the context of a much fuller life which has spiritual and not merely material dimensions.

Williams and Houck ask how Christians in business can use the Bible to help their decision making.[59] There is no detailed guidance in the Bible as to how Christians working in business should make decisions, as business organisation and structures were very different at the time of Christ, the small owner managed business being the norm. Biblical teaching shapes the vision of Christians, including their attitudes and intentions. It is not so much a question of looking at sets of verses, but of being aware of the dominant chords and recurrent themes in Scripture. There may be disagreement between Christians over the interpretation of particular passages of the Bible, and of the relative importance of different sets of teaching, but the overall message of the Gospels is clear.

The Gospel is not a rule book of correct behaviour for Christians in the same way that the *Torah* is for Jews. Christians cannot earn God's favour by their deeds, and there is no utilitarian calculus of spiritual benefits for earthly sacrifice in business or anywhere else. Salvation is beyond human reach, and can only come as a gift of God. What the Gospels proclaim is the boundless love of God, which Christians are to emulate in their unique own human way.[60] Christians are thankful to Christ for his sacrifices on the cross on their behalf, and are inspired in their lives by this example. Christ preached forgiveness and

[59] Ibid., pp. 4–5.
[60] Ibid., p. 6.

did not bear grudges, and nor should they in their daily lives and business dealings. They should treat their superiors, subordinates and associates with respect, and accord them the dignity which God accorded humans by having Christ his son live amongst them. The Christian message is that people are God's representatives on earth and should behave accordingly in order to honour their Creator.

Rules drawn up by Christians in business inspired by these beliefs will surely reflect the Will of God, but it is not a matter of proclaiming in a company's articles of association or mission statement that the business is Christian, as there may be employees of other religions or no religion. The aim of business is not to convert its employees or its customers to Christianity, but to serve its various stakeholders or constituents. A business which subscribes to a code of business ethics, which is not explicitly Christian, but which Christian employees have helped draw up, may serve everyone well, including non-Christian stakeholders. If the rules have been drawn up by people of good will then they will be designed to protect values such as honesty, integrity, fairness and justice.[61]

Williams and Houck address the issue of power in business from a Christian perspective. They point out how power can degenerate into a goal in itself. Yet the desire for power is an important source of motivation for many in management. Indeed, the degree of domination and control over others can be taken as a measure of self-worth. Techniques for manipulating people are seen by some as valid tools for promoting the interests of particular firms. A degree of ruthlessness may be seen as important for business success, with 'weak' people seldom making it to the top. Decisions over issues such as redundancies are seen as tough, but the managers who take the decisions are seen as courageously acting in the company's interest, even when the decisions result in considerable personal and social hardship for those who find they no longer have jobs.

The Judeo-Christian tradition recognises that some individuals must hold power over others, but power is not seen as an end in itself, but rather as a means of serving others. These others may include the company, but this can be interpreted

---

[61] Ibid., p. 18.

to mean the various stakeholders in the company, and not some impersonal legal entity. Power is to be used in a way which helps others realise their unique gifts and talents. The emphasis, in other words, should be on facilitating human development and self-realisation, and on delegating meaningful work to others so that they too can be empowered in relation to their abilities. Williams and Houck quote St Paul's letter to the Philippians: 'Do nothing out of selfish ambition or vain conceit, but in humility consider others better than yourselves. Each of you should look not only to your own interests, but also to the interests of others.'[62] Power should not be abused, as is made clear in John's Gospel, where those who have been given responsibilities for particular tasks are told by Christ to display due humility in carrying them out: 'I tell you the truth, no servant is greater than his master, nor is a messenger greater than the one who sent him.'[63] As this follows a passage which tells of Christ washing the feet of Peter, a task normally carried out by slaves, the importance of humility is evident.

In modern business one prevailing attitude is that 'time is money'. Business executives are usually under pressure to reach performance targets, and as firms slim down the sizes of their workforces, those remaining are often forced to work longer and longer hours. Even though most employees are not officially paid by the hour, they find their remuneration is in practice often linked to the hours worked, as they cannot keep their well paid jobs, or earn performance bonuses, unless they work long hours. In these circumstances, sometimes getting the job done becomes almost as important as the job itself. The corporate culture may also promote the feeling that it is somehow disloyal, perhaps irresponsible, to leave the office before well into the evening. Managers may even feel guilty about going home before their subordinates.

The problem with this is that family relations suffer as executives have no time for anything but their jobs. Their work attitudes tend to carry over into their home lives. Earning money to support their children is seen as more important than actually spending time with the children themselves. The stress on problem solving at the office is carried over into family

---

[62] Philippians 2:3–4.
[63] John 13:16.

relations. Differences of opinion with spouses or children become difficulties to be resolved, with the opinions of the financially dependent perhaps not being given the respect they deserve, and little recognition of their distinctive contribution to family life.

For Christians life is not, as Williams and Houck assert, 'a problem to be solved but a mystery to be lived.'[64] Goal achievement should not eclipse the value of enjoying the moment. Yet there are parallels between the sacrifices which many executives make for the sake of their companies and those that Christians make in the service of God. There is a sense in which both defer benefits by constraining themselves, the business executive in foregoing out of work activities, and the Christian by keeping to the path which is thought to be morally correct in the light of the teaching of the Gospels. Yet just as there is no benefit in immorality, so there is no benefit by putting business development ahead of personal development and in confining life experiences.

The Williams and Houck volume is one of the few studies on Christian business ethics. The field has been surprisingly neglected by both academic theologians with an interest in social ethics and management specialists in ethics within the business school community. To some extent this may reflect almost a hostility to business by those in the tradition of Christian social ethics. Modern British writers such as John Atherton, whose work was discussed in Chapter 3, follow in the footsteps of Tawney with his critique of capitalism and belief in a Christian socialist alternative. Writers such as Brian Griffiths in the United Kingdom or Michael Novak in the United States, both of whose work is also discussed in Chapter 3, are more sympathetic to capitalism, but their concern is with markets and the role of government. Their work is more in the field of political economy than business management. It is the more complex issue of management behaviour which is of central concern in business ethics, where there is a recognition that maximisation and the pursuit of material advantage are not the only explanations for how businesses operate.

There has been some debate on Christianity and enterprise

[64] Williams and Houck, *Full Value*, p. 37.

culture, especially in post-Thatcher Britain, notable contributors being Kenneth Thompson[65] and Paul Morris.[66] Both of these writers are concerned with ideology and political economy however, not with an analysis of internal business decision making, but rather its role in society and relationship with government. Thompson discusses the ideological crisis with the demise of alternatives to capitalism, his main contribution being a useful examination of how the assertion of an individualistic version of enterprise values has upset the communitarian–individualist symbiosis that he believes characterised British ideology in the past. He is, in other words, not so much concerned with corporate or business culture, but how what he calls neo-individualism has permeated many sections of British society. It is evident that this is a development which Thompson regrets, although his critique of the moral underpinnings of Thatcherism is objective, as is his treatment of the religious right, as far as it goes.

Paul Morris's contribution is even more political, the first section being titled 'the Church of England as the "loyal opposition" at prayer or *Guardian* readers talking to *Telegraph* readers.'[67] There is much on the Anglican church's opposition to the market, and the attack by David Jenkins, the former Bishop of Durham, on 'wicked enterprise policies'.[68] As with Thompson, there is reference to Brian Griffiths, and a portrayal of the new Conservatism in Britain as a type of 'theo-economics', their notion being that Christian moral values do indeed encourage enterprise, a view at variance with that of most of the Church of England hierarchy.

There have been similar debates within the Presbyterian Church of Scotland, mostly focused on the merits and drawbacks of market systems, with broad support for the market by

[65] Kenneth Thompson, 'Individual and community in religious critiques of the enterprise culture', in Paul Heelas and Paul Morris, (eds) *The Values of the Enterprise Culture: the Moral Debate*, Routledge, London, 1992, pp. 253–75.
[66] Paul Morris, 'Is God enterprising? Reflections on enterprise culture and religion', in Paul Heelas and Paul Morris, *Values of the Enterprise Culture*, pp. 276–90.
[67] Ibid., p. 277.
[68] Ibid., p. 278.

Gordon Hughes,[69] but some questioning of the justice of market outcomes by Tom Campbell.[70] David Sinclair suggests that although markets should be judged by outcomes, a Christian perspective should focus from the bottom up, that is by examining how the most disadvantaged in society are affected.[71] It is human worth which matters for Sinclair, not simply the prices and values of material goods. Business should be judged by its contribution to the worth of the disadvantaged, including its least well off employees, and not simply by the value of its production.

The Centre for Theology and Public Issues at Edinburgh University instigated a study of Christian financial ethics, which reported through a working group composed of Scottish investment managers, bankers and theologians.[72] The tone is very different to that of much earlier similar studies such as that by the Christian Social Council, a Roman Catholic body, back in 1930.[73] The Christian Social Council study was written by clergy, and it was more theoretical and theological, and arguably less practical. However, it can be compared with the Edinburgh study as it takes a very positive view of investment and its role in modernising business. Although its starting point is a discussion of the traditional prohibition of usury, the contributors, notably Maurice Reckett, draw a distinction between usury, which is condemned on social grounds, as contributing to inequality, and interest, which is seen as indispensable for modern business activity. Investors can accept interest returns, and dividends, but they should make sure that businesses are paying 'just' wages. In modern business ethics terms this can

[69] Gordon A. Hughes, 'The economics of hard choices: justice and the market', in Gordon A. Hughes *et al.*, *Justice and the Market*, Centre for Theology and Public Issues, Occasional Paper No. 21, Edinburgh University, 1991, pp. 1–17.

[70] Tom D. Campbell, 'Markets and justice', in Gordon A. Hughes *et al.*, *Justice and the Market*, pp. 18–27.

[71] David Sinclair, 'Price, value and worth', in Hughes *et al.*, *Justice and the Market*, pp. 33–6.

[72] George Wilkie, (Chairman, Working Group on Finance and Ethics), *Capital: A Moral Instrument*, St Andrews Press for the Edinburgh University Centre for Theological and Public Issues, Edinburgh, 1992.

[73] Maurice B. Reckitt, (ed.), *The Christian Tradition Regarding Interest and Investment*, The Christian Social Council, London, 1930.

be interpreted as implying that Christian investors should be concerned with ethical screening.

The authors of the Edinburgh study see capital as a moral instrument, a means of promoting social justice, as those who control capital, either as investors or fund managers, have considerable power to influence the type of businesses to which capital gets allocated. In other words, those who work in financial services and are making decisions on investments have considerable moral responsibilities. They may need ethical guidance, and for Christian fund managers such guidance can come from the Gospels. A distinction is drawn between the accumulation of wealth and the creation of wealth. The former is seen as a rather narrow materialistic goal, but the latter is a very positive pursuit, as through wealth creation man is fulfilling God's purpose. Jesus himself was not concerned with the acquisition of wealth or its consumption, but for much of his life he worked as a carpenter, taking wood and fashioning it into tables and chairs, as well as yokes and ploughs for farming.[74]

Enterprise is also viewed in a positive light by the authors of the Edinburgh study. God has given man the intelligence, ingenuity and strength to enhance the quality of his own life, that of his family and his neighbours. People are supposed to use their talents, as they are called by God to a life of enterprise.[75] That is not to say that the God given drive in men to improve their lot should be taken to extremes, as there has also to be a place for contentment in life, and time for reflection. The Sabbath provides such a time, and through religious observance man can develop his spiritual life, and have a better perspective on the material. There is the danger of people being possessed by their possessions. Even if Christians do not covet the material goods of others, there is the risk of those in business being devoured by a feeling that they have to catch up with their superiors in terms of material reward.

The Edinburgh study is concerned with practical matters as well as broad principles. The working group on finance and ethics was invited to submit a memorandum to the independent

---

[74] George Wilkie, *Capital: A Moral Instrument*, p. 10.
[75] Ibid., p. 12.

inquiry into corporate take-overs in the United Kingdom. This was submitted in 1990, and is included as an appendix to the study.[76] Particular concern is expressed about the ethical dilemmas posed when take-overs are contemplated. Take-overs are recognised as inevitable under modern business conditions, and are viewed as potentially beneficial rather than simply condemned out of hand. What matters, according to those who submitted the memorandum, is not simply the anticipated financial gains for the company making the bid, but the welfare of all the stakeholders in both businesses. There may be losers and gainers, but the bidder has a moral responsibility to everyone likely to be affected which needs to be taken into account.

The working group recommended that the Office of Fair Trading should have a remit which goes beyond merely considering the competitive effect of take-overs. More stringent rules relating to the registration of shares held in nominee names is also seen as desirable, as those involved in take-overs should be identifiable and accountable. There is also a suggestion that voting rights in companies should be limited to those who have held shares for over a year in the company. This might help ensure that predators cannot simply build up short-term stakes with the intention of then voting for a take-over, in order to realise speculative gains. None of this, of course, is Biblical teaching, and such specific recommendations are inevitably contentious, and indeed may never be implemented. Nevertheless, the recommendations demonstrate the type of conclusions that Christians engaged in finance can come to out of their sincerely held beliefs.[77]

BUSINESS ETHICS IN ISLAM

Although there is an extensive literature on Islamic economics and a considerable amount has been written on Islamic banking and finance, there are few books and articles specifically on Islamic business ethics. This may reflect the limited role which joint stock companies play in most Muslim countries, and the failure of indigenous multinational companies to

---

[76] Ibid., pp. 74–9.
[77] Ibid., p. 78.

emerge in the Islamic World, which can be interpreted as a consequence of the major role which government played in economic activity following independence in many Muslim countries. There is nothing specific to Islam which suggests that the states should control the commanding heights of the economy, as Muslims can subscribe to right wing as well as left wing ideologies. Rather, it was more a result of politically independent Muslim nations wanting to exercise their power to establish at least a degree of economic independence to match their political independence. In other words, the strong role of the state, which crowded out the private sector and inhibited business growth, was a consequence of nationalism rather than religion.

With large business organisations within the state sector, and most private firms small family run concerns, there was little interest by Muslim writers in the business ethics literature which was developing in the West. Those who had been exposed to ethics courses in business schools were largely Muslim employees of Western companies living in, and often with citizenship of, the United States or the United Kingdom. Business ethics courses are not included in the curriculum of the relatively few business schools found in Muslim countries, not because there is any religious objection to such courses, but rather reflecting the fact that private morals are not seen as distinct from business ethics. The difference in the West reflects the separation of business from private lives, which is not present in the culture of most Islamic countries where small family run firms are the norm, and family and business affairs are integrated together. In the West, business ethics courses are concerned with ethical dilemmas facing managers in large companies which are not likely to arise in private life. The ethical dimension is seen as an input into professional and managerial decision making. It may reflect personal values as Sir Adrian Cadbury noted,[78] but it is being applied in a situation at some distance from, or even remote from, family life.

The most notable study of Islamic business ethics to date is by Trevor Gambling and Rifaat Karim.[79] They are both

[78] Sir Adrian Cadbury, 'Ethical managers', pp. 3–9.
[79] Trevor Gambling and Rifaat Ahmed Abdel Karim, *Business and Accounting Ethics in Islam*, Mansell, London, 1991.

accountants by training and profession, Gambling a non-Muslim with an interest in accounting ethics dating from his time as a Professor of Accounting in England, while Karim, a Muslim, lectured in UK and Kuwait Universities before becoming head of an Islamic Accounting Institute in Bahrain. Their book provides an Islamic perspective of Western accounting theory, and develops an Islamic theory of financial management focusing on issues such as business risk. Taking business risks is quite legitimate in Islam, unlike gambling or speculation, *gharar*,[80] which is forbidden, but Muslim investors should not act irresponsibly. Taking a risk to obtain a reward is both necessary and desirable, but an Islamic investor may find it prudent to diversify by building a portfolio of at least seven or more stock, according to Gambling and Karim, so that they minimise the possibility of substantial losses given their family and social responsibilities.[81]

For Gambling and Karim the fundamental principles of Islamic business are *khilafah* and *shura*, the first being the personal responsibility on all Muslims for the resources entrusted to them, and the second being the obligation on resource owners to hear the grievances of those affected by what is done in their name.[82] Investors cannot simply blame management decision makers, and delegate responsibilities, but rather have a duty to take an active interest in the businesses where they have placed funds. For this reason, partnerships on a *mudarabah* or *musharakah* basis are ideal forms of business organisation in Islam. Under the former, one partner provides the capital and the other the management or labour, whereas under the latter, a joint venture arrangement of fixed duration for a specific project, both partners provide some capital contribution to the enterprise.[83] Although such arrangements can extend to many partners, in practice they are best suited for relatively small businesses, as in large entities, the principle of all partners having an active interest may lead to

---

[80] For a discussion of how *gharar* should be translated and applied see Nabil A. Saleh, *Unlawful Gain and Legitimate Profit in Islamic Law*, Cambridge University Press, 1986, pp. 49–52.

[81] Trevor Gambling and Rifaat Ahmed Abdel Karim, *Business and Accounting Ethics*, pp. 123–4.

[82] Ibid., pp. 68–9.

[83] Ibid., pp. 37–8.

disagreements and possibly management inertia if it is impossible to proceed on the basis of agreement.

Under a partnership arrangement, liability is not usually limited unless a separate company is established with its own legal
identity. This concept of a company having an identity has
been subject to debate by Islamic scholars, as the idea of lim-
iting financial liability can be equated with an evasion of responsibility. Yet, as Gambling and Karim stress, to prohibit joint
stock companies on Islamic religious grounds would be to place
Muslims at a considerable disadvantage in the modern business world.[84] In practice, joint stock companies with limited
liability are allowed to operate freely in all Muslim countries,
with Islamic responsibilities defined by the conscience of the
Muslims who own and manage the companies rather than
through laws and government decrees. Companies in Muslim
countries do appear to have their own distinctive codes of
business ethics, and this is more a question of corporate behaviour rather than a consequence of differences in formal
company structure.

It is difficult, and some might suggest inappropriate, to
generalise about business ethics across the ethnically diverse
countries of the Islamic world which are at very different stages
of development. The oil exporting states of the Arabian Penin-
sula are amongst the world's richest in terms of per capita
gross domestic product, with the figures for Kuwait, the United
Arab Emirates, and Qatar being $23 350, $22 470, and $15 140
respectively.[85] States such as Malaysia and Turkey are classified
as newly industrialising countries, with a wide range of modern manufacturing industries, and per capita incomes of $3160
and $2120 respectively.[86] At the other end of the spectrum are
some of the poorest countries in the world such as Bangladesh, Somalia and Afghanistan, with primarily subsistence
economies based on traditional agriculture, and per capita
GDP figures of $220 and below.[87] To assume that a homogenous

[84] Ibid., pp. 70–4.
[85] World Bank, *Atlas*, Washington, 1995, pp. 18–19.
[86] Ibid.
[87] The World Bank estimate for Bangladesh in $220. There are no up to
date figures for Somalia or Afghanistan due to the civil wars and the collapse
of government administration in those countries, but earlier estimates in the
1980s suggested figures of below $100.

set of business ethics prevails in such differing environments is clearly questionable.

Yet there are some similarities in business practices which must owe something to Islam, especially given the strength of religious belief, and the widespread familiarity with the teaching of the *Koran* and the *Shariah* religious law. Trade appears to take on particular forms throughout the Islamic World, the *souk* or *bazaar* mentality being prevalent in business. There have been a number of detailed anthropological studies of *bazaar* economies, most notably the study by Clifford Geertz of market behaviour.[88] He found that *bazaars* could be efficient, especially when goods were heterogeneous and there were high search costs. In such circumstances the ritual of bargaining could result in buyers and sellers establishing close relations, and building up trust in each other. Although both had different interests, the seller to extract as high a price as possible, and the buyer to pay as little as possible, the human contact of the bargaining process created a mutual bond of trust, which was essential for the transaction to be carried out.

Loyalty seems especially valued in Muslim business circles, which extends to relationships between the business and its clients, dealings with other businesses, and relationships between employer and employee.[89] In retail markets Muslim customers seldom shop around but frequent the same establishments and get to know the people they are dealing with well. At the wholesale level retailers stay loyal to their customary suppliers, and do not try to take over their function. There is a much greater respect for different specialisations, which is why vertically integrated businesses are much rarer in the Islamic World than in the West.

The lack of cut throat competition means there are few take-overs or mergers in Muslim countries, but this may also explain why most businesses remain small scale. As many businesses are family concerns, they get handed down from generation to generation, most of the relatively small number of new business starts being the result of family splits or

---

[88] Clifford Geertz, 'The *bazaar* economy: information and search in peasant marketing', *American Economic Review, Papers and Proceedings*, Vol. 68, 1978, pp. 28–32.
[89] Rodney, Wilson, *Islamic Business: Theory and Practice*, Economist Intelligence Unit, Special Report No. 221, London, 1985, pp. 18–19.

divisions. There are few business failures, not only reflecting the small number of new starts, but also the fact that banks are reluctant to instigate bankruptcy proceedings given the prohibition of *riba* or interest under the *Shariah* Islamic law. Most businesses are reluctant to take on long run bank credit in any case, and only borrow to finance stock holdings.

Employers tend to have a paternalistic attitude towards their employees in Muslim societies, and there is much less willingness to delegate or work as part of a team.[90] Despite the authoritarian structures in many Muslim businesses, employees are usually much more secure than their Western counterparts, as there is less of a hire and fire attitude. In times of recession employees are willing to accept wage cuts, enabling the company to maintain its work force. There is solidarity, not only amongst employees but also with the head of the business, whose word will be trusted. When wage cuts occur, the employees know that the head of the business will also be getting less and is sharing the burden. Levels of remuneration of course vary, and indeed inequalities can often be greater than in the West, but there is a feeling that the employees and the employer of the Muslim business are all equal in a more fundamental sense, as disparities in possessions make no difference when they all pray together at the Mosque and submit themselves to Allah.

In small Muslim businesses need is often a more important determinant of pay than performance. The young who live with their parents are often paid little, but employees may receive more on marriage and get wage rises if they have large numbers of dependent children. There is a concept of a 'just wage', the additional payments to those with greater needs not being resented by the unmarried or the childless. There is not usually an annual pay settlement in most Muslim countries, although this practice has gained ground in inflation prone economies such as Turkey.[91] Comparability with other groups of workers is also seldom a issue, as this would imply envy in wage determination rather than need. Few in the private sector are in trade unions, and although in some Muslim countries public sector workers are unionised, collective bargaining in the Western sense is not practised.

[90] Farid, A. Muna, *The Arab Executive*, St Martins Press, New York, 1980.
[91] Rodney Wilson, *Islamic Business: Theory and Practice*, pp. 62–5.

Work and effort are seen as a prerequisite for remuneration in the Islamic World, but all value is not ascribed to labour, as under Marxist analysis, as rewards in the form of rental income on property or returns on invested capital are viewed as legitimate. As in Christianity, there is concern with speculative gains, but this has been an issue much emphasised by Islamic economists, given the explicit prohibition of speculation or *gharar* in the Koran which has already been mentioned. There has been some debate about the legitimacy of stock market investment but most Islamic economists view capital gains as a rightful reward for risk taking and there have been several books written about stock markets in the Islamic World, particularly in Malaysia, which has one of the major emerging markets of South East Asia.[92] The consensus seems to be that it is impossible to legislate against speculation, but the responsible Muslim investor should take an active interest in the underlying fundamentals of the businesses in which he places his funds, and not simply focus on expected stocks to rise, which may result from speculative pressures. Investment horizons should be long-term, rather than merely seeking short-term price gains, but the judgement should be left to the conscience of the individual Muslim acting in good faith.

CONCLUSIONS

Business ethics has emerged as a separate and distinctive discipline, largely drawing on moral philosophy but often also on a case study approach developed in management schools to illustrate the ethical dilemmas which business decision makers face. The literature on Christian and Islamic business ethics is much more restricted, although religious values are implicit in much of the business ethics texts and articles despite the humanist tone. Christian theological commentators, especially those in the field of social ethics, are moving beyond a somewhat simplistic critique of capitalism and a suspicion of

[92] Nublan Zaky Yusoff, *An Islamic Perspective of the Stock Market*, Dian Darulnaim Publishing, Kuala Lumpur, 1992; Saad Al Harran, *Leading Issues in Islamic Banking and Finance*, Pelanduk Publications, Selangor, Malaysia, 1995, pp. 143–51.

markets, to seek a more profound understanding of how Western business works, and the ethical implications of market processes and outcomes. At the same time, valuable lessons and insights can be obtained by studying business practice in Eastern society. Each has its own code of business ethics, which shares both similarities and differences with the practices in the West. There would appear to be much scope for further investigation of business ethics from a comparative religious perspective, especially in a global economy where multinational companies play an increasing role. This study is only a very modest start. Much work remains to be done.

Can any overall lessons be drawn from the comparative study of economics and ethics from the perspectives of Judaism, Christianity and Islam? It can, of course, be difficult to discern the major similarities and differences, given the varying perspectives between and within each religion, and the breadth of ethical issues involving the economy and business.

Nevertheless, several conclusions can be drawn from this study. First, it is clear that beliefs can be a major influence on economic behaviour, as Joan Robinson suggested, and as discussed in the first chapter. Religious belief encourages economic agents to behave in certain ways, as it provides a standard to judge right from wrong. Secondly, religion provides rules to govern economic life, these being particularly well defined in the case of Judaism and Islam. Christianity arguably relies on the conscience of the individual believer as much as rules of social conduct, although self-restraint through conscience is important in all three religions. Thirdly, it is apparent that, although there are differences in worship and approach within and between the great monotheistic religions, the moral concerns in the economic sphere are not so different. Honesty, justice in economic transactions and a concern for the dignity of the poor are hallmarks of all three religions. Fourthly, there appears to be moral concern with the working of modern financial systems, and the misuse of human responsibility in allocating resources. This is apparent from the interest by Islamic economists in a financial system free of *riba*, but there is also concern amongst Christians that the stewardship they have over resources is not being exercised in the modern world as God intends. The ethical investment movement, although by no means confined to practising Christians, illustrates one reaction to these concerns, as does the continuing debate over forms of corporate governance. What many of the authors cited in this book recognise is that guidance on these questions can be found in the oral and written *Torah*, in New Testament scripture, and in the Holy *Koran* and related Muslim writing.

Bibliography

1 ECONOMICS AND ETHICS

Adams, John, 'Economy as instituted process: change, transformation and progress', *Journal of Economic Issues*, Vol. 28, No. 2, 1994, pp. 331–55.

Akerlof, George, 'Gift exchange and efficiency wage theory: four views', *American Economic Review*, Vol. 74, No. 2, 1984, pp. 307–19.

Arrow, Kenneth, 'Extended sympathy and the possibility of social choice', *Philosophia*, Vol. 7, No. 2, 1978, pp. 223–37.

Backhouse, Roger E. (ed.), *New Directions in Economic Methodology*, Routledge, London, 1994.

Blaug, Mark, *The Methodology of Economics*, Cambridge University Press, 1980.

Brittan, Samuel and Hamlin, Alan (eds), *Market Capitalism and Moral Values*, Edward Elgar, Aldershot, England, 1995.

Brown, Vivienne, 'The economy as text', in Roger Backhouse (ed.), op.cit., pp. 368–82.

Burk, Monroe, 'Ideology and morality in economic theory', in Alan Lewis and Karl-Eric Warneryd (eds), *Ethics and Economic Affairs*, Routledge, London, 1994, pp. 313–34.

Burks, A.W., Hartshorne, C. and Weiss, P., *Collected Papers of Charles Sanders Peirce*, Vols. 1–8, Belknap Press, Cambridge, Massachusetts, 1931–58.

Coleman, William Oliver, *Rationalism and Anti-Rationalism in the Origins of Economics: The Philosophical Roots of 18th Century Economic Thought*, Edward Elgar, Aldershot, England, 1995.

Cramp, Tony, 'Pleasures, prices and principles', in Gay Meeks (ed.), *Thoughtful Economic Man: Essays on Rationality, Moral Rules and Benevolence*, Cambridge University Press, 1991, pp. 50–73.

Davis, Charles, *Religion and the Making of Society: Essays in Social Theology*, Cambridge University Press, 1994.

Eide, Asbjørn, 'The right to an adequate standard of living including the right to food', in Asbjørn Eide, Catarina Krause and Allan Rosas (eds), *Economic, Social and Cultural Rights*, Martinus Nijhoff, Dordrecht, 1995, pp. 89–106.

Flemming, John, 'The ethics of unemployment and Mafia capitalism', in Samuel Brittan and Alan Hamlin (eds), op.cit., pp. 45–56.

Goudzwaard, Bob and de Lange, Harry, *Beyond Poverty and Affluence: Towards a Global Economy of Care*, Erdmans, Grand Rapids, Michigan and World Council of Churches, Geneva, 1995.

Gui, Benedetto, 'Interpersonal relations: a disregarded theme in the debate on ethics and economics', in Alan Lewis and Karl-Eric Warneryd (eds), op.cit., pp. 251–63.

Hausman, Daniel M., *Essays on Philosophy and Economic Methodology*, Cambridge University Press, 1992.

Hausman, Daniel M. and McPherson, Michael S., 'Taking ethics seriously: economics and contemporary moral philosophy', *Journal of Economic Literature*, Vol. 31, No. 2, 1993, pp. 671–731.

215

Hay, Donald, Review of Bob Goudzwaard and Harry de Lange, *Beyond Poverty and Affluence: Towards a Global Economy of Care*, Erdmans, Grand Rapids, Michigan and World Council of Churches, Geneva, 1995, in *Association of Christian Economists Journal*, No. 20, 1995, pp. 44–7.

Henderson, Willie, 'Metaphor and economics', in Roger Backhouse, (ed.), op.cit., pp. 343–67.

Hirschey, Mark, Pappas, James and Whigham, David, *Managerial Economics*, Dryden Press, London, 1993.

Hobson, J.A., *Wealth and Life: A Study in Values*, Macmillan, London, 1929.

Hobson, J.A., *Work and Wealth: A Human Valuation*, Macmillan, New York, 1921.

Hoover, Kevin D., 'Pragmatism, pragmaticism and economic method', in Roger Backhouse, (ed.), op.cit., pp. 286–315.

Hutchinson, Terence W., *Changing Aims in Economics*, Blackwell, Oxford, 1992.

Hutchinson, Terence W., 'Ends and means in the methodology of economics', in Roger Backhouse (ed.), op.cit., pp. 27–34.

Hutchinson, Terence W., *The Uses and Abuses of Economics: Contentious Essays on History and Method*, Routledge, London, 1994.

Keynes, John Neville, *The Scope and Method of Political Economy*, Macmillan, London, 1917.

Lewis, Alan, and Warneryd, Karl-Eric (eds), *Ethics and Economic Affairs*, Routledge, London, 1994.

Mansfield, Edwin, *Managerial Economics: Theory, Applications and Cases*, Norton, New York, 1990.

Mitchell, Wesley C., 'The Criticism of Modern Civilisation', *Journal of Economic Issues*, Vol. 29, No. 3, 1995, pp. 663–82.

Moore, E.C., *Charles S. Peirce: the Essential Writings*, Harper and Row, New York, 1972.

McCloskey, D.N., *The Rhetoric of Economics*, University of Wisconsin Press, 1985.

O'Brien, Denis P., *The Classical Economists*, Clarendon Press, Oxford, 1975.

O'Brien, Denis P., *Lionel Robbins*, Macmillan, London, 1988.

O'Brien, Denis P., 'Research programmes in competitive structure', *Journal of Economic Studies*, Vol. 10, No. 4, pp. 29–51, Reprinted in Denis. P. O'Brien, *Methodology, Money and the Firm*, Vol. 1, Edward Elgar, Aldershot, 1994, pp. 277–99.

Pareto, Vilfredo, *Manual of Political Economy*, Macmillan, London, 1971. Translated by Ann Schwier from the French edition published by Librairie Droz, Geneva, 1927.

Paul, E.F., Paul, J. and Miller, F.D. (eds), *Ethics and Economics*, Blackwell, Oxford, 1985.

Rawls, John, *A Theory of Justice*, Harvard University Press, Cambridge, Massachusetts, 1971.

Reder, Melvin, 'The place of ethics in the theory of production', in Michael Boskin (ed.), *Economics and Human Welfare: Essays in Honour of Tibor Skitovsky*, Academic Press, New York, 1979, pp. 133–46.

Rima, Ingrid H., *Development of Economic Analysis*, Irwin, Homewood, Illinois, 1991.

Robbins, Lionel, *An Essay on the Nature and Significance of Economic Science*, Macmillan, London, 1935.

Robinson, Joan, *Economic Philosophy*, C.A. Watts, London, 1962.

Rosenberg, Alexander, 'What is the cognitive status of economic theory', in Roger Backhouse (ed.), op.cit., pp. 216–35.

Rothschild, Kurt W., *Ethics and Economic Theory*, Edward Elgar, Aldershot, England, 1993.

Samuels, Warren J., *The Classical Theory of Economic Policy*, World Publishing, Cleveland, Ohio, 1966.

Sen, Amartya, 'Liberty and social choice', *Journal of Philosophy*, Vol. 80, No. 1, pp. 5–28.

Sen, Amartya, 'Moral codes and economic success', in Samuel Brittan and Alan Hamlin (eds), op.cit., pp. 23–34.

Sen, Amartya, *On Ethics and Economics*, Blackwell, Oxford, 1987.

Singer, Peter, *Practical Ethics*, Cambridge University Press, 1993.

Smith, Adam, *An Inquiry into the Nature and Causes of Wealth of Nations*, Clarendon Press, Oxford, 1976. Edition edited by R.H. Campbell and A.K. Skinner.

Smith, Adam, *The Theory of Moral Sentiments*, Clarendon Press, Oxford, 1976. Edition edited by D.D. Raphael and A.L. Macfie.

Söderbaum, Peter, 'Ethics, ideological commitment and social change: institutionalism as an alternative to neo-classical theory', in Alan Lewis and Karl-Eric Warneryd (eds), op.cit., pp. 233–50.

Usher, Dan, 'The value of life for decision making in the public sector', in E.F. Paul, J. Paul and F.D. Miller (eds), op.cit., pp. 168–91.

Wagner, Adolph, 'The present state of political economy', *Quarterly Journal of Economics*, Vol. 1, No. 1, 1886, pp. 113–33.

Wieland, Josef, 'Economy and ethics in functionally differentiated societies: history and present problems', in Alan Lewis and Karl-Eric Warneryd (eds), op.cit., pp. 264–85.

2 JUDAISM

Aharoni, Yair, *The Israeli Economy: Dreams and Realities*, Routledge, London, 1991.

Brooks, Roger, *Support for the Poor in the Mishanic Law of Agriculture*, Brown Judaic Study, number 43, Scholars Press, Chico, California, 1983, pp. 17–39.

Davies, Eryl W., 'Land: its rights and privileges', in R.E. Clements (ed.), *The World of Ancient Israel: Sociological, Anthropological and Political Perspectives*, Cambridge University Press, 1989, pp. 360–1.

De Roover, Raymond, 'The concept of the just price', *Journal of Economic History*, Vol. 18, No. 4., 1958, pp. 418–34.

Dusenberry, James S., *Income, Saving and the Theory of Consumer Behaviour*, Harvard University Press, Cambridge, Massachusetts, 1949.

Epstein, Isidore, *Judaism*, Penguin Books, London, 1990.

Friedman, Menachem, 'What are the ultra-Orthodox parties all about?', *MidEast Mirror*, 23 June 1992, p. 7.

Furman, Frida Kerner, 'The prophetic tradition and social transformation', in Charles R. Strain, (ed.), *Prophetic Visions and Economic Realities: Protestants, Jews and Catholics Confront the Bishops Letter on the Economy*, William B. Erdmans Publishing, Grand Rapids, Michigan, 1989.

Goodman, Paul, 'Brave new Britain's voice in the wilderness', *Sunday Telegraph*, 5 March 1995, p. 15.

Gordon, Barry, *Economic Analysis Before Adam Smith*, Macmillan, London, 1975.

Gordon, Barry, *The Economic Problem in Biblical and Patristic Thought*, E.J. Brill, Leiden, 1989.

Harris, Abram L., *Economic and Social Reform*, Harper and Brothers, New York, 1958.

Henderson, W.O., *The Rise of German Industrial Power, 1834–1914*, Temple Smith, London, 1975.

Heschel, Abraham Joshua, *The Prophets*, Jewish Publication Society, Philadelphia, 1962.

Kleiman, Ephraim, '"Just price" in *Talmudic* literature', *History of Political Economy*, Vol. 19, No. 1, 1987, pp. 23–45.

Kleiman, Ephraim, 'Opportunity cost, human capital and some related concepts in *Talmudic* literature', *History of Political Economy*, Vol. 19, No. 3, 1987, p. 262.

Küng, Hans, *Judaism*, Crossroad, New York, 1992.

Maimonides, 'Laws regarding gifts to the poor', *Mishnah Torah – Book of Agriculture*, translated by Issac Klein, Yale University Press, 1979.

Martin, James D., 'Israel as a tribal society', in R.E. Clements (ed.) *The World of Ancient Israel: Sociological, Anthropological and Political Perspectives*, Cambridge University Press, 1989, pp. 95–117.

Ministry of Foreign Affairs, *Facts about Israel*, Jerusalem, 1979.

Mitchell, Wesley C., *The Backward Art of Spending Money and Other Essays*, Augustus M. Kelly, New York, 1937.

Mitzman, Arthur, *Sociology and Estrangement: Three Sociologists of Imperial Germany*, Transaction Books, New Brunswick, 1987.

Musgrave, Richard A., *The Theory of Public Finance*, McGraw Hill Kogakusha, New York and Tokyo, 1979.

Neusner, Jacob, *The Economics of the Mishnah*, University of Chicago Press, 1990.

Neusner, Jacob, *Judaism and its Social Metaphors: Israel in the History of Jewish Thought*, Cambridge University Press, 1989.

Noonan, John T., *The Scholastic Analysis of Usury*, Harvard University Press, 1957.

O'Brien, Denis P., *Lionel Robbins*, Macmillan, London, 1988.

O'Brien, George, *An Essay on Mediaeval Economic Teaching*, Augustus M. Kelly, New York, 1967.

Ohrenstein, Roman A., 'Economic analysis in *Talmudic* literature: some ancient studies of value', *American Journal of Economics and Sociology*, Vol. 39, No. 1, January 1980, p. 22.

Ohrenstein, Roman A., 'Economic self interest and social progress in *Talmudic* literature: a further study of ancient economic thought and its modern significance', *American Journal of Economics and Sociology*, Vol. 29, No. 1, 1970, pp. 59–70.

Ohrenstein, Roman A., 'Economic thought in *Talmudic* literature in the light of modern economics', *American Journal of Economics and Sociology*, Vol. 27, No. 2, 1968, pp. 190–2.

Peck, Alan, *The Priestly Gift in Mishnah*, Brown Judaic Study, number 20, Scholars Press, Chico, California, 1981.

Polanyi, Karl, *The Livelihood of Man*, edited by Harry W. Pearson, Academic Press, New York, 1981.

Poliakov, Léon, *Jewish Bankers and the Holy See: From the Thirteenth to the Seventeenth Century*, Routledge and Kegan Paul, London, 1977.

Rubner, Alex, *The Economy of Israel: A Critical Account of the First Ten Years*, Frank Cass, London, 1960.

Sherwin, Byron, 'The US Catholic Bishops' pastoral letter on the economy and Jewish tradition', in Charles R. Strain, (ed.), *Prophetic Visions and Economic Realities: Protestants, Jews and Catholics Confront the Bishops Letter on the Economy*, William B. Erdmans Publishing, Grand Rapids, Michigan, 1989.

Silver, Morris, *Economics Structures of the Ancient Near East*, Croom Helm, London, 1985.

Sombart, Werner, *Der Moderne Kapitalismus*, Dritter Band, Munich, 1928.

Sombart, Werner, *The Jews and Modern Capitalism*, Collier Books, New York, 1962. Translated by M. Epstein from the German original, *Die Juden und das Wirtschaftsleben*, Duncker und Humblot, Leipzig, 1911.

Spengler, J.J., *Origins of Economic Thought and Justice*, Carbondale, Illinois, 1980.

Stellman, Henri, *The Israeli General Election: 23rd June 1992*, The Anglo-Israel Association, London, 1992.

Tamari, Meir, *With All Your Possessions: Jewish Ethics and Economic Life*, The Free Press, Macmillan, New York, 1987.

Wolf, Arnold Jacob, 'The Bishops and the poor: a Jewish critique', in Charles R. Strain, (ed.), *Prophetic Visions and Economic Realities: Protestants, Jews and Catholics Confront the Bishops Letter on the Economy*, William B. Erdmans Publishing, Grand Rapids, Michigan, 1989.

Worland, Stephen T., *Scholasticism and Welfare Economics*, University of Notre Dame Press, 1967.

3 CHRISTIANITY

Andreski, Stanislav (ed.), *Max Weber on Capitalism, Bureaucracy and Religion*, George Allen and Unwin, London, 1983.

Aquinas, Thomas, *Summa Theologica*, Blackfriars in association with Eyre and Spottiswoode, London, and McGraw Hill, New York, 1975.

Atherton, John, *Christianity and the Market: Christian Social Thought for Our Times*, SPCK, London, 1992.

Augustine, Saint, *The City of God*, T. and T. Clark, Edinburgh, 1878. Translated by Rev. Marcus Dods.

Biéler, André, *La Pensée Economique et Sociale de Calvin*, Librairie de l'Université, Geneva, 1959.

Cortés, Juan Donoso, *Essay on Catholicism, Liberation and Socialism*, Lippincott, New York, 1962.

Dempsey, Bernard W., *Interest and Usury*, Dennis Dobson, London, 1948.

De Roover, Raymond, 'The concept of the just price: theory and economic policy', *Journal of Economic History*, Vol. 18, No. 4, 1958, pp. 418–38.

De Roover, Raymond, 'Monopoly theory prior to Adam Smith: a revision', *Quarterly Journal of Economics*, Vol. 65, No. 4, 1951, pp. 492–524.

Duchrow, Ulrich, *Global Economy: A Confessional Issue for the Churches*, World Council of Churches Publications, Geneva, 1987.

Gordon, Barry, *Economic Analysis Before Adam Smith*, Macmillan, London, 1975.

Gordon, Barry, *The Economic Problem in Biblical and Patristic Thought*, E.J. Brill, Leiden, 1989.

Gorringe, Timothy J., *Capital and the Kingdom: Theological Ethics and Economic Order*, Orbis Books and SPCK, New York and London, 1994.

Grant, Frederick C., *The Economic Background of the Gospels*, Oxford University Press, 1926.

Griffiths, Brian, *The Creation of Wealth*, Hodder and Stoughton, London, 1984.

Harris, Abram L., *Economics and Social Reform*, Harper and Brothers, New York, 1958.

Hay, Donald, *Economics Today: A Christian Critique*, Apollis, Inter-Varsity Press, Leicester, 1989.

Hybels, Bill, *Christians in the Marketplace*, Hodder and Stoughton, London, 1993.

Meeks, M. Douglas, *God the Economist: The Doctrine of God and Political Economy*, Fortress Press, Minneapolis, 1989.

Miranda, José, *Marx and the Bible*, Orbis Books, New York, 1974.

Mitzman, Arthur, *The Iron Cage: An Historical Interpretation of Max Weber*, Transaction Books, New Brunswick, 1969.

Moltmann, Juergen, *Theology of Hope*, Harper and Row, New York, 1967.

National Conference of Catholic Bishops, *Economic Justice for All: Pastoral Letter on Catholic Social Teaching and the US Economy*, Washington, 1986.

Niebuhr, Reinhold, *Christian Realism and Political Problems*, August M. Kelly, New York, 1953.

Noonan, John T., *The Scholastic Analysis of Usury*, Harvard University Press, 1957.

Novak, Michael, *The Spirit of Democratic Capitalism*, Madison Books, Lanham, Maryland and Institute of Economic Affairs, London, 1982.

O'Brien, George, *An Essay on Mediaeval Economic Teaching*, Augustus M. Kelley, New York, 1967.

Oresme, Nicholas, *The De Moneta and English Mint Documents*, London, 1956.

Pelikan, Jaroslav, *Luther's Works*, Concordia Publishing House, St. Louis, 1959.

Preston, Ronald, *Religion and the Ambiguities of Capitalism*, SCM Press, London, 1991.

Preston, Ronald, *Religion and the Persistence of Capitalism*, SCM Press, London, 1979.

Rima, Ingrid Hahne, *Development of Economic Analysis*, Irwin, Homewood, Illinois, 5th ed., 1991.

Sleeman, John, *Economic Crisis: A Christian Perspective*, SCM Press, London, 1976.

Stivers, Robert L. (ed.), *Reformed Faith and Economics*, University Press of America, Lanham, New York and London, 1989.

Strain, Charles R. (ed.), *Prophetic Visions and Economic Realities: Protestants, Jews and Catholics Confront the Bishop's Letter on the Economy*, William B. Erdmans Publishing, Grand Rapids, Michigan, 1989.

Tawney, R.H., *Religion and the Rise of Capitalism*, John Murray and Harcourt Brace, New York, 1926 and Penguin Books, London, 1938.

Viner, Jacob, *Religous Thought and Economic Society*, Duke University Press, Durham, North Carolina, 1978.

Weber, Max, *The Protestant Ethic and the Spirit of Capitalism*, 1905, English translation, Allen and Unwin and Scribners, London, 1930.

White, John, *Money Isn't God: So Why is the Church Worshipping it?* Inter-Varsity Press, Leicester, 1993, (1st ed., 1977).

Wogman, J. Philip, *Christians and the Great Economic Debate*, SCM Press, London, 1977.

Wogman, J. Philip, *Economics and Ethics: A Christian Enquiry*, SCM Press, London, 1986.

Worland, Stephen Theodore, *Scholasticism and Welfare Economics*, University of Notre Dame Press, 1967.

4   ISLAM

Aghnides, Nicolas P., *Mohammedan Theories of Finance*, The Premier Book House, Lahore, 1961.

Ahmed, Akbar S., *Postmodernism and Islam*, Routledge, London, 1992.

Ali, Abdullah Yusuf, *The Holy Koran: Text, Translation and Commentary*, That es-Salasil, Kuwait, 1988.

Al Harran, Saad, *Islamic Finance: Partnership Financing*, Pelanduk Publishing, Selangor, Malaysia, 1993.

Amirahmadi, Hooshgang, *Revolution and Economic Transition: the Iranian Experience*, State University of New York Press, 1990.

Amuzegar, Jahangir, *Iran's Economy under the Islamic Republic*, IB Tauris, London.

Aryan, Hossein, 'Iran: the impact of Islamisation on the financial system', in Rodney Wilson (ed.), *Islamic Financial Markets*, Routledge, London, 1990, pp. 155–70.

Bani Sadr, Abdulhasan, *Work and the Worker in Islam*, Hamdami Foundation, Tehran, 1980, originally published in Farsi by the Payam Azadi Press, Tehran, 1978.

Batatu, Hanna, 'Iraq's underground Shi'i movements: characteristics, causes and prospects', *Middle Eastern Journal*, Vol. 35, No. 4, 1981, pp. 577–94.

Chapra, M. Umer, *Islam and Economic Development*, International Institute of Islamic Thought and Islamic Research Institute, Islamabad, 1993.

Chapra, M. Umer, *Islam and the Economic Challenge*, Islamic Foundation, Leicester, 1992.

Chapra, M. Umer, *Towards a Just Monetary System*, Islamic Foundation, Leicester, 1985.

Choudhury, Masudul Alam, *The Principles of Islamic Political Economy*, Macmillan, London, 1992.

Choudhury, Masudul Alam, and Uzir Abdul Malik, *The Foundations of Islamic Political Economy*, St. Martin's Press, New York, 1992.

Cragg, Kenneth, *Counsels in Contemporary Islam*, Edinburgh University Press, 1965.

El Ashker, Ahmad, *The Islamic Business Enterprise*, Croom Helm, London, 1987.

Haq, Inamul, *Principles and Philosophy of Democratic Socialism in Islam*, unpublished paper, Karachi, 1966.

Hilal, Mohamed, 'Ethical and social foundations of Islamic science and technology', in Klaus Gottstein (ed.), *Islamic Cultural Identity and Scientific-Technological Development*, Nomos Verlagsgesellschaft, Baden Baden, 1986, pp. 81–92.

Hosseini, Hamid, 'From *homo economicus* to *homo Islamicus*: the universality of economic science reconsidered', in Cyrus Bina and Hamid Zangeneh, (eds), *Modern Capitalism and Islamic Ideology in Iran*, St. Martin's Press, New York, 1992, pp. 103–20.

Ibn Khaldûn, *The Muqaddimah: An Introduction to History*, Princeton University Press, 1958. Complete three volume English translation by Franz Rosenthal. An abridged English version by N.J. Dawood for Princeton University Press, 1967.

Ibn Taimîyah, *Public Duties in Islam: the Institution of the Hisba*, Islamic Foundation, Leicester, 1992, translated from the Arabic by Muhtar Holland.

Iqbal, Zubair, and Abbas Mirakhor, *Islamic Banking*, IMF Occasional Paper No. 49, Washington, 1987.

Islahi, Abdul Azim, *Economic Concepts of Ibn Taimîyah*, Islamic Foundation, Leicester, 1988.

Issawi, Charles, *An Arab Philosopher of History*, John Murray, London, 1950.

Kahf, Monzer, 'Zakat: unresolved issues in contemporary *Fiqh*', in Abdul Hasan Sadeq, Ataul Huq Pramanik and Nik Hassan, (eds), *Development and Finance in Islam*, International Islamic University Press, Selangor, Malaysia, 1991, pp. 173–90.

Khan, M. Fahim, *Essays in Islamic Economics*, Islamic Foundation, Leicester, 1995.

Khan, Waqar Masood, *Towards an Interest Free Islamic Economic System*, Islamic Foundation, Leicester, 1985.

Kuran, Timur, 'Economic justice in contemporary economic thought', in K.S. Jomo, op.cit., pp. 49–76.

Kuran, Timur, 'The economic system in contemporary Islamic thought', in K.S. Jomo (ed.), *Islamic Economic Alternatives*, Macmillan, London, 1992, pp. 9–47.

Mahdi, Muhsin, *Ibn Khaldûn's Philosophy of History*, George Allen and Unwin, London, 1957.

Mallat, Chibli, 'Muhammad Baqer as-Sadr', in Ali Rahnema (ed.), *Pioneers of Islamic Revival*, Zed Books, London, 1994, pp. 251–72.

Mannan, Muhammad Abdul, *Islamic Economics: Theory and Practice*, Hodder and Stoughton and the Islamic Academy, Cambridge, 1986.

Maunier, R., 'Les idées économiques d'un philosophe arabe au XIV siècle, Ibn Khaldûn', *Revue d'Histoire Économique et Sociale*, Vol. 6, 1913, p. 409ff.

Mayer, Ann Elizabeth, 'Islamic banking and credit policies in the Sadat era:

the social origins of Islamic banking, in Egypt', *Arab Law Quarterly*, Vol. 1, Part 1, 1985, pp. 32–50.

Mez, Adam, *The Renaissance of Islam*, Luzac and Co., London, 1937.

Milani, Mohsen M., *The Making of Iran's Islamic Revolution*, Westview Press, Boulder, Colorado, 1988.

Montgomery Watt, W., *Islamic Fundamentalism and Modernity*, Routledge, London, 1989.

Naqvi, Sayed Nawab Haider, *Economics and Ethics: An Islamic Synthesis*, Islamic Foundation, Leicester, 1991.

Naqvi, Syed N.H., *Individual Freedom, Social Welfare and Islamic Economic Order*, Pakistan Institute of Development Economics, Islamabad, 1981.

Naqvi, Sayed Nawab Haider, *Islam, Economics and Society*, Kegan Paul International, London, 1994.

Presley, John R., *Directory of Islamic Financial Institutions*, Macmillan, London, 1988.

Rahman, Afzalur, *Economic Doctrines of Islam: Banking and Insurance*, Muslim Schools Trust, London, 1979.

Sacks, Wolfgang, 'Progress and development', in Paul Ekins and Manfred Max-Neef (eds), *Real Life Economics: Understanding Wealth Creation*, Routledge, London, 1992, pp. 156–61.

Schirazi, Asghar, *Islamic Development Policy: the Agrarian Question in Iran*, Lynne Rienner Publishers, Boulder, Colorado, 1993.

Siddiqi, Muhammad Nejatullah, *Insurance in an Islamic Economy*, Islamic Foundation, Leicester, 1985.

Siddiqi, Muhammad Nejatullah, *Muslim Economic Thinking: A Survey of Contemporary Literature*, Islamic Foundation, Leicester, 1981.

Spengler, Joseph J., 'Economic thought of Islam: Ibn Khaldûn', *Comparative Studies in Society and History*, Vol. 6, 1963–64, pp. 285–6.

Weiss, Dieter, 'Ibn Khaldûn on economic transformation', *International Journal of Middle Eastern Studies*, Vol. 27, 1995, pp. 29–37.

Wilson, Rodney, *Banking and Finance in the Arab Middle East*, Macmillan, London, 1983.

Wilson, Rodney, *Economic Development in the Middle East*, Routledge, London, 1995.

Wilson, Rodney, *Islamic Business: Theory and Practice*, Economist Intelligence Unit Special Report, No. 221, London, 1985.

World Bank, *World Development Report*, Oxford University Press, 1981.

World Bank, *World Bank Atlas*, Washington, 1995.

World Bank, *World Tables*, Johns Hopkins University Press, Baltimore, 1994.

Zangeneh, Hamid and Ahmad Salam, 'An analytical model of an Islamic banking firm', in Cyrus Bina and Hamid Zangeneh, op.cit., pp. 201–11.

5 BUSINESS ETHICS

Al Harran, Saad, *Leading Issues in Islamic Banking and Finance*, Pelanduk Publications, Selangor, Malaysia, 1995, pp. 143–51.

Andrews, Kenneth and Kay, Donald (eds), *Ethics in Practice: Managing the Moral Corporation*, Harvard Business School Press, Boston, 1989.

Andrews, Kenneth R., 'Ethics in practice', in *Harvard Business Review, Ethics at Work*, Harvard University, Boston, 1991, pp. 39–44.

Baida, Peter, *Poor Richard's Legacy: American Business Values from Benjamin Franklin to Donald Trump*, William Morrow, New York, 1990.

Bowie, Norman E., 'Business ethics as a discipline: the search for legitimacy', in R. Edward Freeman (ed.), *Business Ethics: the State of the Art*, Oxford University Press, New York, 1991, pp. 17–41.

Cadbury, Sir Adrian, 'Ethical managers make their own rules', in *Harvard Business Review, Ethics at Work*, op.cit., pp. 3–9.

Campbell, Tom D., 'Markets and justice', in Gordon A. Hughes *et al.*, op.cit., pp. 18–27.

Casson, Mark, *The Economics of Business Culture*, Clarendon Press, Oxford, 1991.

Clarke, Michael, *Fallen Idols: Elites and the Search for the Acceptable Face of Capitalism*, Junction Books, London, 1981.

Cohen, Adrian L., 'Bankruptcy: who sacrifices', in Andreas R. Prindl and Bimal Prodhan (eds), op.cit., pp. 83–94.

Cowton, Christopher J., 'The development of ethical investment products', in Andreas R. Prindl and Bimal Prodhan (eds), op.cit., pp. 213–32.

Datastream, London, September 1995.

DeGeorge, Richard, 'Will success spoil business ethics?', in R. Edward Freeman (ed.), op.cit., pp. 42–56.

Donaldson, John, *Business Ethics: A European Casebook*, Academic Press, Harcourt Brace Jovanovich, London, 1992.

Donaldson, Thomas, 'Multinational decision marking: reconciling international norms', in John Drummond and Bill Bain (eds), op.cit., pp. 137–8.

Donaldson, Thomas J., 'Rights in the global market', in R. Edward Freeman (ed.), op.cit., pp. 139–62.

Donaldson, Thomas J. and Freeman, R. Edward (eds) *Business as a Humanity*, Oxford University Press, New York, 1995.

Drummond, John and Bain, Bill (eds), *Managing Business Ethics*, Butterman Heinemann, 1994.

Eiteman, David K., Stonehill, Arthur I. and Moffett, Michael H., *Multinational Business Finance*, Addison Wesley, Reading, Massachusetts, 1995, 7th edition.

Fadiman, Jeffrey A., 'A traveller's guide to gifts and bribes', in *Harvard Business Review, Ethics at Work*, op.cit., pp. 29–35.

Freeman, R. Edward (ed.), *Business Ethics: the State of the Art*, Oxford University Press, New York, 1991.

Gambling, Trevor and Karim, Rifaat Ahmed Abdel, *Business and Accounting Ethics in Islam*, Mansell, London, 1991.

Geertz, Clifford, 'The *bazaar* economy: information and search in peasant marketing', *American Economic Review, Papers and Proceedings*, Vol. 68, 1978, pp. 28–32.

Goodpaster, Kenneth E., 'Ethical imperatives and corporate leadership', in R. Edward Freeman (ed.), op.cit., pp. 98–108.

Goodpaster, Kenneth E. and Matthews John B. Jr, 'Can a corporation have a conscience?' in Kenneth Andrews and Donald Kay, (eds), op.cit., pp. 155–67.

Hall, William D., *Making the Right Decision: Ethics for Managers*, Wiley, New York, 1993.

Hartley, Robert F., *Business Ethics: Violations of the Public Trust*, John Wiley, New York, 1993.

Hartman, Edwin M., 'Donaldson on rights and corporate obligations', in R. Edward Freeman (ed.), op.cit., pp. 164–6.

Harvey, Brian (ed.), *Business Ethics: A European Approach*, Prentice Hall, New York, 1994.

Heelas, Paul and Morris, Paul (eds), *The Values of the Enterprise Culture: the Moral Debate*, Routledge, 1992.

Holden Meehan, http:/www.bath.ac.uk/centres/ethical/Holden Meehan.

Hughes, Gordon A., *et al.*, *Justice and the Market*, Centre for Theology and Public Issues, Occasional Paper No. 21, Edinburgh University, 1991.

Hughes, Gordon A., 'The economics of hard choices: justice and the market', in Gordon A. Hughes *et al.*, op.cit., pp. 1–17.

Lynch, James J., 'The future shape of ethical banking', in John Drummond and Bill Bain (eds), op.cit., pp. 175–8.

Mahoney, Jack, 'How to be ethical: ethics resource management', in Brian Harvey (ed.), *Business Ethics: A European Approach*, op.cit., pp. 32–55.

Moore, Jennifer, 'What is really unethical about insider trading?' in Andreas R. Prindl and Bimal Prodhan (eds), op.cit., pp. 113–42.

Morris, Paul, 'Is God enterprising? Reflections on enterprise culture and religion', in Paul Heelas and Paul Morris (eds), op.cit., pp. 276–90.

Muna, Farid A., *The Arab Executive*, St. Martin's Press, New York, 1980.

Nash, Laura, 'Ethics without the sermon', in Kenneth Andrews and Donald Kay (eds), op.cit., pp. 243–57.

Paine, Lynn Sharp, 'Ethics as character development: reflections on the objectives of ethics education', in R. Edward Freeman (ed.), op.cit., pp. 67–86.

Pastin, Mark, 'Ethics as an integrating force in management', in John Drummond and Bill Bain (eds), *Managing Business Ethics*, Butterman Heinemann, 1994, pp. 76–88.

Pointon, F.W., 'Conflicts of interest for lending bankers', in Andreas R. Prindl and Bimal Prodhan (eds), op.cit., pp. 70–3.

Prindl, Andreas R. and Prodhan, Bimal (eds), *Ethical Conflicts in Finance*, Blackwell, Oxford, 1994.

Prodhan, Bimal, 'Ethics, finance and society', in Andreas R. Prindl and Bimal Prodhan (eds), op.cit., pp. 1–22.

Reckitt, Maurice B. (ed.), *The Christian Tradition Regarding Interest and Investment*, The Christian Social Council, London, 1930.

Saleh, Nabil A., *Unlawful Gain and Legitimate Profit in Islamic Law*, Cambridge University Press.

Sherwin, Douglas S., 'The ethical roots of the business system', in Kenneth Andrews and Donald Kay (eds), op.cit., pp. 144–55.

Sinclair, David, 'Price, value and worth', in Gordon A. Hughes *et al.*, op.cit., pp. 33–6.

Thompson, Kenneth, 'Individual and community in religious critiques of the enterprise culture', in Paul Heelas and Paul Morris (eds), op.cit., pp. 253–75.

Yusoff, Nublan Zaky, *An Islamic Perspective of the Stock Market*, Dian Darulnaim Publishing, Kuala Lumpur, 1992.

Wilkie, George, *Capital: A Moral Instrument*, St Andrews Press for the Edinburgh University Centre for Theological and Public Issues, Edinburgh, 1992.

Williams, Oliver F. and Houck, John W., *Full Value: Cases in Christian Business Ethics*, Harper and Row, San Francisco, 1966.

Wilson, Rodney, *Islamic Business: Theory and Practice*, Economist Intelligence Unit, Special Report No. 221, London, 1985, pp. 18–19.

World Bank, *Atlas*, Washington, 1995.

Index